GETTING HERE

GETTING HERE

From a Seat on a Train to a Seat on the Bench

Peter Ney

iUniverse, Inc.

New York   Bloomington

Getting Here
From a Seat on a Train to a Seat on the Bench

iUniverse books may be ordered through booksellers or by contacting:

iUniverse
1663 Liberty Drive
Bloomington, IN 47403
www.iuniverse.com
1-800-Authors (1-800-288-4677)

ISBN: 978-1-4401-7138-3 (pbk)
ISBN: 978-1-4401-7140-6 (cloth)
ISBN: 978-1-4401-7139-0 (ebook)

Printed in the United States of America

iUniverse rev. date: 11/19/09

To Betty

Contents

ACKNOWLEDGEMENTS

Without Betty, this memoir would not have been written. First of all, if she had not shared my life for the last sixty years—who knows what that life would have been like. Second, without her encouragement, I know the book would not have been written. Third, she was an eyewitness to most of the events told here—she read the first draft of each chapter as it came out of the printer and compared her memories with mine.

Very special thanks and gratitude go to Marilyn Baseman, my editor and Betty's childhood friend, who worked tirelessly to correct my fractured syntax. Marilyn's suggestions were invaluable, notably her idea for the subtitle—From a Seat on the Train to a Seat on the Bench. Marilyn, please know that your friendship, patience, and creativity are much appreciated.

Any editorial errors appearing in the book should be attributed to the author's stubbornness, not to any oversight by the editor.

INTRODUCTION

My Jewish ancestors lived in Western Germany, in the territory of Rheinland-Pfaltz, for over 200 years in relative peace and prosperity with their predominantly Christian neighbors. However, regional political bodies periodically placed limitations on Jews by imposing discriminatory taxes on them and by restricting their occupations, travel, and construction of houses of worship. This relatively peaceful and safe environment changed dramatically shortly after my birth in 1931.

In 1750, in the tiny village of Odernheim, near Krauznach in Rheinland-Pfaltz, a wedding took place. As was the Jewish tradition at that time, Jews generally had no surnames. Mendel ben Josef—"ben" indicating he was the son of Josef—married Jonannete Mayer, whose family used the modern style of a surname. Jonannete's father, Izak Mayer, was the head of the Odernheim Jewish congregation.

In 1752, Jonannete gave birth to a son, Kiebe ben Mendel. As a young man, consistent with his desire to be assimilated into the greater society, he adopted the name Josef Ney. Thirty years later, the Napoleonic Code of 1804 would have compelled him to have a surname in any case. Josef married Bella Anselm, and they moved to Lochenmostel where, on March 24, 1776, Bella bore a son, also named Josef.

Little did they know of or concern themselves with the dramatic and world-changing events occurring across the Atlantic Ocean in the United States of America during young Josef's first year of life.

The French Revolution of 1792 resulted in periodic military occupations of the Rheinland-Pfaltz by French troops under the command of a distinguished officer, Michael Ney, who later became Napoleon's chief of staff. If Michael was a relative, the family never found the thread. In 1806, Napoleon formally annexed the area to France. Napoleon had decreed that, in France, Jews had full rights of citizenship; these rights were now extended to residents of the annexed territories.

Josef Ney, the father, died in 1838 in Niederkirchen, probably unaware of how the American Revolution had permanently changed the world.

In 1818, the younger Josef Ney, a forty-two-year-old widower, married twenty-five-year-old Johannette Bock. A year later, my great-grandfather, Abraham Ney, was born on February 20, 1819.

In December 1854, Abraham married Amelia Gimbel. She was the sister of Adam Gimbel, who had left his family home in Niederkirchen to make his fortune in America and with his seven sons had founded the Gimbel Brothers chain of department stores. Like Adam, Abraham and Amelia also had seven sons: Karl (1855), Gustav (1859), Nathan (1860), twins Josef and Isaak—my grandfather—(1863), Emanuel (1865), and August (1867). All were born in Niederkirchen.

The family moved to Kaiserslautern, where Abraham established a horse-trading business. He died on July 23, 1900; Amelia survived him by eleven years.

August, the youngest, moved to Nuremberg, where he started a metal business. Gustav moved to Ulm, where he married Louise Moos. Louise's maternal grandfather, Raphael Einstein, was the brother of David Einstein, the grandfather of physicist Albert Einstein.

Isaak continued the horse business. In 1890, he married Henrietta Mandel, who had been born on November 18, 1865 in the neighboring town of Albisheim. They moved to a relatively large house he had bought at 12 Glockenstrasse and operated his business in the acreage behind the house, where he constructed twenty horse stalls around a cobblestone courtyard.

Their first child, Johanna, was born on August 21, 1893. Within two years, on December 21, 1894, my father, Markus Alfred, was born;

five years after that, on September 21, 1899, Isaak and Henrietta's youngest child, Kurt Paul, was born.

My father, because of his father's horse business and his family chores, became a proficient horseman, often riding in Kaiserslautern festivals and parades. When he was a teenager, a horse kicked him in the face, leaving a scar on his upper lip. This gave him a dashing appearance, suggesting that he had been a member of a university or military dueling society. Though Jews in the Rheinland Pfaltz area retained most citizenship rights even after the Prussians defeated the French and took back the German territories, this would not have been possible for a Jew at that time.

My father often described his high-school graduation paper, "Man in the Modern Society," in which he wrote with great pride about living in that pinnacle of civilization and described the recent technological advances of the time—the telephone and, most remarkably, the airplane. He wrote about the excitement in Kaiserslautern when, as a teenager, he saw his first airplane flying over the town. He was convinced that he was living in the greatest period of technology, culture, and civilization—and that it would continue far into the future, certainly through his lifetime.

Germany invaded France in August 1914. On August 8, 1914, Markus Alfred, not yet eighteen, was one of the first in Kaiserslautern to volunteer for the 23rd Infantry Regiment. He immediately was issued a uniform and rifle. As he marched out of town with the other volunteers, flowers in the barrels of their rifles and the cheers of the residents ringing in their ears, his greatest concern was that Germany would defeat the French before he could demonstrate his heroism for the Fatherland. My father had, by his enlistment, completed the process of assimilation begun when Kiebe ben Mendel had adopted the surname Ney. He considered himself a German first and a Jew second. He soon would learn that not all Germans agreed with his rankings.

Within weeks of his enlistment, Alfred lay wounded outside the French town of Lille. He was in excruciating pain, with shrapnel in his right upper leg. He described the battle scene as one of pure horror, with dead and wounded men scattered on the ground. The latter, screaming in agony and fear, were pleading for help. The scene did not resemble the vision of heroism and glory he had imagined as he marched out of Kaiserslautern to the cheers of his neighbors.

His leg was saved, but it had been shortened by about six inches. He was hospitalized for more than a year, spending the first six months of 1915 in the War Recuperation Center in Munich. He developed a relationship with Paulita, a nurse, who wrote an inscription in his copy of a militaristic, patriotic epic poem, *Knight, Death, and the Devil,* asking him to think of her sometimes. To help him remember, she pasted her picture in the frontispiece.

After his discharge from the recuperation center, Alfred was awarded the Iron Cross for heroism. He returned to his parents' home in Kaiserslautern for about eighteen months, where he learned to walk unassisted. In December 1916, he accepted employment as a bank clerk in Nuremberg. He worked there until June 1918, when he joined the metal-trading business of his father's brother, August, also in Nuremberg.

He worked for his uncle as an apprentice or journeyman for a few years, learning the metals business. In 1920, Alfred asked his uncle for an interest in the business, and in response to his uncle's refusal, he started his own business—Alfred Ney Metalworks. His brother, Kurt, joined him in the business.

My father built a modern metal refining factory on Industriestrasse in Nuremberg, with "Alfred Ney" emblazoned in large letters across the top of the building. He developed a trademark using the letters *A* and *N* with smoke coming from the vertical of the *N*. The business became successful, and my father was recognized as a very eligible bachelor in Nuremberg Jewish society.

He liked to tell the story that he was one of the first to have a zipper installed in his trousers and was always happy to demonstrate the operation of this advanced technology at parties, to the delight of both the men and women in attendance. Alfred was engaged at least once before he met my mother, and he broke that engagement so clumsily that he had to leave town and spend several weeks at a resort.

My mother, Gretl, the younger child of Oscar and Tina Schwarzmann, was born on April 30, 1909, in Wertheim. Oscar had established an international leather-trading firm. Proficient in many languages, he served in the army as an interpreter and interrogator of prisoners of war. He was popular with the prisoners, who gave him many drawings as gifts.

My mother's older brother, Rudi, joined his father in the leather business. Living a very privileged life, Gretl completed her formal education in a finishing school in Lausanne, Switzerland, where she was supposedly learning business skills but instead became a proficient skier.

After her schooling, Gretl worked in her father's office, where one of her duties was to take the mail to the post office. On one of these trips, she ran into my father, whom she had previously met at a party. He was fifteen years older than she was. These meetings, on her way to the post office, occurred with some regularity, and developed into a courtship.

In 1929, Alfred and Gretl had an elaborate engagement celebration and attended a New Year's Eve costume party to welcome 1930. They were married June 30, 1930, in a formal black-tie–and-tails wedding that featured a multi-course lunch, dinner, and dancing to a live band. They celebrated their honeymoon in Venice.

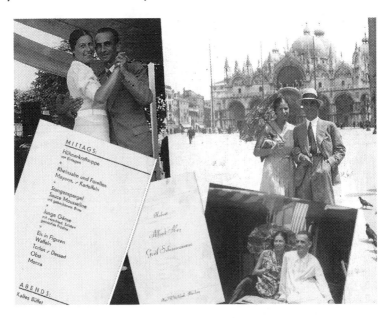

On November 11, 1931, thirteen years to the day after Germany was defeated in World War I and two years before Adolf Hitler became Chancellor of Germany, I was born—the adventure began.

– 1 –

Happy Birthday

Wroooom! Wroooom! Wroom, Wroom, Wroom! I turned away from my view of *Die Burg*—the castle and its surrounding chest-high stone wall with the hoofprints embedded in its top. My father had explained that these were made several centuries ago when *Der Ritter*—the knight on his mighty horse—leapt across the moat surrounding the castle to perform a heroic deed. As I turned, I saw many excited people rushing to the curbside. I, too, was drawn to the sound of drums, but just as the bugles started, my parents held me back.

"This is not for us," my father said in an unusually sharp tone. Through spaces in the crowd, I saw boys in their late teens marching four or five abreast, with long drums extending from their waists to below their knees, playing two long beats and three short ones. After three rows of drummers, there were three rows of buglers. All the boys were dressed alike. Each had a white shirt with a black bandana tied around the neck, and a brown leather strap that ran across the shirt from the left shoulder to the right waist where it was attached to a belt. The uniform was completed with short tan pants, white knee-high socks, and a red, white, and black armband.

I struggled to break free and join the cheering crowd at the curb. "This is not for us," my father said again, more severely than before. All the color had drained out of his face.

I turned to my mother for help. She looked terrified. "Why not? Why not for us?" I screamed. "You don't understand! You don't understand! Everyone else understands. See how they are cheering at the music, and now see the flags coming ..."

They dragged my struggling six-year-old body out of the Old City of Nuremberg. Eventually, we got to our apartment at 13 Kaulbach Platz.

I was so disappointed in my parents, because they just did not understand, though they tried to explain why the parade was "not for us." It had something to do with being Jewish. I understood none of this. As they tried explaining what being Jewish meant, all I understood was that it was not good and kept me from being part of what others enjoyed.

The day had been planned as an outing with my parents to the medieval part of my hometown, Nuremberg. It was a real treat to be with my parents instead of my nurse, Annie, who usually had the responsibility of keeping me amused while my father took care of his business and my mother shopped and met her friends at various cafes. My mother would often relate her activities at the evening meal, which was served by a maid. Sometimes, the tone changed, as when my father would speak of going to the American Consulate or to the police station to get one important paper or another. Periodically, there was discussion of the ever-important number. How could a number be so important?

I was very excited when the day started with a visit to the marketplace, a large cobblestone square occupied by wooden tables that displayed all sorts of treasures. I first was attracted to the figures made with dried apples, figs, and pears connected by sticks. These figures were caricatures of farmers, musicians, doctors, lawyers, peddlers, and mothers with children. I was warned to look but not touch. Other tables were filled with toys. Many had soldiers in varied colored uniforms. There were tanks, warships, and all sorts of airplanes. Nuremberg was the toy manufacturing capital of Germany. Since many of those manufacturers were customers of my father's metal refining factory, he brought home many toys for me. My favorites were cars—replicas of real autos.

Standing on one side of the market square were the Catholic cathedral and the Jewish synagogue. I knew I had some connection to the synagogue, but I remembered being inside it only once or twice. I did not know I had an ethnic connection to the whole market square, whose space was created in 1341 when Charles IV authorized the destruction of the Jewish community. The cathedral was constructed on the spot where the original synagogue had been razed.

The synagogue I saw then, during the last days of its existence, had been built during the previous century in a period of flourishing Jewish integration into German society. Hanging on the other buildings surrounding the square were many long, vertical, bright red flags; each had a white circle with the swastika inside.

My parents, as did most Jews in Germany at that time, considered themselves Germans. Only superficially connected to their Jewish heritage, they were fully integrated into the German social structure, with full civil rights—until unexpected events unfolded.

I think my parents were in denial. Although they had applied for immigration to the United States, they hoped against hope that the recent Nazi acts of official anti-Semitism were a phenomenon that soon would pass. They reasoned that in Germany, a country of culture and science, the madness of Nazism could not survive. Jews had contributed to the highest levels of education, medicine, literature, science, theater, cinema, business, and music; those contributions would not be destroyed. Or would they?

At the marketplace, my parents showed me a fountain with the figure of a boy a little older than I was, holding a goose under each arm. Each goose had a stream of water cascading from its beak. In front of the cathedral, there also was a fountain—this one resembled the spire of a miniature cathedral. My parents pointed to a metal ring linked through the fence that surrounded the fountain. They told me the legend of the ring, which I have long forgotten. The medieval city of Nuremberg had no shortage of legends. There were myths around each corner: magic rings, flying horses, and barons that rode cannonballs.

From the market, we went to the castle. *Die Burg* was a medieval structure surrounded by a very deep moat. We crossed the drawbridge and went to the castle's biggest attraction, an iron, life-size human figure hinged on each side: the Iron Maiden. It stood open, revealing the long spikes that would penetrate the body of a person placed inside when the iron halves closed. It frightened me so much that my father had to assure me that we now lived in such a modern, civilized country that the *Jungfrau*—maiden—and the other torture instruments on display, like the rack and the molten metal pouring ladles, would never be used today.

I was reminded of the time my mother had to calm me when I became terrified at hearing the story of Hansel and Gretel pushing the old witch into the cast iron oven. She also had assured me that it was just a story and would never happen today.

After the war, when I saw pictures of the extermination camps, I saw a similarity in the design of those oven doors and the oven door in my copy of *Hansel and Gretel*. Is it possible that children all over Germany were dreaming about the creatures created by the Brothers Grimm and their compatriots?

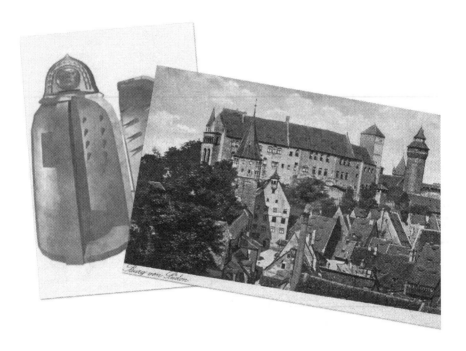

As we left the castle, my mind still on the Iron Maiden, I became distracted by the hoofprints left on the outer wall by the legendary knight, and forgot my fears.

I don't remember having any friends as a young boy. My only regular playmates were two sisters, Lori and Lotte, who lived in the apartment above us. They were both older than I and had already started school. After they came home from school, they would lower a basket on a rope from their balcony to me. Sometimes, we would exchange toys, messages, or treats. One of my last memories of them is playing in the snow on my wooden sled in the small grassy area in front of our apartment house.

In our apartment, my favorite amusement was riding up and down the long hallway on a toy car that I propelled with my feet. The hallway was dimly lit, and along one side were several large wardrobes. For a long time, I saw the Iron Maiden in spaces between those wardrobes. The Maiden, and the witch being shoved into the cast iron oven, populated many of my nightmares.

A story I remember hearing frequently was *Strumpelpeter*, the story of a young boy with my name who was unclean, had unkempt long hair and uncut fingernails, and was rejected by society because of his filthy condition. My favorite story was *Till Eulenspiegel*, the tale of a prankster who tormented the authorities.

I did not see my grandparents often. My father's father had died before I was five. My grandmother sold the horse business and moved from the house in Kaiserslautern to live with her sister in Frankfurt. The house, with its horses, stalls, and courtyard, continued to reside faintly in my dim memory.

My mother's father and her brother had a successful international leather and hide business. Her parents and her brother's family, including his twins, a boy and a girl, were able to immigrate to Switzerland. I saw these grandparents for the last time on a mysterious trip I took with my mother on Lake Constance.

Very early one fall day, my mother was dressed more fashionably than usual in a flowing white dress and white shoes. She was a striking, dramatic beauty with eyes that sparkled with excitement. Her pitch-black hair, with its center part, was tightly pulled back and secured in a pinned knot at the back of her head. When she dressed me, I looked like a little gentleman in long pants, white shirt, necktie, jacket, and cap.

"Where are we going, Mutti?" I asked.

"We are going for a boat ride. Is that not exciting? There will be a surprise," she said, "as we will see people we have not seen for some time."

We took a short ride to a town on Lake Constance that formed part of the German–Swiss boundary. Pleasure ships toured the lake, stopping at towns on both sides of the border. My mother spoke to the ticket agent as if she had just gotten the idea to take the boat ride. "This is such a beautiful day for a boat ride. Can my son and I get a ticket? Would one be able to leave the ship at any stop along the way?" The agent was only too happy to sell a ticket, but warned her that the stops along the way were short and you would have to purchase another ticket to complete the tour if you were not on the ship when it departed.

We left the ship at a stop on the Swiss side, and whom should we meet but my grandparents! They gave me a board game called "Trip through Switzerland," and we spent the day together. I remember there was a great deal of serious discussion between my mother and her parents. They made sure I was otherwise occupied, with ice cream, Swiss chocolate, and my game.

My grandfather, a very serious man, had a shaved head in the German style. He spoke many languages fluently and had been a decorated soldier in the First World War, acting as an interpreter during the interrogation of Turkish, British, and French POWs. He had many interesting drawings that had been gifts from those soldiers.

As the afternoon stretched on, I said what turned out to be my last goodbye to these grandparents, and my mother and I took another ship to complete the tour around Lake Constance. As we were leaving the ship, I remembered that my mother had placed my game on the overhead luggage rack and started screaming for it. She, of course, wanted to abandon the game because it was a dead giveaway that we had gone to Switzerland, which she was not permitted to do. If she had taken me along as a decoy, I was a total screaming failure.

I had expected to start school earlier but that had not yet happened. Now, again, there was discussion that I would be starting school. It was not the public school but one referred to as "the Jewish school."

One afternoon, Annie, my nurse, took me out for an excursion that required a ride on the trolley car. Our destination was an enormous field, larger than any sports stadium I had ever seen. Very high flagpoles ringed the field. At one end of the field was a three-tiered stone block stage with a high stone wall in back topped by a large stone swastika.

The field was almost empty except for a few guards and clean-up people. There also were a few couples meandering in the grass, some walking their dogs.

Annie obviously had come to meet one of the guards. He was there with a rifle, wearing a uniform and a steel helmet. I was sent to play with the soccer ball we had brought along. After about an hour, Annie gathered me up and we rode home on the trolley car.

I never saw Annie again. I was never certain if Annie had been discharged or if the laws that were coming into effect at that time had prohibited her from working for Jews. The field that Annie had taken me to was where thousands of soldiers assembled in Nazi rallies. It became an iconic image of Hitler's rise to power and was memorialized in Leni Riefenstahl's film *Triumph of the Will.*

One of my favorite periodic activities was accompanying my father to his factory. We would ride there in his shiny, almost new, Opel sedan. A few times, I was permitted into the manufacturing portion of the factory.

Tough-looking men in work clothes were pouring molten metal into forms. Because of the fires and molten metals, I was not allowed to get too close. There were carts that traveled on tracks, and a few times I was allowed to ride short distances. My favorite activities were in the office where I spent my time with Miss Krist. She gave me a metal, tree-like desk stand, which had three levels of circular disks with metal clips that held many rubber stamps, a stamp pad, and scrap paper. Many of the stamps had my father's name: Alfred Ney. The stamps with the company name, AN Metalworks, had the logo with the smoke coming out of the vertical of the *N*, like a smokestack. Others said "Balance Due" and "Paid In Full." Some stamps were rectangles, others were circles and ovals. I enjoyed rubber-stamping almost as much as driving my car down the hall of our apartment. Miss Krist was so nice. She always talked to me and offered me chocolates.

My parents owned a small tract of land, "the Garden," on the outskirts of Nuremberg, at the end of the trolley line. The Garden had a small wooden structure. Shutters decorated with little heart cutouts were on its windows. We spent many weekend days there. My parents often invited their friends to sit in the sun, eat, drink beer, and play cards. The Dietenhofers were there frequently. Ellen was my mother's closest friend. They would bring their son, Theo, intending that we become friends. Sometimes, Ellen's parents, the Frankens, came along.

As that year progressed, the discussions at the Garden became more hushed and very serious. Everyone spoke of sponsors, relatives in America, quota numbers, affidavits, and medical examinations. One afternoon, a new subject occupied the discussion. Unbelievably, it had to do with hair styling. Each of the group had a folded white card that had been issued the previous week. On the front was a large capital *J* in classic German type, and the holder's name was written in fancy official script. Each man's middle name was written as "Israel" and each woman's middle name was written as "Sara." But what caused the most discussion were the photographs on the inside of the women's identity cards: each woman had been forced to have her picture taken in profile with her ear exposed.

Most of our visits to the Garden were on weekends when my father drove us. I remember the last visit. It was during the week, and my mother and I took the trolley car to the end of the line. We were the only ones in the Garden. My mother cut flowers, and I picked strawberries.

As we left, we saw a trolley car waiting to start its return trip. My mother called for me to hurry. As we ran to catch the trolley, my basket of strawberries spilled in the street with some rolling onto the tracks. I stopped to pick them up, but my mother told me to leave them since they now were dirty and therefore inedible. We made it to the trolley in time, but I could not get the picture of the spilled strawberries on the trolley tracks out of my mind. On the trolley, I thought about my mother and her not understanding that the strawberries could have been washed rather than left in the street to rot.

As fall approached, I was excited about starting school. I was supposed to have started the previous year, but my entry to the school suddenly was cancelled at the last minute. Overhearing my parents discuss this, I understood it had something to do with my being Jewish, whatever that was. The school I was taken to appeared quite different from the one I was to have gone to last year. It was on the second floor of what looked like a warehouse.

My first day of school was filled with the excitement all German first-graders experienced. I had been given a backpack made of thick, rigid leather with shoulder straps and all sorts of clips and rings. It had that wonderful new leather smell. I was careful to adjust the straps perfectly. The biggest thrill was the large decorated cone filled with candy and school supplies, which all German students took to school on the first day. My class had about seventeen students.

I look back at the class photograph taken that day, with me standing next to the teacher, and I wonder what happened to them all. Some of the students look out of the picture as if they want to tell me.

We used two textbooks that had been approved by the authorities. The first lesson's illustration, in the reading book *With Us In Nuremberg*, was of two boys in front of the castle giving the Nazi straight-arm salute, with the caption "Heil Hitler." The next lesson showed six-year-old boys in single file with drum and fife, carrying a flag, coming through the main gate of the castle, which was festooned in flags. The caption for this lesson was "Raise the flag high." The third lesson, illustrating a massive military parade through the streets of Nuremberg, was "A festival, a long parade, flags in the parade, flags in all the streets." The rest of the book was devoted to non-political subjects like circuses, workers, ice cream, and sandmen.

The frontispiece of the arithmetic textbook had a drawing of Hitler accepting flowers from a young boy and girl, with two smiling SS men looking on. The caption was "One Leader – One People." On the inside cover, there was a six-by-ten chart of men in different uniforms. Some of the pages were illustrated with military exercises and Hitler Youth activities.

My teacher, Dr. Einstadt, was a distinguished-looking man who obviously had been teaching for many years. What I did not know was that we were privileged to have this learned professor only because he no longer was permitted to teach at the university.

My seventh birthday was approaching on November 11. It meant a lot to me. What presents would I receive? Something to do with cars, I hoped.

Two days before my birthday, the level of depression and anxiety in my house rose to an even higher level than normal. I overheard some discussion between my parents. They spoke about an assassination in Paris. Would this be a pretext for an action? What reprisals would be taken? I, of course, understood none of this, except that it was something bad.

I do remember my parents making elaborate preparations in their bedroom. They laid out underwear and clothing very carefully. When I was put to bed, my parents seemed to hug me more intensely than usual. I was read a cheerful story about a boy who had a wonderful birthday. As I lay in my bed, I saw that a bench had been placed along its side. Was this where my presents would be placed?

I was half-dreaming, half-awake when I heard loud, deep crashing sounds that sounded like barrels bouncing down stairs. As I was waking, I heard glass breaking. The room was flooded with light as my mother rushed in. She was wearing her nightclothes, her hair was in disarray and a look of terror was on her face. She rushed to my bed and scooped me into her arms. *Could this have something to do with my birthday?* I wondered. The sounds of crashing and breaking glass continued as I glanced down at the bench next to my bed. There were no presents on it.

My mother carried me into the hallway where I saw men in brown uniforms holding axes and rushing past us down the hall to my parents' bedroom. As we passed our living room, I saw our tall bookcases pulled from the wall and lying at crazy angles, supported by some of the other pieces of furniture.

My father, standing in the room and facing one of the uniformed men, was holding his Iron Cross in his open palm. Another uniformed man was screaming at my mother, telling her to leave the apartment. We went out to the stairway landing and took the stairs up toward other people. We climbed until we could go no further because of the families who were sitting on the stairs in front of a gate made of large boards, blocking entry to the apartment house attic. I saw Lori and Lotte sitting on the stairs with their mother. I waved, but they did not respond. I thought of my birthday presents that were now downstairs in the apartment. Would they be safe?

The people on the stairway did not speak. The only sound from them was some sobbing. The crashing sounds from below continued for what seemed a long time. When the noise started to subside, I saw my father making his way up the stairs to join us. My parents whispered to each other. Of the four or five family clusters, there was only one other with a father.

When no sound came up the stairway, some of the people started to speak. "Do you think it is safe to go down?" A slow procession started down the stairway. After a few minutes, my parents led me down the three or four flights to our apartment. Its front door was open. My mother picked me up again, surely because my feet were bare and glass littered the floor. The living room looked like a windstorm had hit it. All the furniture was upset, with the fallen bookcases blocking our entry into the living room. Part of one bookcase had been built into a liquor cabinet, and the contents of the broken bottles had run over the scattered books and onto the oriental carpet. Much of the furniture had been hacked to pieces. The chandelier had been smashed.

We went into my room and found it had not been disturbed. At first glance, my parents' bedroom looked undisturbed. The covers on the large bed were as they probably were when my parents jumped out of bed. The clothing that had been carefully laid out in anticipation of the expected emergency was still neatly in its place, unused because they had had no time to get dressed. My mother told me I would sleep in their bed this night in "the moat," which is what I called the small space between the two mattresses.

As I started to climb onto the bed, my mother screamed and pulled me off. The light fixture at the head of the bed had been smashed and the sheets were covered with broken glass. I waited, wrapped in a blanket and dozing in a chair, as my parents picked the glass out of the bed and changed the sheets. I awoke on a bright day, lying in "the moat," wondering if what I remembered had actually transpired, or, I hoped, was just a dream.

I heard my mother on the telephone. "How is Fritz? Good, he was not taken. Thankfully, neither was Alfred. I begged him to stay inside this morning, but he went to the factory. Your parents' home has been completely destroyed? Where are they staying? Most of our damage was in the living room. Bring them here; they can stay with us." She spoke, as she had for some time, in very short cryptic phrases. You never can tell who is listening.

I looked out the window and saw several columns of smoke rising into the bright sky. It had not been a dream! Suddenly, I was filled with terror. I heard my father come into the apartment. I ran out to meet him, hoping he could provide some security. He told my mother the factory had not been damaged. Evidently, they were told that the factory, identified as "war critical," was in the process of being aryanized. The synagogue was burned to the ground.

The German government passed emergency legislation exempting the damage of that night from insurance coverage and fining the Jewish community for causing such damage and disruption of national order.

That night, November 9, 1938, became known as *Kristallnacht*, the night of broken glass. The nightmarish events that took place in Nuremberg were repeated all over Germany. They served as a wake-up call for the world to see Germany's intentions, which would ultimately lead to the Second World War. Ironically, the Berlin Wall, dividing Germany after the war, came down on the fifty-first anniversary of Kristallnacht, unifying Germany again.

PARIS PRESS SCORES NAZIS

'World Astonished' at Reprisals, Says One Newspaper

Wireless to THE NEW YORK TIMES.

PARIS, Friday, Nov. 11.—The French press, which was almost unanimous in condemning the Polish-Jewish assassin who shot Ernst vom Rath in the German Embassy here, today just as severely reproves the outbreak of anti-Semitism that has followed this incident in Germany.

"The world is astonished," says the Petit Parisien, "that a civilized nation like Germany should permit such terrible reprisals against victims whose only relationship to the murderer is one of race. Even that could be explained if these acts had been committed by uncontrollable mobs. But Goebbels [German Propaganda Minister] has been somewhat slow in issuing a call for order and it is apparent that for nearly twenty-four hours nothing has been done to prevent the disturbances.

"Unless this exhibition ends quickly it bids fair to tarnish the reputation for discipline and honor that the Nazi regime is always claiming as its own exclusive attribute."

13

A policeman came and took a report of the damage. He assured my parents this was the work of hoodlums and would not be tolerated. A worker from my father's factory arrived. My father gave him some of the damaged furniture to repair for his own use. He thanked my father profusely and expressed sorrow at what had happened. Evidently, he did not load his truck properly, because one of the chests of drawers fell off, smashing to smithereens, as he drove away on the curve of Kaulbach Platz. I felt so bad that this worker would not be able to use the chest. My feeling reminded me of the strawberries that had spilled as my mother and I were running to catch the trolley from the Garden.

The next day, I did celebrate my seventh birthday with my parents. My main present was a model electric highway, the *Autobahn,* the German turnpike system, then under construction, undoubtedly with military utility in mind. My toy set up as a large figure eight. There was an overpass where the highway crossed. The controls were contained on the back of an Esso station. The two metal cars were very realistic Auto Union models. I loved it. I excitedly invited Lotte and Lori down to show this wonder to them. They were very sad. They had had no word of their father.

A few days later, my father brought home a package that was even larger than the *Autobahn.* He handed it to me, telling me it was a present. I was disappointed when I excitedly removed the wrapping paper to discover a new brown leather suitcase. It had the same leather smell, which I had liked so much, as my school backpack.

"Why do I need a suitcase?" I asked. My parents attempted to explain that I would soon be going to England with many other children and would meet a very good man, Stephen Wiseman, in London.

"You are not going with me?" I asked.

"No, but we will meet you there soon." They tried to reassure me.

I started to cry. "Why? Why? What did I do wrong?" I screamed.

"No, my darling, you did nothing wrong. You are going for your own good." My mother started to cry.

"How could this be for my good?" I asked, now sobbing. I opened and closed the catches and locked and unlocked them with the tiny keys that had been tied around the handle.

Many times over the next few weeks, the suitcase was packed and repacked with brand-new clothing. My mother had gotten a long spool of white tape that had "Peter Ney" repeatedly embroidered in red every few inches along its entire length. There must have been a hundred Peter Neys on that tape. She sewed my name into each piece of clothing that was going into that suitcase.

Ellen Dietenhofer's parents, the Frankens, lived with us for several days. I heard them speak of a relative, Herr Stephen Wiseman, who lived in London and was arranging to get the Dietenhofer family to England. The Frankens, who were very grateful to my parents, stated several times that they would not leave unless my family could come also.

I could sense my parents' panic and desperation as my father frequently went to the American Consulate. There always was the subsequent discussion of the quota numbers, sponsors, and affidavits that all had to come together like some surreal ballet. My father also had to go periodically to the main police station to get official papers stamped. Once, going with him to get my passport, I noticed that this newly expanded building had the latest technology. I was fascinated by a continuously moving elevator that had no doors. The passengers would jump on or off when the compartment was approximately level with the floor. I suppose there were big plans for the police building.

When I received my passport, I was repeatedly told that I must never lose it. It had my picture in it. I wrote my name below the picture in block letters. A circular stamp imprint of an eagle clutching a swastika was placed over the corner of the picture and my name. A large purple *J* was stamped on the green page.

Lotte and Lori came to say goodbye. They still did not know what had happened to their father. They gave me an autograph book with a padded cover decorated with tiny blue, red, and yellow flowers, and each wrote a sentimental message on the first two pages. I put the book into the suitcase along with a "Peter Ney" rubber stamp, a stamp pad, postcards addressed to my home in Nuremberg, and stationery that had a drawing of a gnome printed at the top of each sheet. I promised my parents I would write often.

The next day, I took the suitcase, which had been packed so many times, into the highly polished Opel. My parents and I drove to Frankfurt to see my grandmother.

My grandmother's apartment, which she shared with her sister, seemed very dark. My parents appeared very sad and agitated. Everyone sat in the dining room.

I was on my knees, on a dining room chair, staring at some small dark medicine bottles. The one that fascinated me the most had a glass stopper topped by a heart. As I reached out for this attraction, both my parents reprimanded me. "That is not a toy; it is your grandmother's medicine! How can you be so foolish?" My grandmother came to my defense. "Leave him be. Not tonight." They immediately looked at each other, calmed down, and held me tightly. I was totally confused by the changed attitudes.

My confusion continued as I lay in bed staring at the ceiling in the dark room. What was so important about this night? Did it have anything to do with the events of the night before my birthday?"

– 2 –

Exodus

The railroad station in Frankfurt was gigantic, with its arched roof extending over more than a dozen tracks. From the crest of the arch hung the enormous German flag. The smell of burning coal, smoke, and circling steam mixed with the sobbing of parents and children who were crowded into a waiting hall and slowly moved to one end of the first platform.

"Now, when you get to England, be certain to take the train to London," my father instructed. " 'Uncle' Stephen Weisman will be waiting for you at Liverpool Station." My parents had told me this many times during the past few weeks and repeatedly during our last evening, at my grandmother's apartment. Not understanding the difference between England and London, I was more concerned with figuring out what I had done wrong by fingering my grandmother's brown glass medicine bottle with the heart-shaped stopper. My parents' statements that I was going to London or England for my own good did not seem believable. I desperately wanted to trust their assurances that they would join me there "very soon," but none of it rang true.

That morning, at my grandmother's house, my father had given me a silver pencil "as a remembrance." He showed me how this pencil would expose different colors of lead as the back was turned. I had never seen anything like it. As I turned the back, out popped a black lead; as I turned again it was red, then green, then blue. I promised my parents and grandmother that I would make wonderful drawings with this pencil. But why did he say it was "a remembrance?" Would I not see them soon in England?

Now, I was standing with my parents on a platform in a crowd of other parents and children who all seemed to be dressed in their very best. I was wearing brand-new clothing, and the other children looked as though they were, also. I and all the other children had cardboard shipping labels attached through a buttonhole in our overcoats, as if we were packages being shipped to an unknown destination. My mother, like many other women, was wearing a fur coat and a hat with a veil. "Why? Why?" I asked.

"For your good," was the only reply.

The loudspeakers continually blared, "Go there! Stay here! Go there!" Now, there was noticeable movement in the crowd. "All adults must remain where they are. When ordered, all children with authorization for the *Kindertransport* will board the train on platform three."

Kindertransport? I wondered. *What could that mean?*

I held in my pocket the four-color silver pencil my father had given me that morning "as a remembrance." With my other hand, I picked up my new suitcase. My mother hugged me and kissed me. She told me I would be safe and they would soon see me in England. *What did "soon" mean? When would we be together again?* With the crowd of other children, I made my way to the train with my suitcase swinging back and forth. It was much too large for me.

I found a window seat in one of the train's compartments, and I could see my parents sobbing on the platform two tracks away. *Why was this happening? If they were so sad for me to leave, why did they put me on this train? Did it have something to do with my misbehavior with my grandmother's medicine bottle? Was this about the event just before my seventh birthday, about a month ago, when I was awakened in the middle of the night and taken by my mother through our apartment with its smashed furniture to the attic of the apartment house? Was I leaving because my parents never wanted me to watch the parades and rallies with all the flags, drums, and bugles?*

I always felt that my parents didn't get it—when all the other people on the street were cheering wildly, my parents were so solemn, pulling me away. Now, they still didn't get it. They were sending me to

England or London, wherever. They just don't get it. How could they be so wrong? How could this be good for me?

The train started to move. I looked at the sad figures of my parents and felt a sense of relief that I now would not be able to see them sobbing. Sounds in the aisle broke into our compartment. "Any of you vermin who has any valuables, turn them over immediately." A burly man in a uniform continued, "If we find any of you scum has kept valuables, the whole train will be turned back." For emphasis, he grabbed some suitcases from the overhead rack, opened them, and dumped their contents on the floor.

I clutched my silver pencil inside my pocket. My heart was beating wildly; I could hardly breathe. The compartment was in chaos. *Silver sounds valuable,* I thought. I carefully pulled the pencil out of my pocket and slipped it into the waistband of my trousers and into my underwear. The teenagers in the compartment solemnly stared forward.

My mind raced. *Did my parents know how lonely and frightened I was? I had promised them that I would be good and not cause problems. What was I doing keeping the pencil in my underwear? How would I find Uncle Stephen, as I had promised my parents I would? Would I disappoint them again, as I had by playing with my grandmother's medicine bottle?*

The train wound its way through the German countryside. I stared out the window, my thoughts more on the past than on the unknown future. The other occupants were much older than I—teenagers, perhaps. They sat mostly in silence, and when they did speak with one another, it was in whispers. No one spoke to me nor I to any of them. Periodically, the men in uniform yelled at other passengers on the train. My suitcase was undisturbed, sitting on the overhead shelf. I felt my silver pencil, still safe in my underwear. I decided that I had the responsibility to keep my suitcase and pencil safe. That was one thing I would do right.

Thoughts of my perceived misbehavior with my grandmother's medicine bottle; my parents' sadness at the station; their promise to meet me soon; the events of the night just before my seventh birthday, when my parents and I were chased out of our apartment, returning to find our furniture smashed—all swirled in a disorganized whirlpool in my head.

Then, the train slowed down, with no town or train station in sight. Everybody became absolutely quiet and tense. Even the yelling from "the uniforms" stopped. The only sound was the shrill grinding of the train's brakes on the steel wheels. After the train came to a full stop, I saw that a group of "the uniforms" had started to collect alongside the train. The clanging of the coupling and the bump of the cars indicated that the engines were being changed. The steam and smoke of the engine swirled backward, partially obscuring the group of laughing men in uniform. After what seemed like an eternity, the train started to roll ever so gently. All the uniformed tormenters seemed to have left the train. There now were no adults visible.

A great cheer went up from the teenagers, who seemed to know what had happened. They shouted, *"Die Grenze!"*—The border. The train rolled on very slowly as the teenagers' shouts became angry curses directed at their hated *verdammte Vaterland*—damned Fatherland. I didn't understand their rage. Just then, the slowly rolling train stopped again. Silence again enveloped the passengers.

As I looked out, I saw groups of women in white uniforms standing next to the train. They smiled and gestured for us to open the windows; then, they served us the best-tasting hot chocolate and cookies I'd ever had. I realized that I had not eaten since leaving Frankfurt many hours ago. Although my mother had packed some sandwiches and fruit in my suitcase, I had been afraid to take the suitcase down from the overhead shelf.

The ladies had red crosses on their white uniforms. Their language was strange but their speech was kind, in sharp contrast to those men with the red, white, and black armbands with the *Hakenkreuz* who had left us. We now were in the Netherlands.

The train traveled for several hours before it stopped at what I was told was the Hook of Holland—what a funny name. The sun was going down. I mailed my parents a postcard, postmarked January 5, 1939, from the Hook, telling them I was fine and had made the trip with many of the children who had been in the waiting hall. I also wrote, "Now going on a ship. Greetings and Kisses your Peter."

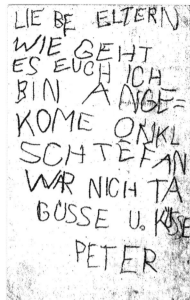

We boarded the ship as adults checked the numbered tags on our coats against names and numbers on tablets they were holding. I don't remember much of the sea voyage; I think I slept through most of it. Waking up at dawn, I saw the activity as the ship was docking. We *Kinder* of the *Kindertransport* were lined up on deck and our papers were checked as we departed the ship.

Many decades later, I learned that the *Kindertransport* was the product of emergency legislation enacted by the British government in reaction to *Kristallnacht*. It gave unescorted Jewish children from Germany, Czechoslovakia, and Austria sanctuary from Nazi persecution. Between December 1938 and September 1939, through the singular generosity of the United Kingdom, ten thousand children found refuge in England. Of these, only a thousand were ever reunited with their parents. These efforts are now commemorated in Vienna's railway station, Berlin's railroad station, London's Liverpool Station, and with a plaque in Parliament.

In deep gratitude
to the people and Parliament
of the United Kingdom
for saving the lives of
10,000 Jewish and other children
who fled to this country
from Nazi persecution
on the Kindertransport
1938 - 1939

Before it is too late...
GET THEM OUT!

I became aware that I was in England because now I could not understand a word that was being said, and remembered my father's instruction: "When you get to England, take the train to London to meet Uncle Stephen Wiseman." Well, here I was in England, but I didn't see any train or Uncle Stephen. Names were called out, and cabins were assigned in what ordinarily was a summer resort but in January was being used to house the children.

I kept listening for my name, expecting someone to show me the train I was supposed to take. When my name was not called, I took it upon myself to look for the train and meet Uncle Stephen Wiseman; and so, I wandered off into the English countryside. I don't know how long I wandered. I remember thinking, as I walked, that I had promised my parents that I would meet Stephen Wiseman and not cause any problems. I had failed on both counts. I could not find my way back to the camp even if I had wanted to—I was hopelessly lost.

I was so confused. I could not tell reality from dreams or, more likely, nightmares. I felt that I deserved what was going to happen to me, which surely would not be good. Herr Wiseman undoubtedly had told my parents that I failed to meet him as I was supposed to, and now my parents would be even angrier with me than they were when I had played with my grandmother's medicine bottle.

The next thing I remember is being awakened by a policeman who was wearing a funny hat. He obviously knew by my clothing and tag that I was from the children's camp. When I got back to the camp, I wrote my parents a postcard, postmarked January 6, saying that I had arrived safely but Uncle Stephen was not there.

Several days later, I was in a warm playroom wondering what would happen next, when, for the first time, someone called out my name. I was relieved that my existence finally was recognized. Perhaps, I did belong to something.

Uncle Stephen had found me, and I was driven to New Herlingen School, a boarding school in Kent. Perhaps my exodus was back on track. My failure to meet Uncle Stephen and my wandering away from the camp had now been remedied.

Anna Essinger, a Jewish teacher in Germany whose foresight had recognized the need for a boarding school for unescorted children fleeing the country, had founded the New Herlingen School. The name of the school was later changed to Bunce Court. Many of the children who were never reunited with their parents received their entire education, through high school, at Bunce Court.

I found out, many years later, that Stephen Wiseman had been waiting for his charge in vain at Liverpool Station. Not wanting to alarm my parents in Germany, he had telegraphed, "Train arrived on time." True, but not quite the whole story. My parents interpreted the telegram, as intended, as reassurance that everything had gone according to plan.

I don't remember ever speaking to any of the other kids at the school. I was going to be here only a short time, as my parents had told me they would meet me here shortly. Or would they? Perhaps not. The day after I started my English lessons, I was instructed to write to my parents. I took out the stationery my parents had packed in my suitcase for such an occasion. I used the rubber stamp with my name and stamped the letter just above the picture of the gnome. The envelope was postmarked January 10, 1939. The letter read:

Dear parents
How is it going? Today I had English for the first time.
Greetings and kisses
Peter

A note from the director of the school followed my letter, assuring my parents that I was adjusting well.

I had addressed the letter to my old address in Nuremberg, "German". I wondered if it would reach them, because by now, according to their promise, they would be on their way to meet me.

On February 25, the director of the school wrote my mother with the bad news that I was very ill with scarlet fever and whooping cough and had been taken to an isolation hospital where no one could visit me, even if someone had been interested.

I sweated and coughed constantly, so my hospital gown and sheets were always wet. My skin itched but the nurses, who constantly cleaned me and changed my gown, sheets, and dressings, told me I was forbidden to scratch. I knew terrible things would happen to me if I disobeyed. After what seemed like an eternity, the itching and sweating went away, and I felt better. But I worried that even if my parents were now coming to join me, as they had promised, they would not be able to find me. I gave up on ever seeing them again. I wondered, *would I be going back to the school? Was my suitcase with my silver pencil safe at the school?*

I could now understand and speak English. I wrote letters to my parents in English. The nurses treated me like their little prince. We joked around, played games, and I laughed for the first time in a long time. I particularly remember one of the nurses, Trish. She had reddish hair, freckles, and what I considered a beautiful overbite. I enjoyed hugging her and, especially, her hugging me back. I loved the smell of her hair. Sometimes, when she sat on my bed, the hem of her dress exposed her knee, and my fantasies traveled up the mysteries of her thigh. I began to appreciate that girls were better to be around than boys, a principle I still maintain.

One day, Trish and another nurse came in smiling, saying they had a surprise for me. With one at the foot of the bed and the other at the head, they wheeled me up to a window in another room. I got onto my knees and looked out the window—and I saw my parents climbing the stairs that permitted them to look through the window directly into my eyes. Just as in the Frankfurt railroad station four months earlier, their eyes brimmed with tears. Their lips mouthed: "P e t e r." Although I could not hear my parents, I knew this time that someone had called my name with love. I desperately wanted to believe that my longing to belong had been fulfilled.

I stayed in the hospital until the middle of April, then went back to the school until June, when I moved into a house on Alba Gardens with my parents, the Frankens, and the Dietenhofers.

And, by the way, seventy years later, I still have the silver pencil.

– 3 –

War in Our Time

We Will Hang Our Wash on the Siegfried Line

After I had left Germany, my parents were in a panic, attempting to secure their escape and worried about my welfare, while caught in a bureaucratic nightmare. Their confidence in their cultured society, that the Nazi regime would soon be rejected, was shattered. As a prudent safety measure, in 1936 they had applied for immigration to the United States.

Because immigration to the United States was severely restricted, they were assigned a quota number that took on life-and-death proportions. Prospective immigrants were granted permission to enter the United States in numerical order until the annual quota for that nationality was filled. If an applicant's number was not called before the nationality quota was filled, that applicant had to wait for the following year's quota. Applications for these prized numbers had increased dramatically as more repressive measures against Jews had been imposed. I remembered overhearing many discussions my father had with Jewish friends about mysterious numbers that I could not understand.

To complicate the process further, the calling of the number had to coincide, within a small window of time, with the issuance of the German exit permit. In addition, my father had to "aryanize" his business, which meant he had to "sell" it to an Aryan.

Since it was a metal refining plant and had military utility, my father would not be granted permission to leave the country until he had fully trained his successor, August Hetzel. All money paid for the business was taxed at 100 percent. That was not of much consequence, though: although my parents could ship their furniture out of the country, they were prohibited from taking any liquid assets in excess of the equivalent of about ten dollars. Hetzel renamed the business "Alt und Neu Metalworks"—Old and New Metalworks—so he could retain the Alfred Ney Metalworks trademark with the smoke rising from the vertical of the *N*.

Finally, in the spring of 1939, my parents were granted permission to leave Germany. However, their United States number had not yet come up. Where could they go? Stephen Wiseman, who had been waiting for me in vain at Liverpool Station, came to their rescue again and arranged for a one-year entry into the United Kingdom with himself as guarantor for our support. My parents shipped all their furniture to the United States, to be placed in storage in Philadelphia where our sponsor family lived.

A condition of our entry into England prohibited my parents from gainful employment. Stephen Wiseman felt a responsibility for his relatives, the Frankens and their family. Because of the Frankens' gratitude to my parents following Kristallnacht and their daughter Ellen's close friendship with my mother, he generously took on the additional financial responsibility of our family. We were entirely financially dependent on Stephen Wiseman during our year in England.

The eight of us lived in a small but adequate house at 26 Alba Gardens, in Golders Green, a section of London predominately inhabited by German Jewish refugees.

During the summer of 1939, I was looking forward to entering a public school in September. This would have been a first for me. But on September 1, 1939, two months before my eighth birthday, Germany invaded Poland and Britain declared war on Germany. My entry into the public education system was delayed once again.

Those first days of September were filled with excitement. A lot of energy was expended with very little accomplished. Trucks rumbled into the intersection at the end of Alba Gardens, and men in uniform unloaded wooden building materials and sheets of corrugated metal.

The residents of the street gathered around a soldier who was giving instructions.

Each family was to dig a hole 4 ½ feet wide, 6 ½ feet long, and 4 feet deep in our backyards. When the hole was completed, we would be given building materials to complete the air-raid shelter as described in a mimeographed sheet the soldier distributed. We also were to tape all our windows, as illustrated on the sheet.

On that first day of World War II, the eight residents of 26 Alba Gardens, none of whom had ever attempted any productive physical labor, enthusiastically started to dig a hole using shovels, picks, and even kitchen utensils. We were now in the war. Our patriotic fervor was evident as the eight of us, regardless of age, threw ourselves into our duties. Even though we were just digging a hole, it became a glorious act for England, leading to the defeat of the hated Germans.

My mother, with Ellen Dietenhofer and her parents, began working on the blackout window coverings once it became apparent that we had only two makeshift shovels that could be used to work efficiently on the shelter.

Ellen's son, Theo, and I were assigned the job of taping all the window glass from corner to corner, top to bottom, and side to side with strips of gummed-paper tape, so that each window had the appearance of a brown Union Jack. While taping the windows, with patriotic music from the radio in the background, we told each other tales of what we would do to any German soldiers we could catch. As would be expected, the handiwork of two eight-year-old boys was not the neatest, but we were hopeful that it would keep any shattered glass, resulting from exploding bombs, from slicing us to pieces.

After a few hours of digging, my father and Ellen's husband, Fritz, had dug out an irregular rectangular hole that was only about a foot deep. It was starting to get dark, and since the blackout curtains were not completed, we would not be able to have any lights on within the house. Ellen and my mother prepared a hasty dinner by the fading light. We finished our meal in the dark, and everyone went to bed early since we could not see. The completion of the shelter and blackout curtains would have to wait until dawn.

A truck with a loudspeaker rumbled down the street and announced that at 8:30 AM everyone was to report to the corner where we would be issued gas masks, which, we learned, we would always have to keep with us. We also were cautioned to be certain that no light from the house was visible from the street. Anyone in violation would be subject to serious penalties. Since we in 26 Alba Gardens were not even close to blacking out our windows, we complied by keeping the house totally dark.

At the crack of dawn, Fritz and my father again started digging the hole for the air-raid shelter. Theo and I wanted to help, but there was only a coal shovel and a garden spade available; it had been determined early on that the kitchen utensils could not be utilized. However, we watched, and whenever the diggers took a break, we took up the shovels of our respective fathers. As we struck the earth with our shovels, using the full force of our bodies, we sang *There'll Always Be an England* at the top of our lungs.

At 8:00 AM, the eight of us gathered in the front of the house and walked as a group to the corner, where a crowd had already gathered. Our neighbors were lined up in a queue in typical British fashion. Men in uniform fitted each individual with a gas mask, issued in a cardboard carrying box that had a twisted wood fiber cord for hanging it from the neck or shoulder. I placed the cord around my neck, and then, because the wood fiber cord was very scratchy, I carried the box under my arm. We were instructed on how to place the mask on our faces and breathe through the mask. Everyone had a great deal of difficulty putting on the masks; we were told to practice until we could put it on within a minute. We were told that we were to have the mask with us at all times, which was a real problem with that scratchy cord. This was beginning to sound like serious business.

After several days of digging the shelter, we encountered several large rocks. The first protruded from one of the sides of the hole, about two feet from the surface. There was no way to move it, so we designated it a bench. Large immovable rocks were uncovered in several areas of the hole. It became clear that we would never reach the required four-foot depth, and therefore we would not be issued the six-foot corrugated metal sheets that would form the sides and roof of the shelter.

Fritz and my father scavenged some scrap lumber and attempted to construct a roof over the shallow hole. They hoped this would provide some protection if we were to crawl under it in the event of a bombing raid. They placed wood timbers diagonally across the hole, and laid plywood on top. Fortunately, the fragility of our shelter was demonstrated before a real air raid, when Fritz threw a hammer onto the roof and the roof immediately collapsed into the hole.

I received some bad news that first week of September: The school I had excitedly anticipated attending, as my first normal public school, would not open. The authorities had determined that its modern steel-and-glass structure would be unsafe in the event of an air raid.

All of the children who were scheduled to attend the school were reassigned to other schools. Theo and I were reassigned to La Sagesse, a Catholic convent school run by an order of French nuns. As far as I knew, Theo and I were the only Jewish students among the transfers from public school into the otherwise Catholic student population. We also were the only ones who spoke no French and had no familiarity with Latin. Le Sagesse was constructed of large stone blocks and resembled a Renaissance church. It looked so powerful and imposing that I was sure it could take a direct hit and the students and nuns would survive. Thus my concerns were not of the German bombs, but the French nuns in their frightening black habits.

Most of the academic classes were taught in French; the daily religious classes were in Latin. We transfers were intermingled with the regular students. Daily, the whole student body was assembled in a church-like building with row upon row of benches. The fact that I could not understand any of the Latin, which comprised the majority of the religious service, was not my most serious problem, though. I worried about appearing as a perennial outsider by standing or sitting when all the others were kneeling; and I didn't know how or when to make the unfamiliar sign of the cross. I became expert at watching the other students and using their slightest movement as a tip-off indicating what I was expected to do.

During one day's religious service, we had a particularly terrifying silent movie shown to us. It centered on the crucifixion and what would happen to sinners and non-believers. I knew I was a non-believer, and what was in store for me was hardly pleasant. For most of my life, experiences like these taught me that being Jewish might not be a real advantage.

One day, I experienced severe panic when I had to go to the bathroom during class. I did not know how to ask permission or directions to the bathroom in French, and the nun did not immediately understand my newly acquired English. When she finally granted me permission, my urgency had become an emergency.

I left the room in a run with no idea where I should be going. I found myself in a dimly lit hallway, surrounded by very large statues that I assumed were important religious, possibly divine, persons. My desperation was so severe that I relieved myself next to one of the statues. I was certain that now there would be no salvation for me. I was destined to live for eternity in flames and smoke, just like those sinners in the movie.

In addition to getting acclimated to school, I faced the constant anticipation of air raids and air-raid drills. The first one took place before our blackout curtains were finished. We never knew if it was real or a drill. When the wail of sirens sounded, we all got up in the dark, carried our gas masks, and negotiated the stairs to assemble in the pantry—our substitute temporary air-raid shelter.

After about ten minutes, we became concerned that the Frankens were not with us. What could have happened to them? After the all clear sounded, we found them still in their room trying to get their gas masks on. Happily, they had not succeeded, as it would have been impossible for them to safely walk down the darkened hallway and staircase wearing their gas masks. We had developed a gallows humor, which found the predicament of the old people attempting to put gas masks on in the dark before coming down to the pantry hilariously funny.

Barrage balloons, large blimp-like shapes filled with gas and held to the ground by steel cables, now were floating in the sky over the city. They were part of the British air-defense system, designed to discourage low level and dive-bombing raids.

As winter approached, the blackout curtains were completed and installed, the air-raid shelter was abandoned, and the sloppy window taping was replaced by neater Union Jack patterns. We settled into normal wartime life in London, with the families gathered in the living room in front of the fireplace—the only source of heat in a British house. The radio in the room was always on to follow the war news and listen to patriotic songs.

My primary interest was to complete my collection of pictures of warplanes that came with Players cigarettes, my father's only luxury. I had almost filled the album that was distributed by the Players Company.

I frequently played with Theo on the sidewalk in front of the house. One of our favorite pastimes was floating sticks and paper on the runoff in the gutter. Nina, an English girl who lived in the corner house, often played with us. I felt privileged that such a pretty girl would play with us refugees. When she was around, I always hoped that Theo would be called into the house. Siegfried, a refugee teenager, sometimes joined the group as well. I hated Siegfried, first for competing for Nina's attention, and second for his Germanic name and what I perceived to be a German accent. I frequently tormented him, and hoped to embarrass him in front of Nina by singing the early war song, *We Will Hang Our Wash on the Siegfried Line*, in reference to the German fortifications. One day, he had had enough and proceeded to beat me up. I thought the beating was worthwhile, though, because Nina showed a great deal of concern for my bloody nose.

For years, as I heard about the massive air raids on London, I fantasized about saving Nina from a burning corner house that had been bombed. I never found out if she survived the war.

– 4 –

Coming to America

My mother was biting her lower lip, and her face had that combination of anger, frustration, and fear I had learned to recognize as a signal for me to stay out of the way. It was not a good sign, so I went into the living room—leaving her to stare out the kitchen window at the falling snow. I leafed through my collection of airplane cards from Players cigarettes.

"How will we get to Liverpool tomorrow in this snow?" she asked.

"I'm sure the trains will be running," my father said, to reassure her. "I have heard nothing on the radio about train or air interruption."

"Don't talk like a fool!" my mother angrily responded. "Do you think the radio would broadcast that no flights could take off, and let the Germans know they could bomb London without any resistance? And how do you think we will get to the train station in this snow?" she added as a postscript. "Do you propose we walk?"

My father also took the hint, and walked away in frustration. He kept out of the way, checking our passports, papers, and tickets, for what seemed like the hundredth time.

"Lady, make sure you have everything. I assure you I won't be coming back," the cabby said authoritatively in his cockney accent as he drove away from the curb. The snow had been falling for days, and on each side of the street there were mounds taller than people.

"We must be on the train to Liverpool in two hours. Will you get us to the station in time?" my mother asked worriedly. After all the waiting, would a snowstorm prevent us from getting to the United States?

"Mum, I'll get you there, but I can't guarantee the trains will be running in this weather," the cabbie replied.

I looked out the window at 26 Alba Gardens and knew this would be my last view of the house that my parents and I had shared with two other families for almost a year. I thought of the air-raid shelter we had built in the backyard in the first few days of the war; and how, whenever we hit hard earth or a rock while digging, we had agreed that this would be a good place for a seat and had dug around the obstruction. The shelter, built half below ground and half above, was now covered with snow and looked more like an Eskimo's igloo than a formidable war-like structure of corrugated steel.

I know I'll never see it again. I wonder who will use it. Will we ever have to build another? My thoughts then wandered to leaving Nina. I looked at the sky and saw, through the fog and light snow, the barrage balloons tethered by long cables which were intended to shear the wings off any low-flying German bombers.

My parents discussed the possible consequences of our missing the ship in Liverpool. Would our precious visas still be honored? We had waited a year for our immigration number to come up. Would this be all in vain because of the snowstorm?

We shared the railroad compartment with my uncle Kurt, his fiancée Cilly, and her daughter Ruth. They had lived in another part of London, but their immigration numbers had come up at the same time as ours. There also were three British sailors who regaled us with stories of their ship being torpedoed out from under them and their eventual rescue. This terrified fifteen-year-old Ruth.

My mother had prepared sandwiches at our house in London; we finished them on the train, arriving in Liverpool very late at night. Outside the station it was pitch black—no streetlights, no traffic. We had paid the cabby in London with the last of our money, so even if taxis had been running, without headlights, we could not have afforded one. At this stage of our trip, we were literally penniless.

England had been at war for four months. From the first day, blackout curtains had to be used to prevent all interior light from escaping to the outside; automobiles were not permitted to drive with their lights on; and street lamps were turned off. Air-raid wardens, who were men too old for military service, relished giving orders, in their British style military helmets, to enforce these regulations.

It had stopped snowing, but the mounds of snow, sometimes visible by moonlight, towered higher than any of the six of us. My father carried our only marketable possession, a portable typewriter in its case. Since we could not see, frequently one or all of us fell into a pile of snow. After a short while, we were all laughing hysterically. The scene of four adults and two children walking in blackness without a destination, falling into snow drifts, struck us all as hilariously funny, even though we didn't know what this night or the long-term future held for any of us.

We all were starting to feel very chilled. "Would a hotel let us stay in the lobby just to get out of the cold?" my parents wondered. Even if we had found a hotel with an available room, we could not have paid for it.

My mother, who spoke the best English in the group, was designated as spokesperson, in case we found anything promising. We passed a building and could hear the faint singing of *We'll Hang Our Wash on the Siegfried Line.* It was the song, referring to the German fortifications at the French frontier, that I had used to torment the teenager in Alba Gardens. In the darkness, someone felt a wall that led to a large doorway. My mother was sent on her mission.

"We are lucky!" my mother excitedly announced. "We have found a hotel! They are so full they have even rented out their broom closets, but they will let us stay in the lobby, if we can find any space."

We crowded through the door, and when all of us were in the blackened foyer, and the outside door was closed, my mother opened the blackout curtain to reveal the pandemonium in the lobby. British sailors, and a few soldiers, were spread over the lobby like a human carpet, with not a sober man among them. Their song had now melded into *The White Cliffs of Dover.*

Finding a piece of furniture to sit on was an impossibility; finding a space on the floor would be a luxury. A thoroughly drunk petty officer offered his loveseat to my mother "for the little chap." He ordered some of the sailors to squeeze together to let some of us sit on the floor. After he arranged for our accommodation, he promptly threw up and passed out, disappearing behind the back of the loveseat.

"Where am I?" I asked. "In one of the finest hotels in Liverpool—the Adelphia Hotel," an adult responded.

After a few more war songs, I drifted off to sleep wondering if the Adelphia Hotel had any connection with our going to Philadelphia, rather than New York where everyone else seemed to be going.

The six of us and some of the sailors headed for the pier area as dawn broke. We found our pier and crowded into what seemed like a large shack with windows on three sides. As I looked out, in the fog of dawn, it appeared as if we were high above the water and the concrete pier. *Where was the ship?* After what seemed like forever, I could make out a gigantic, dark shape. As it approached, I saw it was a ship with a very large cannon jutting out above its prow.

The ship inched next to the pier. A figure crouched outside the railing near the prow, holding onto the icy railing with one hand and using the other hand to throw a line to men standing on the concrete pier below. The man, who had appeared above us, must have slipped on his icy perch and lost his grip, tumbling to the freezing water below. His paperboy cap floated behind him. I did not see him being pulled from the water, but the adults assured me he definitely was safe.

A walkway extended from the end of our structure to a large opening in the side of the ship. We got in a long line and walked slowly along the gangplank into the blue-gray ship. "Did anyone see the name of the ship?" people asked repeatedly. No one answered, though, because there was no name on the prow. The ship, with its exterior military appearance, took on a new character as we entered; we found ourselves in the lap of luxury. Crystal chandeliers, dark polished wood furniture, ornate carpets, and an elaborate stairway greeted us. My father opened the drawer of a writing desk and pulled out a sheet of stationery. "Welcome to the HMS *Georgic*," he announced.

The cabins had been converted to more utilitarian, military-style accommodations, with steel stacked bunk beds. We were delighted to be on board. At noon, we heard the gong of an old-style luxury ship announcing lunch. The dining room was as ornate and luxurious as the salon. To top things off, a printed menu was at each place setting. Most of the passengers were fleeing for their lives, Europe was immersed in a world war, and we were being served lunch by dark-suited waiters—a real "Ship of Fools."

As we awoke the next morning, assuming we had headed out to sea during the night, everyone commented, "What a wonderful ship; I could not feel a thing." We found our way to the deck, and, as we looked over the side, we discovered we were still tied to the pier. We stayed moored for two days, and my parents were delighted since the passage had been paid for, and the longer we were on the ship the longer we were fed and housed. We had no idea, though, how we would support ourselves in America.

On deck, I discovered horse stalls quartering about thirty horses. The crew explained that, as a precaution, the British thoroughbred bloodlines were being sent to America for safe keeping in case England was invaded. There was a persistent rumor that we were not yet starting our voyage because part of the British gold reserves would be coming with us to America, for safekeeping.

During our two-day stay, while the *Georgic* was tied to the pier, a memorable family picture was taken. This photo portrays our group lined up by height: I was in front, wearing my school cap; followed by Ruth; her mother, Cilly; a friend of my father's who happened to be on the ship and owned the camera that took the picture; Kurt; and my mother and father. If the picture had not been taken then, it never would have been taken, because once the ship headed out to sea, there never was a time when our group was uniformly well enough to smile for a picture. Several months later, each family received a copy of the picture, which we all treasure. My mother inscribed the back, "Trip to Freedom."

On the third day, the engines quivered and shook the whole ship. The large bulkhead doors between sections below deck were closed and sealed. Now, the only way to get from the front of the ship to the rear was to go up and over one floor at a time. I always got lost trying to navigate back to our cabin. I was on deck as the ship cleared Liverpool harbor and saw the litter of half-sunk hulls of ships, victims of U-boat attacks. I still remember a ship split in half with all the floors exposed.

We had been told that we would be traveling in convoy, but during the entire trip we never saw another ship. To avoid U-boats, we took a zigzag course, heading into the stormiest part of the North Atlantic. Everyone, including the crew, was seasick, so the orderlies constantly had to clean the carpeted hallways. The passengers tried to spend as much time as possible on deck for air, but the vision of the rolling sea did not help matters. Sometimes, the waves broke across the decks, and water rushed down the stairways. Rumors circulated that a torpedo had hit us. At night, there was no light on, inside or outside the ship. We traveled in total blackness except for the moonlight.

After a day at sea, my thoughts turned to Nina, whom I knew I would never see again. I went to the lounge where, in each desk, there was stationery inscribed, "Cunard White Star *Georgic*."

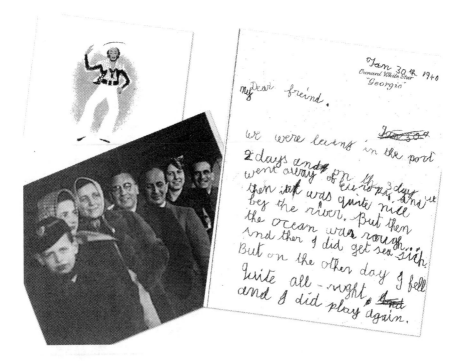

I started the letter, "Dear freind." I described our two days in port and our trip in the rough ocean. I squeezed "My" in front of the "Dear freind" to make the letter more affectionate. The letter was never sent; I believe it was because the price of the postage stamp would have been considered a frivolous expenditure that my parents could ill afford.

Late one afternoon, after our tenth day at sea, the ship's engine slowed. We had gotten so used to the steady noise and trembling of the ship's steel structure that the change was like a loudspeaker announcement. What was happening? I saw three crewmembers throw a rope sea ladder over the side, not far from where I was standing; as I looked over the railing, I saw a small ship, far below, bobbing up and down in the waves. Its flag had red and white stripes with a blue field in its upper left-hand corner I recognized the flag of the United States.

Several men in uniform climbed up the ladder and went to the bridge. Some of the adults said one was the pilot who would guide the ship the rest of the way. We watched as the sun set, and soon the darkness of night enveloped us again. We were sure we must now be near New York.

The news, which spread like wildfire through the ship, was encapsulated in a single word that everyone knew the meaning of and shouted repeatedly—"Light!" The excitement that word engendered is hard to believe unless you have experienced total darkness outside at night for four months. It was as if Thomas Edison had reinvented the light bulb.

All the passengers surged on deck to see this wonder for themselves. I looked across the bow of the ship to marvel at the glow of lights as the ship lurched forward toward this phenomenon. After about an hour, I could see the glow was made of tiny pinpricks of light. It became apparent, as the ship drew closer, that the lights were coming from the tallest buildings I had ever seen.

My parents, engaged in intense conversation, were discussing new worries. Since it was Sunday, would the ship be unloaded today? Would the immigrants have to go through Ellis Island? Would my father pass the physical with his leg that had been severely injured in the World War? Would our sponsors renege on their obligation?

My mother, yet again, was biting her lip with that expression of anger, frustration, and fear. My father repeated what he had cabled our sponsors, "Promise faithfully never to be a burden." The cable's stilted wording was the result of its having been composed, word for word, from a German-English dictionary.

"Look, look, there she is! Look in the fog! See her?" I saw the silhouette of the lady with her arm held high, holding a lit torch. Tears of joy were in the eyes of each passenger. I don't believe a native-born American could ever experience quite the emotion every immigrant feels on seeing this lady.

The ship docked at the Cunard White Star pier amid considerable excitement. Immigration officials boarded the ship, and all passengers were told to wait in the lounge area until their names were called. The anxiety of the refugee passengers, including my parents, was at a feverish pitch since anything could still go wrong. As we stood in front of the immigration officials who examined our papers, even I was trembling.

We had given them our German passports, with the German eagle clutching the swastika on the cover and the large purple *J* on the inside page, and they stamped the last page of each passport with a stamp that covered the entire page. That was a good sign, and my parents seemed relieved. The officials had written something on each of the stamps. As soon as they handed the passports back to us, they asked us to return them. My parents panicked! The officials had mixed up my parents' passports and only had to correct the names they had filled in on the last pages. My parents were almost in tears as, once again, they received their passports with permission to disembark.

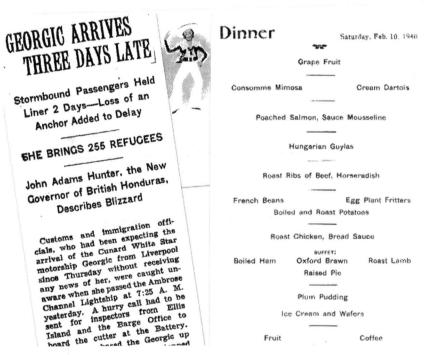

The 255 refugee passengers could hardly believe they had actually made it and were being admitted to the United States. Cargo and luggage were being unloaded as we made our way down the gangplank. Kurt, Cilly, and my parents discussed how to get in touch with friends who would house us for a few days.

As we waited on the pier for my parents' friends, I noticed black men working. I had never before seen a black person. I excitedly pointed out this phenomenon to my parents, shouting, "Look! Look! See the *Neger!*" the proper German word for a black person. My parents had the good sense to shut me up, though it reminded me of the times when I was dragged away from the exciting parades in Nuremberg, and I thought, "They still don't get it when there is something exciting to see."

I saw many blacks as we drove in my parents' friends' car through Manhattan and the edge of Central Park. It was Sunday, and the men were dressed in what I later learned were called "zoot suits." These were outfits in spectacular colors of light blue and pink, with baggy pants cuffed tight at the ankles. Coming from England, where all the men I'd seen were white and dressed in black, I was certain this was one sight the other passengers in the car had to see immediately because it certainly would be gone by tomorrow. None of the adults' assurances could convince me this was not a one-day event.

We stayed in my parents' friends' basement for a few days until we could go to Philadelphia to meet our sponsors. This indeed was a marvelous country! Our hosts had been here only two years and they had a car and were living in a house.

– 5 –

Boardinghouse

My parents and I stood on the porch at 3833 North Seventeenth Street in Philadelphia awaiting the arrival of our "lifts." The truck turned up the narrow street loaded with two enormous wooden containers that looked to me as large as two small rooms.

The construction of lifts, wooden shipping crates, had become a substantial industry in Germany during the late thirties and boomed after Kristallnacht, when Jews panicked and fled, facing the reality that there would be no future for them or their children in Germany.

The problem confronting most of the Jewish emigrants was finding a country that would admit them. Here, my parents' foresight paid off. Years previously, my parents had applied to the United States for immigration visas and had obtained a sponsor—a cousin of my father's mother who lived in Philadelphia, and who had generously agreed to be financially responsible for us so that we would not become public charges. The United States had very limited immigration quotas and it took years to get to the front of the line.

The Nazis, who wanted the Jews to emigrate, implemented policies that would support the economy by permitting Jews to take their furniture and clothing with them and use their assets to purchase transportation out of the country. However, Jews were strictly prohibited from taking with them any jewelry, artwork, or money beyond the equivalent of ten dollars per person. Before they could obtain permission to emigrate, they were subject to various special taxes and fees levied on the value of all their liquid assets. Penalties amounting to 100 percent of assets remaining at the time of departure had to be paid to the German government. My father had paid for steamship tickets to New York and the cost of packing and shipping the lifts to Philadelphia. However, it had taken almost a full year for our family to follow our furniture to Philadelphia and storage costs had accumulated in that time. These fees had to be paid before we could get our furniture.

Although we were very grateful to our sponsors, the Mandels, for their assistance, it had quickly become evident that this childless couple was not prepared to offer any long-term hospitality to us foreigners. Mrs. Mandel made it clear that we must live independently as soon as possible. I don't think they had anticipated our arriving without any assets whatsoever.

It must have been the most painful and degrading day of my father's life when he went to see Ellis Gimbel, head of Philadelphia's Gimbel Brothers Department Store. Ellis's father, Adam Gimbel, had immigrated to the United States from Germany in the nineteenth century, settling in Vincennes, Indiana, where he opened a general store and fathered seven sons, who founded the Gimbel Brothers Department Store chain. Adam's sister, Amelia, had married my great-grandfather, Abraham Ney.

Wearing his best suit and highly polished shoes to his appointment with the very important head of the large department store, my father made sure to bring a photograph he had taken of the grave monument of his grandparents, Abraham and Amelia. Although Ellis Gimbel had not answered my father's plea to sponsor our immigration to America, as the Mandels had, my father believed that Ellis would be interested in his family history. He hoped that this interest might translate into some help.

When my father returned from the meeting, he explained that Ellis had expressed absolutely no interest in the photo of his aunt's tombstone, but had agreed to give my father enough money to bail out our furniture and pay for two months' rent. My mother wanted to turn the rental into a boarding house, both to bring in some money and enable her to take care of me when I was not at school. I'm sure

Ellis thought he would never see his two hundred dollars again, but my father insisted that this was a loan to be repaid as soon as possible.

So, here we were, watching the flatbed truck, with the two large wooden containers, slowly rumble up Seventeenth Street and stop in front of our house. The truck blocked the narrow street, and two muscular black men jumped out of the truck cab on our side. The sight of black people still fascinated me. The white driver came around the truck and handed my father a sheaf of papers, while the black men started to pry open the wooden timbers that made up the top of the first crate. I could see into the crate, since the house was quite a bit higher than the street, and I spotted rectangular cushions that I had last seen, more than a year ago, on our couch in Nuremberg. When one side of the container was removed, I saw parts of familiar furniture stacked vertically. All the spaces between the furniture were filled with cushions, pillows, and rugs. As the furniture was brought up the steps, my parents directed the men to various rooms. The men also carried up boxes of pots and pans, clothing, soap, and cleaning products. It seemed that nothing salvageable had been left behind.

I found toys, games, and books that I had not seen for about eighteen months. Although they seemed familiar to me, I had forgotten that I had played with most of them. The only item I immediately connected with my past was the big red box containing "The Autobahn." This consisted of two small cars and about thirty pieces of pressed metal track—some straight and others curved—which would set up in a figure eight with a bridge crossing over the midpoint in the track. The track would let two cars go in opposite directions; the speed controls were on the back of a pressed metal gas station. My father had also packed a transformer that could accept 110-volt U.S. current for the electric-powered track. The Autobahn had been my present for my seventh birthday, the day after Kristallnacht, and of course I wanted to set it up immediately, amid the disorder of moving in, just as I had on my birthday a year and a half earlier in Nuremberg, amid the disorder of our smashed furniture.

My parents convinced me to wait until we were settled and then set it up in their bedroom, where I was to sleep on a couch with a raised head. The other bedrooms were to be rented out to provide our family with income for the first time since my parents had left Germany.

As I remember, we got boarders very quickly. Like us, they were refugees from Germany: the Feder brothers Paul, in his fifties, and George, in his forties; and Werner Schlesinger, who was in his twenties. My mother cooked breakfast and dinner for them and did their laundry. My parents, although impoverished, appeared genuinely happy starting over in the United States where there was now some permanency after years of uncertainty.

Every day, my father went out looking for a job. Initially, he sought to capitalize on his past experience, and he looked for employment with metal companies, but he had no success. Becoming desperate, he started to look for menial jobs. He still dressed as he had as a factory owner in Germany, wearing a dark suit, white shirt with necktie, and polished shoes. Once he was gone all day, which was a good sign; when he returned, he had a few dollars that he had earned doing odd jobs.

One day had been bittersweet. In his normal executive dress, he had applied for a job at a sweatshop where shirts were manufactured. He told us that the owner, without looking up, had said, "See that nail on the wall? Hang your coat on it and go to that ironing board and start ironing that pile of shirts." My father had never used an iron before. He lasted all day on his feet, doing the best he could, and was paid a welcome few dollars; however, he was not asked to come back.

After about two weeks of frustration, having had only a few hours work in addition to that one day spent ironing newly manufactured shirts, my father had a second appointment with Ellis Gimbel. This time it resulted in his employment as a stock clerk in the china department at Gimbel's department store, where his work consisted of pushing a stock cart and tending to displays. I never heard him complain about having descended in two years, at the age of forty-six, from being a successful businessman with his own factory to working as a stock clerk for a minimum wage. He remained hopeful that eventually he would secure employment in his line of work.

I looked forward to attending Grover Cleveland Elementary School, the first time I would go to a "normal" public school, just like a "normal" kid. In Germany, the Nuremberg laws had prohibited me from attending a public school. In England, Stephen Wiseman had appropriately enrolled me in the New Herlingen boarding school until my parents could arrive. The school year was just about over when I moved with my parents to Alba Gardens; then just before the new school year was to start the war began. The authorities determined that the modern glass and steel school I had been assigned to was unsafe in the event of an air attack; therefore, some other students and I were assigned to La Sagesse Convent, a catholic school administered by an order of French nuns.

My first week at Grover Cleveland, however, was quite a shock.

I knew I was expected to make friends, and I had seen other kids play together; also, I had heard stories and learned to read enough to know that normal children had friends and playmates. I had had few playmates, though, and I decided I was not normal.

In Nuremberg, aside from our periodic elevator games and a few days playing in the snow, I had had very little contact with the two girls in the apartment above ours, who were a few years older than I was. Our respective parents were concerned for our safety and did not frequently permit us to play outside the apartment house. In England, I had played with Theo, who thought of me as a younger newcomer he could not be bothered with; and we had known Siegfried and Nina as well.

That first day at Cleveland Elementary in Philadelphia did not start well. I was dressed in my very best clothes from Germany when my parents took me to school: dark long pants, white shirt with necktie, a cap, and, worst of all, new shoes that had buckles.

We walked past some tough-looking kids in slovenly clothes; some wore knickers. I noticed that the boys were in two separate groups: White boys like me on one side of the schoolyard, and, across the schoolyard, dark-skinned boys. I could feel the hostility from the whites as we walked to the principal's office. He was a very nice, short man who listened attentively to my parents struggling with their English as they explained my fragmented educational history. Based primarily on my age, he decided that I would start in the third grade. My parents kissed me goodbye with the admonition to be good and cause no trouble. I knew it would not be a good day if any student saw this.

I was taken to Miss Whitaker's third-grade classroom where class was already in session. I stood in front of the class with Miss Whitaker at my side. Her hand was on my shoulder. She explained that I had just arrived from England, and hoped my classmates would welcome me. I was directed to take a seat in the back while snickers drifted across the room, descending on me like a black cloud.

Miss Whitaker sat down at the piano, announcing, "do, re, mi," as she played three notes. Using a pointer, she indicated a series of horizontal lines with dots on them. I had never seen anything like this before and became filled with terror.

I had left Germany knowing only German. Within six months, I had learned English; then, at La Sagesse Convent, I had been forced to learn French and Latin to communicate with the French nuns who were my teachers. Now, I again was faced with an incomprehensible language.

What could it possibly mean? I knew a doe was a deer, and as the class recited "fa, re, so, mi, do," I was certain this was a story about the forest, inhabited by animals, birds, and perhaps, a hunter. My classmates seemed hostile; I certainly was not going to raise my hand, ask a stupid question, and bring more attention to myself. Aware of my promise to my parents that I would not cause any trouble, I decided to try figuring it out for myself. I never did learn to read music.

Recess was painful. My funny clothing, particularly those buckled shoes, brought more ridicule my way. When I spoke, although in fluent English, I had a distinctive English accent, which gave me a distinctively non-masculine image. My first day at a "normal" school was decidedly not a success.

I quickly learned to lose my English accent and attempted to adopt a Philadelphia style of speech. Most people who leave that city work very hard to lose their ugly accent; I was probably the only person in history to actually try to speak like a Philadelphian.

The clothing was another problem; there absolutely was no way my parents could buy me any new clothing. My mother tried hard to modify the offensive buckled shoes by cutting the buckle and strap off and hoped that I could keep the shoes from falling off my feet. Since my parents had sent clothing and shoes in various sizes for me, I ended up wearing shoes that were either too large or too small to avoid the modified buckled shoes.

During my first week at school, I had permanently destroyed my image with the tough boys on the playground. During the second week, I thought perhaps I could get some favorable attention from a few of the girls. Since I had never seen any "negroes" before arriving in the United States, I treated them like a curiosity—and stared. One girl in a group jumping rope had lighter skin than the others; I thought she was very pretty. I was trying to show my interest by chasing her across the schoolyard when one of the dark-skinned girls shouted, knocked me to the ground, punched me, and repeatedly scratched my face. I was very embarrassed having to explain my scratched face to my parents. The last thing I wanted was for my parents, who never did get it, to intervene at school on my behalf.

During my fourth week at Cleveland Elementary, the principal entered Miss Whitaker's classroom with a girl about five years older than the rest of us students. She wore a dark green *Loden* coat, which identified her to me as another refugee. Miss Whitaker introduced her to the class and we were told that she spoke no English. Since I was the only other refugee in the class, I hoped she would be seated next to me and I would be assigned to help her get adjusted. Perhaps, though,

Miss Whitaker had heard about my social success in the schoolyard, because she declined to give me the opportunity to guide the girl who, it turned out, was severely retarded.

My home life in the boarding house was no better than my life at school, although it did have the advantage of being safe from the shame of being beaten up by a girl. The primary purpose of the boarding house was to give us a basic income while giving me a mother at home when I was not at school, so I felt it was my fault, in a way, that three additional men were living in our home and sitting at our dinner table. I had to stay out of the way of the boarders. But, I had discovered radio and was in another world from the time I came home from school until they returned from work.

Each hour in late afternoon was divided into four fifteen-minute segments of serial stories. At four in the afternoon, I was glued to the radio for the start of *Jack Armstrong: The All-American Boy*. If only I could be All-American, my problems would be solved. He never got beaten up by a girl, or wore funny clothes that people made fun of because his parents could not afford to buy any replacements, or spoke with a funny accent. He didn't live in a boarding house, and, best of all, he was All-American, not a refugee! Immediately following was *Terry and the Pirates*. Terry's battles with America's enemies in Asia put him in the company of beautiful and exotic women. Sometimes, even the enemy was beautiful and exotic like the Dragon Lady.

The dialog and sound effects created a world so realistic that the stories and characters came to life in my mind. The eight stories between 4:00 PM and 6:00 PM were the highlight of my day, a chance to escape the reality of my school and home.

Two favorites, *Little Orphan Annie* and *Captain Midnight*, had generous sponsors who sent premiums to their listeners upon receipt of a label and a dime. *Little Orphan Annie* was sponsored by the Quaker Oats Company, which would send a complete airplane cockpit, with some assembly required from the cardboard sheets that arrived in the mail. It took quite some time to convince my mother that Quaker Oats was essential to my health, and send in the required label and ten cents. *Captain Midnight's* sponsor was the maker of Ovaltine, a drink filled with essential vitamins, and guaranteed to make you tall and strong. Unless my mother bought Ovaltine, I would be doomed to be beaten up by girls for the rest of my life. Also, possibly of equal importance, I would not be able to get the seal that was under the screw-on top of the jar and was required to get the secret decoder ring for decoding the Captain's secret message which concluded each day's broadcast. I never could get all the Ovaltine crystals to dissolve in either cold or hot milk, but it did make me tall—I was a six-foot three-inch teenager—although not strong.

I willingly suspended reality to follow Superman, the man of steel who was faster than a speeding bullet, more powerful than a locomotive, and always fighting on the side of justice and the American way. Lois Lane was always at his side, unaware that Clark Kent, a wimp like me, had only to step into a phone booth to rescue her, or the city, from criminals or dictators.

I thought a radio was the greatest luxury I could wish for. After the boarders got home, my parents' radio dial was immediately turned from my serials to world news. Everyone in the house, except my mother who was busy preparing dinner, clustered around the radio to listen to the deep voice of Gabriel Heater, who told us the bad news of the German advance through Europe. Sometimes the radio was tuned to Nathan Fleisher, a Yiddish newscaster. None of our boarders knew Yiddish, but these German-Jewish refugees were able to understand the program because Yiddish used derivations of German. In spite of the terrible news, the fractured German provided amusement to the group. Eastern European Jews had preceded them to America by a generation and, therefore, were economically far more secure than the German refugees who deluded themselves into thinking they were culturally superior to the Eastern European Jews, who still used Yiddish as a living language.

The only escapes from my restricted life in the boarding house were the radio, comic books, and the Saturday matinee movies. Whenever I could lay my hands on a dime, which I earned by delivering groceries for the corner grocery store, I bought a comic book or went to a Saturday matinee. There was always a double feature and at least one western serial that ended with the hero or heroine in an impossible situation. Since I was sure there was no way for them to survive, I hoped against hope to return the following Saturday. I also discovered that you could stay in your seat after you had seen both features and watch them all over again. That kept me at the movies from 10:00 AM to 6:00 PM—what a bargain!

I remember always going to the movies alone, with one exception. Friends of my parents, who had a son my age, had recently arrived from Europe and were at our house on a Saturday. I was excited to show this newcomer the wonders of America. We saw the two features more than two times, and everyone was frantic when we returned to the boarding house at 8:00 PM. It seemed like an eternity before I was permitted again to see a Saturday movie.

Once, I came home from the movies and proudly announced that the following week I would return with five dollars. A man who sat next to me in the movies had whispered that he would give me a present of five dollars if I would meet him in the back of the movie house the next Saturday. I never did tell my parents that he had started his conversation by reaching over and squeezing my upper thigh. Even with that omission, I was restricted from going to the movies—this time until I was over ten years old.

Comic books were considered a corrupting influence on minors at that time, so I hid my treasures in the bench that I had used as a toy chest in Germany. The bench was a black carved antique, which had sustained a hatchet mark during Kristallnacht. Some of the carvings were particularly interesting: bare-breasted women with two sets of breasts. As a teenager, I stored material more corrupting than comic books in that appropriately carved bench.

On my tenth birthday, my parents, the boarders, and some of my parents' friends celebrated with cake and ice cream in our dining room; no children my age were present. The boarders made a large cardboard card commemorating my birthday, with poetry and clippings cut from newspapers and glued on the card. The only presents I really wanted were a dog or a radio, both of which were impossible. My mother gave me a very small wooden toy dog as a substitute. The boarders and my parents also gave me a few dimes and quarters for my movie pursuits.

One Sunday morning after my tenth birthday, while I was straddling the porch railing with the cardboard airplane cockpit from the Little Orphan Annie sponsor in front of me and the control stick between my legs, an announcer on the radio, which was tuned to world news as usual, stated that the regular program was being interrupted. My parents heard the ensuing news in shock and hysteria. Pearl Harbor had been attacked. The war had found us again!

During this time, I went to Sunday school. My parents were not religious and had attended synagogue probably only twice a year, but because our dire circumstances were due to being Jewish, they used some convoluted logic to decide that their only son should have a rudimentary Jewish education leading to a bar mitzvah. My father talked to the rabbi about our circumstances and joined the congregation at reduced dues, but it was still a financial hardship for my family.

I tried to learn Hebrew and biblical history, but I felt even more out of place in Sunday school than in public school. In public school, I had the embarrassment of funny speech and odd clothing, but all the kids came from very poor families. In religious school, it was obvious that I was the poorest in the class. The students wore what seemed like very fine clothing and were dropped off and picked up by their parents in automobiles. I rode the subway both ways. The boys in the class talked with the teacher about the University of Pennsylvania football games they had seen. Their world was so far removed from mine that I could not comprehend my fellow students' lives—or the material covered in class. I could not wait until my bar mitzvah was over and I never had to go to a synagogue again.

It became apparent that if I were to have any friends, they would have to come from the refugee community, which was scattered throughout Philadelphia. My parents found another German-Jewish family with a son my age. Although he lived a subway ride away, Ralph Hirsch and I became friends.

I had my bar mitzvah in November 1944. My parents had a social event at the boarding house with about fifty guests, but only two were my age. One was Ralph and the other was the beautiful daughter of one of my mother's girlfriends from Nuremberg who now lived in New York. A celebrity guest of honor signed my guest book with this note, "Have faith in yourself, your country, your God, and, above all, observe the Golden Rule. Ellis A Gimbel."

My father was a very principled gentleman who defined a gentleman as a man who never hurts another unintentionally. He probably did not make that up but borrowed it from someone else. He was honest, truthful, and loyal without compromise and lived by those principles, trying to impart them to me, his only son. When I displayed improper behavior, he never raised his voice or hand to me, but tried instead to explain to me the error of my ways. Although I both respected and resented my father's rigid Germanic principles, I know that many of them became imprinted within me in spite of my strong desire to free myself of them.

My parents' primary concern was that I get a good education so I could be successful, which meant that I be able to support a family—if I were to have one. I am certain they were panic-stricken by my mediocre scholastic performance. The teachers always told them I was just not performing up to my potential, as demonstrated by objective tests that were becoming widely used at that time. My parents blamed it on laziness. They did not hide their disappointment from me, and repeatedly explained to me that they worked hard for my benefit and the least they expected from me was to succeed in school. My report card, at the end of my first semester in a normal public school, was marked "Satisfactory" in all areas but two: "Handwriting" and "Does not play well with others" were noted as needing improvement. Those marks followed me over the next few years, until report cards no longer had a place to enter "Needs improvement." It was a genuine relief to me, forty years later, to learn that I was dyslexic, and although my handwriting improved, the other need for improvement has continued up to the present.

I never can recall my father living in the past or comparing his life as the owner of a successful business in Germany with his status as a stock clerk at Gimbel Brothers department store. My mother, on the other hand, fondly reminisced about her life of leisure in Germany, although she frequently added that much of her life there had been meaningless, frivolous, and totally unrealistic.

My father talked very seriously to me about my vow to never go to religious services ever again. He told me I had a duty to all the oppressed Jews in the world never to deny my Judaism. At a minimum, I should not work on the High Holidays, and I should go to services at least once for each of the two holy days. What a responsibility—millions of oppressed Jews—for a thirteen-year-old, even though, according to Jewish tradition, the bar mitzvah ceremony marks the day when a boy becomes a man. *What kind of man?* I wondered. I was certain my parents would have described me as a lazy dreamer.

– 6 –

Awakening

Shortly after my bar mitzvah, to my great delight, we gave up the boarders. To make up for the lost income, my mother went to work at a factory that made ornamental bows for ladies' shoes. We moved to a second-floor apartment in a converted house and, best of all, I had my own room where I kept my treasured radio and could post maps on the wall using pins and flags to record the progress of the war.

It was 1944, and I was now finishing the second semester of the seventh grade at Gillespie Junior High School, a gothic structure just one block from the boarding house. My social life did not improve and I still felt like an outsider. We students were seated alphabetically in class, and one day Leitha Newton, the girl next to me, surprised me by starting a conversation. "Will you be going to the after-school dance next week?" she asked.

Thoughts raced through my head, as no one—boy or girl—had ever started a conversation with me, except to threaten me with bodily harm. Leitha, without doubt, was the prettiest girl in the school; I had better not mess up this opportunity! I did not know how to dance and was even awkward at walking. If I told her I would go, she undoubtedly would discover I could not dance, so I confessed.

She responded by inviting me to come to her house that Friday night so she could teach me how to dance. I was so excited I could barely speak. She wrote down her address and phone number. My head was spinning. I hoped I could remember every detail of those matinee movies, especially the scenes with Humphrey Bogart and Lauren Bacall—perhaps it would help if I took up smoking.

I explained to my parents that this nice girl had offered to teach me dancing on Friday and I needed carfare to get to her home. They looked at each other, acknowledging that I was getting older. They asked all sorts of questions: Was she Jewish? Where did she live? What did her parents do? Was she a good student? It was as if they could not believe that their refugee son would be invited to the house of an American unless something was wrong.

On the trolley to Leitha's house, I was more nervous and scared than on Kristallnacht or my arrival in England. She met me at the door, looking even better than she did at school. I had expected to meet her parents, but it was obvious that no one else was in the house. She took my hand and led me to the living room sofa. "When is she going to turn on the music for my dancing lesson?" I wondered. In an instant she had her arms around my neck. I was a slow learner but not that slow!

For the next two hours, we were all over the sofa and floor panting, groping, struggling with our own and each other's clothing until we lay breathless and exhausted on the floor. To top off the evening, she leaned over and gave me the most delicious goodnight kiss.

My head was spinning on the trolley ride home. I had never experienced an evening like that even in the movies. Humphrey Bogart probably would have approved but, surely, my parents would not. Before entering the apartment, I tried to straighten my clothes. I was greeted by my father calling out for me to come into my parents' bedroom.

"How was your dancing lesson?" he asked.

"Just fine," I responded, while thinking, *If he only knew.*

"What are her parents like?"

"Oh, very nice," I lied. Thank God the room was dark so he and my mother could not see my guilty face.

As the war drew to a close, educators and social scientists evidently were determined to avoid the evil of warfare in the future. To this end, they decided, we must all just learn to live together in harmony. Therefore, "Social Living" was instituted at Gillespie Junior High

School as a core curriculum, replacing most of the basic, important, traditional subjects.

The classrooms were decorated with cutout paper figures of strange-looking people dressed in folk costumes. One cutout couple, wearing wooden shoes, supposedly represented the Netherlands, although they didn't look like any of the people I saw when I had passed through Holland on the Kindertransport. None of the people I had seen were wearing wooden shoes or brightly colored print clothing; they were dressed in very dark clothing. The men I saw wore brimmed hats, not tasseled caps like the cutout man wore. I had my doubts that the school had any of the figures right.

I definitely was not a good student; nonetheless, I did have a certain curiosity. What I wanted to learn, although I found English and History worthwhile, was how airplanes flew, how chemicals reacted, and most important of all—how the radio worked. The school still offered some typing, cooking, and sewing classes for girls and wood and metal shop for boys, but it no longer offered any true mathematics or science classes.

I had trouble sitting still during the social living classes that supposedly were teaching us how to get along; I had neither the background nor the natural ability for wood or metalworking. Before being seriously injured, I was saved by kindly Mr. Michener, the shop teacher who also taught printing. He came to my rescue by getting me excused from the social living classes so I could spend that time in his printing shop. He also was responsible for managing the school theater and gave me the key to the stage room, from which I could look down on the stage and operate the theatrical lights. Anything was better than learning how to be sociable: those "Peter does not play well with others" entries on my early report cards rang true at the time, and continued throughout my life.

I enjoyed the print shop, where I eventually learned enough from Mr. Michener to hold down a printing job. I used the time in the stage room reading material that surely was not morally uplifting.

I knew there was an interesting world outside the school building, and, realizing that no one knew where I was due to the schedule Mr. Michener provided me with, I soon discovered I could escape. My parents gave me lunch money which I spent taking the subway to downtown Philadelphia. I would wander aimlessly through the downtown streets, meandering into the markets, department stores, railroad stations, Leary's bookstore, and other sights remarkable to a tall gangly teenager.

I also discovered the Franklin Institute, a truly exceptional interactive scientific museum. In the main lobby, there was a gigantic white marble statue of Benjamin Franklin, a fellow printer, who became a personal hero of mine as I learned more about his life. The Institute consisted of multiple floors filled with interactive displays. I could push a button to activate an electric fan, and the air current would lift the model airplane that was in the case. A large pendulum swung from the top floor into the center of the circular staircase, illustrating the rotation of the earth. One of my favorite displays was a Link Trainer, an enclosed airplane cockpit that simulated flying and was used to train military pilots. I spent many Saturdays or Sundays at the Institute, with my parents' approval, making full use of the membership they had paid for.

On one of my weekday wanderings in central Philadelphia, on a narrow street near City Hall, I came across an outstanding cultural center: the Troc. The theater's marquee was a gigantic semi-circle of bare, flashing light bulbs. A ticket booth was in the center with swinging doors on either side. On the far side of the doors hung eight-by-ten-inch glossy photos of some of the most beautiful women I had ever seen, dressed in feathers, lingerie, or strategically placed rhinestones.

The sign in the ticket booth read: "Balcony 25 cents" and "Orchestra 50 cents." Since I was tall for my age, I received my ticket stub, in exchange for my quarter, with just a sideways glance from the bald, overweight, unshaven ticket seller. My heart was pounding as I swung open the first set of doors and entered the lobby. Its walls were covered with more photos of women standing, sitting, or lying on sofas. Some provocatively looked over their shoulder.

I climbed the stairs to the balcony in darkness and opened the door to Nirvana. The show had started. Because of the darkness, and because I found it difficult to take my eyes from the stage, I could barely find a seat. My heart sank as I looked at the stage and saw a man dressed in pants too short for him, shoes three sizes too large, and a green and yellow sailor's hat. He was speaking to the audience, which I observed, once my eyes became adjusted to the light, was very sparse. As the comedian ended one bad joke after another, the audience responded with tepid chuckles. I felt cheated. Where were the beautiful, exotically dressed or, more to the point, undressed women? If my parents found out how I had wasted my lunch money, I would never survive the guilt that would be heaped on me.

Finally, the comedian was finished. There were a few more chuckles, and some unenthusiastic, scattered applause.

The stage became totally black. Rhythmic music started. *This must be what I came for*, I thought. I could barely breathe in anticipation. A large picture frame was illuminated from behind and there was the silhouetted form of a nude female in it. The woman started to brush her long hair to the rhythm of the music. She then sat on what appeared to be a sofa and slipped a stocking slowly and sensually up her raised leg. Next, she appeared to fasten the stocking onto a garter belt, and, changing her position in the frame, she repeated the procedure with her other leg. The rhythm of the music increased as she stood up, and as she walked to the edge of the frame, her face appeared in the spotlight that had been aimed at the frame's outer edge.

She was beautiful, I thought, with blonde hair framing that face with the dark lips and eyes. Because I was so entranced, I'm sure I did not even blink. A leg now appeared at the outside of the frame. As she bent her leg again and again in time with the music, I noticed she was wearing extremely high heels. Now, she stood at the edge of the frame, exposing one side of her body outside the frame while her other half was silhouetted within it. The music's tempo and volume increased as she danced around the stage with her hair swaying. One after the other, she raised her long stockinged legs, perched on such incredibly high heels, and swung them to the music while arching her back and looking at the audience over her shoulder. I could have sworn she mouthed a kiss to my section of the balcony. Between her legs was a triangle of sparkling rhinestones. Her breasts appeared to be bare but were always screened by her long gloved hands.

When her dance ended, I prayed there would not be another comedian coming out, as I was looking forward to another dancer. I knew there would be more, because there were all those black and white photos at the front of the theater. No, it wasn't a comedian. Instead, the house lights came up, and hawkers came down each aisle selling magazines, popcorn, candy, and—most incredible of all—spectacles that gave the wearer the ability to see through clothing, guaranteed!

I saw that the meager audience was scattered throughout the orchestra. It seemed an eternity until the house lights dimmed again. Another comedian! The time was flying by and I had to get back home before my mother came home from work. Finally, another dancer appeared. Her specialty was very large feathers.

I knew I had to leave; this was one adventure my parents could never find out about. When I let myself think about my deceit, the guilt was oppressive, but not great enough to keep me from immediately planning my return to this forbidden pleasure palace.

I became a regular attendee, growing more familiar with the names of the stars at the Troc than the stars of the Philadelphia Phillies, Athletics, or Eagles. I saved my lunch money and arranged my ambiguous school presence with Mr. Michener's unintended assistance. Although the English and history classes were corrupted by the social living concept, I sometimes did show up. I stopped attending the social living classes, though. When I could not afford the Troc, I spent the time in the stage office or print shop.

My parents, unaware of my non-existent academic progress, constantly impressed on me the importance of a good education. Our dentist's son, who had achieved such high grades that he now was employed as a research scientist with General Electric, was held up as a model of success. "His future is secure," my father repeatedly told me. The implication was that secure employment was the ultimate goal. Several times, I had met Joachim the prodigy. We called him "Einstein." I thought he was a very strange-looking, oddly behaved young man and consoled myself with the knowledge that even though I was not excelling in school, Leitha would never have asked him to her house for "dancing" lessons. Nor would he be found at the Troc.

I developed an interest in drawing and fantasized about a possible career in art; perhaps my consumption of comic books could be put to good use. My parents' concern for my future career was pushing me in a direction I recognized as disastrous for me. Working like Joachim, in a lifelong career with colleagues in a research environment, seemed to me like imprisonment, to be avoided at all costs. I started to spend much of my time in the stage office, copying cartoon characters and advertising art, with a particular emphasis on lingerie and hosiery. I discovered that art gave me a great deal of freedom.

My parents approved of my drawing, and even proudly showed my drawings of partially dressed women to their somewhat embarrassed friends. I researched mail order courses that promised riches for cartoonists who could live anywhere, mail their work to the publisher, and receive payment by return mail. Making a living without associating with fellow workers seemed ideal, with the added bonus of getting approval for drawing near-naked women. I also considered creating a comic superhero. Of all the super powers I desired, invisibility was my favorite—not too surprising for someone who felt socially challenged.

My personal heroes were the heroes of the Sunday and daily comic sections and the artists who created them: *The Spirit*, by Will Eisner; *Terry and the Pirates*, by Milton Caniff; *Prince Valiant*, by Hal Foster. Their artwork was excellent and their story lines were incredible. Their appeal to me was the consistent theme of damsels in distress being rescued by the hero. I voraciously consumed these strips, and practiced imitating them.

For several years, I attended the Graphic Sketch Club, a free art school founded in 1898 by Samuel S. Fleisher, a Philadelphia philanthropist whose estate still supports the school that exists as the Fleisher Memorial, the oldest free art school in the country.

When I arrived on a Saturday morning, with my black portfolio under my arm, I climbed the stairs to the second floor where I was given a very large sheet of charcoal paper in exchange for my dime. I clipped the paper onto my portfolio and stayed until early afternoon drawing casts, portraits of other students, or chairs, under the direction of very good, patient instructors. This was my first experience in art training and I will be grateful forever for those wonderful Saturdays.

Although Mr. Michener never knew how I was spending the time when I was not going to classes, he knew that Gillespie Junior High School, with its emphasis on social living, was a total waste of time for me. I had come to the same conclusion, but did not have a clue how to get out of there. Mr. Michener proposed a solution for me: apply to the highly regarded, academically superior Central High School, which started in the ninth grade.

That sounded good, as it would get me out of Gillespie with its damned social living and I might really learn something. There were disadvantages, however: There would be no more Troc, and Central was an all-boys' high school. More importantly, though, the school's very high academic standards would require discipline and hard work. My formal education, up to that point, had been chaotic at best.

My parents enthusiastically approved the proposal. I don't know how Mr. Michener did it, but even with my mediocre scholastic record I was accepted for admission to the January 1946 class of this highly competitive school.

During April 1945, on the map on my bedroom wall, I moved the Allied flags of the United States, Britain, and the Soviets closer and closer to Berlin, where only one Nazi flag remained. On April 12, when my mother and I were walking from a dry cleaner shop toward our home, we heard an unusual buzz of excited but subdued conversation on the street. In a few minutes, we learned that President Franklin D. Roosevelt, a personal hero and protector in our home, had died. We were not the only ones on the street that had tears rolling down our cheeks. "What will happen to us now?" my mother asked no one in particular.

On May 8, I removed that last swastika from my wall map. Car horns blew continuously; people cheered. As night fell, I leaned out of our second floor window and waved to the people running and jumping in celebration.

About two months later, I found my father seated at our dining room table with his back to me. His body was shaking. I asked what was going on, but he waved me off. I had never seen my father cry before or since. He repeated over and over again, in German, "Why? Why? She was only an old woman." In his hand was a pink postcard from the International Red Cross, expressing their sympathies for my grandmother's death, in 1941, in the Theresienstadt concentration camp.

The war in the Pacific continued. There was great speculation about an imminent invasion of the Japanese islands, until August 6, when all radio broadcasts were interrupted and newspapers brought out special editions announcing the dropping of an atomic bomb on the Japanese city of Hiroshima. The total vaporization of an entire city and population was described. Drawings appeared in the paper, attempting to explain how this new weapon worked. I appreciated that this was a new era, and saved the newspapers. Nine days later, the Japanese surrendered. The war was over! That night I again looked out our second floor window, this time seeing more cars now with streamers flying. I rushed downstairs and picked up the streamers which I kept as souvenirs of this great day.

That was a year of momentous transformation for the world, the country, and for me personally: I became a naturalized American citizen.

– 7 –

Quirk

Sitting in the subway car, I found myself shaking to the rhythm of the steel wheels' clickity-clack as they raced along the tracks. My shaking increased with excitement as I anticipated my first day at Central High School. No one there would know that I was born in Germany, grew up in a boardinghouse, used to wear strange clothes, or had been taunted, just a few years ago, for speaking English in an effeminate manner. Also, no one would know that I had not gone to classes for the past year. It felt that this was my last chance to give my parents some reason to be proud of me, and it seemed like a wonderful opportunity for a fresh start—perhaps even worth the sacrifice of the Troc. As I thought of my past, sitting on that subway, I hoped I could fake my way through this new beginning.

My social life at this time was almost non-existent. I yearned to shed my German-Jewish background. My parents had a very fearful view of the world, which was not surprising after what they had been through. Every weekend, dressed in a dark suit, starched white shirt with tie, and highly polished shoes, my father was the epitome of an old-world gentleman—a contrast to his weekday appearance, that of the menial laborer he now was. My mother, a lady of leisure in Germany where she spent her afternoons at coffee shops with friends, had been reduced to cleaning other people's toilets. Eventually, she graduated to a higher standard of work in sweatshops making shoe ornaments and inspecting hairnets.

I was ashamed of my background—not only because I was poor, felt uncomfortable in my environment, and had a heritage associated with the enemy of my adopted country—but also because my parents' value system had its origins generally in Europe, and particularly in Germany. I hated everything connected with Germany, not only for the obvious reason of its present politics but also, primarily, for its society's rigid standards and conventions.

Growing up, I constantly battled with my parents as they attempted to instill in me an appreciation of their social standards, which they believed outlined the only way to live a proper life. I felt as if I was expected to follow standards that were written in a secret code to which I was never given the key. For instance, they thought I always dressed improperly—too informally—for their standards. They also thought that the subjects I was interested in were frivolous, but to me, they were critical in my attempt to become what I desired most to be: an American.

My companions outside of school consisted exclusively of the children of my parents' refugee friends. I accepted them only because there was no alternative. Ralph, Herbert, and I frequently went to public swimming pools in the summer, with the objective of meeting girls. We occasionally succeeded and would make awkward romantic advances if the girls' parents were not home. Once, we were in a girl's basement with her and her two friends and were proceeding with our clumsy groping, when a shaft of light from the opening of the upstairs door frightened the three of us so much that we raced out the back door and ran at full gallop for several blocks. We were certain we would be sent to prison if we were apprehended.

I had no interests in common with Ralph or Herbert, but we often went together to a social club established by the German-Jewish refugees in a converted residence on Broad Street near the Girard subway station. The adults exchanged information about immigration and citizenship laws and, after the war, talked about restitution benefits from Germany. The older men played their German card games of 66 and Schacht. Ralph and Herbert were unenthusiastic about going, but persuaded by my continual hope that we would meet girls our age, they agreed to come along.

I was looking for girls who were like the happy-go-lucky girls in the movies. In other words, I was looking for Americans. But the girls we met at the club all had the same German-Jewish background I did. After the war, young people who had spent time in the camps and had experienced unspeakable horrors started to appear in the club. As much sympathy as I felt for these young people when I overheard fragments of their life stories, I had nothing in common with them. If I wanted happy-go-lucky, it was not to be found at the German-Jewish social club.

I thought about this on the subway ride. Finally, the subway reached its destination: Olney Avenue, the end of the line. I was hopeful that this was the beginning for me. The doors hissed open and the car emptied. Many boys my age were in the departing crowd. As I walked up the steps to the street, I wondered if I had paid too great a price to get out of Gillespie Junior High and its social living program: Central High was an all-boys school.

On that January day of 1946, as I walked down Olney Avenue, passing the Widener School for the Handicapped, I resolved to make this new beginning a success. As usual, I was walking alone while all around me boys were walking down the gently sloping avenue in groups of two, three, or more.

Central High School stood at the top of a hill that was visible only when you got to the bottom of Olney Avenue. The great seal of the school shone over its entrance. The building appeared new and modern compared with all the other schools I had attended. As an entering freshman, I had been instructed to report to the auditorium. I was about forty minutes early, and only a few students were clustered in groups around the auditorium.

Before I selected a seat, a thin, grey-haired man approached me and asked me how much basketball I had played. I told the truth: I had never, ever, played basketball. It was obvious what had prompted the question: I was the tallest boy in the incoming freshman class, at least eight inches taller than the grey-haired man, who turned out to be the basketball coach. He asked for, and received, my promise that I would report for basketball tryouts after school in two weeks.

Trying to remain anonymous, as had become my custom, I took a seat in the middle of an empty row halfway back from the stage. I discovered the writing leaf, locked it in front of me, laid down my brand new, three-ring notebook, and opened it to the first page. It was pristine with only one exception: I had noted the coach's name and the date of basketball tryouts. It was truly ironic that the first entry in my high school notebook would be related to team sports, the activity that interested me the least.

The auditorium filled with bodies of eager boys and the sound of excited conversation. No one had taken a seat on my row. A hush quickly fell over the auditorium as a tall, thin man in a black suit walked to the podium.

"I am Dr. Cornig, the president of Central High School. You are about to enter the long tradition of this excellent institution with its high academic standards that you will be expected to uphold." He reminded us that we were the first entering freshman class following the end of the war and at the dawn of the atomic age. He told us of the responsibilities that came with attendance at this prestigious institution, which was equipped with the latest laboratories, including a planetarium funded by a Philadelphia soap manufacturer.

Generous contributions of the school's alumni augmented the public funds that made these facilities possible. The name Barnwell came up repeatedly. Mr. Barnwell had created a foundation that provided prizes for academic excellence. Small books, with gold lettering on their red—or "crimson," as I was to learn—covers, were passed out to the students. The book gave the history of the school, dating back to 1836; the role of the Barnwell Foundation, which supplemented the public funds provided to this public high school; the honor code we were expected to live by; a list of the honors and academic prizes that were available; and the words to the school song, which emphasized the honor of going to school under the crimson and gold and assured us that we would remember our high school days more powerfully and with greater affection than our college days.

This certainly was impressive; however, I wondered, *would I be able to survive without any real preparation?*

I kept my promise to the basketball coach and appeared at the tryouts. The coach was extremely patient and attempted to teach me the rules of the game and some of the techniques of dribbling, shooting, and passing. He apparently had tremendous faith in height overcoming lack of skill. His faith proved to be misplaced.

The classes, instructors, and facilities were remarkable. The school's planetarium and the physics, chemistry, and biology laboratories looked the way I imagined facilities at most universities. At the time I entered Central High, all the teachers were male, they always dressed in dark suits with white shirts and neckties, and they all looked old—over fifty. They had advanced degrees and most were addressed as Doctor.

Our class was the first to enter high school after the conclusion of World Word II. Because of the academic nature of the school, the majority of the students planned to go to college. We soon became aware that we would face stiff competition in securing admission to college because the returning veterans, with their G.I. Bill subsidies, were swamping the colleges. Also, many of Central's students, perhaps a majority, were Jewish, and some of the elite colleges and universities still had quotas restricting the number of Jews who could enroll.

So, with practically no preparation from junior high school, I faced a rigorous curriculum and a very competitive student body. As it turned out, between my lack of academic training at Gillespie and my attendance at an art school after high school, the three and a half years I spent at Central High School made up my entire academic career.

My first year at Central was not the disaster it could have been. I earned diverse marks: A in social studies; Bs in English, gym, art, and German; and C in mathematics. I worked harder at my schoolwork than I had ever worked at anything before.

I still went to the social club on weekends, perennially hopeful of meeting fun girls; my search proved unfruitful, though, as more and more refugees arrived from displaced persons camps after the incredible hardships of the concentration camps.

During high school, I became more interested in pursuing a career as a cartoonist. The working conditions seemed ideal: I could work anywhere, in isolation; I could mail in my masterpieces, and I would receive a check from the magazine. Three or four published cartoons each month could give me a comfortable existence. If I could establish a career as a cartoonist before graduating from high school, my parents' anxiety over my lack of marketable skills would be relieved.

I continued my Saturday morning art classes and my visits to the Franklin Institute, the Philadelphia Library, and Leary's bookstore, a Philadelphia treasure I had discovered on my wanderings downtown while I was still at Gillespie. Every conceivable type of book was jammed into this multi-story, narrow brick structure. I enjoyed many visits to

Leary's, mostly rummaging through books on radio, which had been a passion of mine since the days at Gillespie when I was addicted to the daily fifteen-minute dramatic serial shows: *Jack Armstrong, Terry and the Pirates, Little Orphan Annie,* and, on the weekends, *The Shadow* who knew what evil lurked in the hearts of men.

Of course, I also was interested in how-to books on cartooning, drawing, and painting. I bought some of these with the hope that they would make me a successful cartoonist. I also carefully studied my idols' comic strips: Milton Caniff's *Terry and the Pirates* and Will Eisner's *The Spirit.* They truly were works of art and literature, produced daily, usually by one person who both wrote the story and drew the pictures. It became obvious to me that I would never be able to produce artwork equal to these masters; as a teenager, I did not have the life experiences needed to write adventure stories like theirs.

Now that the war was over, my father was able to secure work in his field, as a night shift supervisor at Bers & Company. His work was physically demanding, but the new job greatly improved our financial status. After about two years, he was transferred to the day shift, and he bought a used car from the company, paying for the 1946 Ford sedan in cash. He never would have considered paying for it any other way. The father of one of my classmates had bought a new Buick, and I asked my father why we hadn't gotten a fancier new car.

He put on his jacket and told me to come with him. We took the subway to downtown Philadelphia, got off at Market Street, and walked a few blocks to the Philadelphia Savings Fund Society, a bank founded by Benjamin Franklin. My father told me to look up at the skyscraper. "That building looks pretty expensive, doesn't it?" he asked. Of course, I had to agree.

"You have your savings account here and they pay you 2 percent for storing your money safely. So, how do you think this bank gets the money to build that tall expensive building?" he continued. "Let me explain. The bank makes all the money to build this expensive building, pay all the people who work in there, and also pay you the interest on your savings account, by lending money to people like your friend's father, so they can buy cars they can't afford." I had a lot to think about on the subway ride home, and never in my life borrowed money for a car.

In the first semester of my second year at Central, a young instructor, Joe McCloskey, joined the English Department. He was a returning veteran and I believe the school waived its advanced degree standard for him. Without that young instructor's three years of training, I am convinced my life would have taken a very different and much less fulfilling turn. He taught us the elements of grammar, composition, and creative writing. That was the first and last exposure I had to instruction in these academic areas, and it stuck with me. Exceptional teachers in American and English literature, with several semesters devoted to Shakespeare, were invaluable elements of my education.

During that same semester, a very attractive woman joined the faculty. She was only six or seven years older than the students. Her presence doubled the population of female faculty members; the other woman was an art teacher. Our new teacher had a habit of sitting on her desk, in the front of the room, crossing and uncrossing her legs. I was so fascinated by her distracting habit that, try as I might, I cannot remember what subject she taught. She disappeared after one semester.

The best that can be said of my endeavors in science and mathematics is that I was consistent: I earned straight Cs from beginning to graduation. This certainly was not the fault of the teachers or the result of a lack of interest in these subjects. I was simply lost from beginning to end. It did seem obvious that I should not pursue an engineering or scientific education in college, limitations which, I found, limited my career options.

After one year with Bers, my father earned a one-week vacation, but my mother got no vacation from her job at the sweatshop. She insisted that my father needed to take a real vacation.

He had not purchased a car yet, so we took a bus to Atlantic City. As soon as we got off, we searched for the rooming house where my father had made reservations for three nights. Our accommodations consisted of a third-floor room, just under the attic, with a bathroom down the hall. We would have a three-block walk to the beach.

On the second afternoon, after my father had returned to the room, I was climbing the stairs past the second floor when I heard a woman calling my name. I turned and saw that the door to one of the rooms was slightly ajar.

The woman called again, "Peter, come here. I have something to show you." I pushed the door open and saw a woman, probably in her forties, dressed in exotic lingerie and smoking. I closed the door behind me, hoping that no one would see me in this woman's room. "Come over here, Peter, and let me have your hand." She took my hand and placed it on her breast. "Does this feel good to you, Peter?" With that, she took the cigarette and touched the glowing end to the back of my hand, laughing as I quickly pulled back my hand. "See, now you have learned life's important lesson: for each pleasure, a price must be paid," she said laughingly. I retreated out the door and up the stairs to our third-floor room, hoping my father had not heard anything. He hadn't.

When we returned home, my mother's primary concern was that we were as red as lobsters. We assured her that we had just been in the sun and that we did not have sunburn. "How stupid could you be? You will be sick for days. What a fine way to spend the remaining days of your vacation!" my mother went on, scolding us incessantly, even though the trip had been her suggestion. She never asked if we had a good time.

This was the beginning of my mother's struggle with menopause-related mood swings. She got continually worse. Her irrational, angry outbursts and long periods of stony silence were directed primarily at my father, although frequently I also became the target. My father and I tried to avoid any situation that might displease her, but walking on eggshells did not solve the problem. Eventually, I stayed out of the house as much as possible, but there was no escape for my father. He and I never discussed my mother's condition, as I assume he thought I was too young to handle this situation.

My mother avoided displaying her anger or behaving irrationally when she was in the company of others, so my parents' friends always thought of her as an incredibly kind and competent woman.

Money was always a problem in our family; if I wanted to go to movies, with or without a girl; or buy books or drawing supplies, I had to work and earn some money after school or during summer vacation.

In the summer of 1947, just before my sixteenth birthday, when I was still too young to work at a regular job, my father thought I might make a good self-employed salesman. Unfortunately, he was again disappointed.

At that time, every restaurant had an ashtray at each table. He had seen a gadget that he thought had some possibilities: an ashtray with a spring-loaded arm that would rise when a button was pushed. This could alert the waitperson that service was requested, thus avoiding the waving, yelling, or finger snapping that were the accepted methods of calling for service. My father and I were convinced this was a world-shaking idea with a potential market of thousands of restaurants.

Most owners or managers, however, were too busy to talk to a fifteen-year-old kid who wanted to sell them something. I gave up after struggling for two weeks without one sale. I never tried selling again.

That summer was also the first time we went on a one-week family vacation. Economy was the guide. We ended up at "Peters Place" in the Pocono Mountains, not too far from Philadelphia. At that time, most resorts in that area had a policy of no Jews allowed. This was publicized by phrases in their advertising: "Church Nearby," "Restricted Clientele," or "Christian Community." We selected Peter's Place partly because of the absence of such notices, but primarily because of its price. They had advertised that they had a swimming pool, hiking trails, and activities for all ages.

It turned out that the swimming pool was a muddy pond with a diving board at one end; the hiking trails supported a stroll around the pond or along the highway; and the family activities were a collection of board games stacked in the living room of the large boarding house. Each family had a room with toilet privileges down the hall.

As we drove into the driveway in our used two-door Ford sedan, I noticed an attraction that was not in the brochure: two sisters, the younger one about my age. There also was a boy about three years older than I. All three seemed very pleased to see me. I considered that a very good sign. After helping to take my parents' luggage up to our musty room, I went outside and found all three waiting for me.

The girls, Ginny, the younger, and Julie, the older, were on the diving board; Michael stood off to the side while I awkwardly tried to engage the girls in conversation. Ginny suggested we go for a swim after lunch; I enthusiastically agreed. The prevailing medical wisdom at that time was that you must wait one hour after eating before going swimming, so we agreed to meet at two thirty.

I joined my parents for a walk around the property, advocating for going to the dining room promptly when it opened at noon. When I told my parents of my afternoon swimming plans, my mother immediately warned me that I must wait one hour after lunch before going into the water.

Lunch consisted of sandwiches made of baloney and cheese encased in white, gummy bread. A bowl of lettuce, celery, carrots, sliced tomatoes, and onions, and a bowl of potato salad—not the German style my mother very proudly prepared, but a creamy style with lots of mayonnaise—completed the main course. My parents never said this vacation was a mistake, but my mother's displeasure is revealed in the photo I took. After lunch and the obligatory one-hour wait, I was standing on the greasy diving board when Ginny and Julie arrived. I dived into the water and they followed. It was so muddy that when I was underwater and wanted to grab one of the girls' legs, I could not even see their shadows. Michael joined us about twenty minutes after we had entered the water.

Getting out of the pond without getting covered in the mud that extended several feet to the scrubby grass proved to be a challenge. I opted for pulling myself up onto the diving board, but could not avoid getting my feet covered with mud on the short walk back to the "hotel" which had an outside cold water shower next to the front door.

Michael invited me to get dressed in his room. I had brought my clothes downstairs, knowing that my parents were either napping in our room or walking around the grounds. Since I did not have a key to our room I accepted. He assured me that he had extra towels. When we got to his room, Michael said he would dry my back. Although I thought it somewhat strange, I complied with his invitation to lie on my stomach on his bed. As he knelt behind me, I heard the girls giggling in the next room. I told him to hurry up drying my back.

The noises from the next room became more inviting, so I got up, foregoing any more thorough drying of my back by Michael, and hurriedly dressed.

"Come in," one of the girls responded to my knock. "Peter, we have a surprise for you," Ginny said, and pulled back her unbuttoned shirt. The girls were wearing identical jeans and plaid shirts. Neither of them had buttoned her shirt.

Next, Julie opened hers and asked, "Which do you like better?"

Not wishing to offend either and totally shocked by the scene, I assured them they were the most beautiful sights I had ever seen. My predicament: *What do I say? What do I do?*

Ginny, reading my mind accurately, invited, "You may touch, if you like."

During the next two days, I followed Ginny and Julie like a puppy with my cheap Kodak Brownie. I took innumerable pictures of them, which in my mind were glamour shots. The girls were, of course, fully dressed in the pictures; at that time, no photo lab would develop or print pictures that contained any nudity.

Our first family vacation ended in three days, with my parents constantly concerned about what embarrassment they might be exposed to if our religion was discovered, as all the other guests were non-Jews. My mother was also particularly concerned with the hotel's lack of cleanliness, which she said was a breeding ground for germs, and she constantly worried that we would get sick. As we drove away from Peters Place,

I thought, "Now, that was a pretty good experience." Ginny and Julie had exchanged their New Jersey addresses and phone numbers with me; however, none of us ever made any attempt to renew our friendships.

Several years later, we went to Grossinger's, in the area of the Catskills known as the Borscht Belt, which catered to Jewish guests with five meals of traditional Jewish food a day and Yiddish comedians at night. My parents, like most German-Jewish refugees, neither spoke nor understood Yiddish and were unfamiliar with the Eastern European Jewish food that was served, so they felt just as uncomfortable as they had at Peters Place.

In 1948, I took two classes at summer school, thereby advancing from Central High School's class 193 to 192. My graduation now would be scheduled for June 1949 rather than December. If I had not qualified for a June graduation, my entry into any of the smaller colleges that began classes only once yearly would have been delayed by a full year. Although I had no plans for college, I was in a hurry.

When I reached my sixteenth birthday that November, I started working after school as temporary help for the Christmas season at Gimbel Brothers department store. On the first day, I reported to the office in the basement where part-time employees received their assignments from two tall women behind a glassed-in counter. The temporary employees, lined up at the counter, were assigned a department and issued a card to insert into a time clock, recording their time in and out.

When I got to the front of the line, the two women looked at each other knowingly and asked me to come into the office. They assigned me to the personal property desk, where the employees checked their belongings while at work. I thought I might have gotten this plum job because they had heard I was related to Ellis Gimbel, the president of the store, but I quickly suspected that they gave me the job for their own amusement.

Candice and Barbara, who looked about ten years older than I, appeared very glamorous to me. The high-heeled shoes they always wore enhanced their height and the shapeliness of their legs. It never escaped my notice that, when they stood behind the counter, they would put one foot up on a railing, requiring them to raise their tight skirts and expose the upper part of a thigh. Noting my fascination, they laughed between themselves, and joked with me about my interest in their legs. Sometimes, when there was no activity in the office, they stood at the counter and invited me to stand between them while they guided my hands along the upper parts of their thighs. They laughed hilariously as they observed my reaction.

They also enjoyed watching my response to the female employees who checked their personal belongings at my window. They always gave me reviews of the girls' appearances, particularly their breast size. I suspected that Candice and Barbara secretly encouraged some of the girls to flirt and go out with me, as they always seemed to know when I met one of the temps outside of work, and they wanted a complete report.

Since my job was related to the administration of all part-time help, it did not end in the second week of January when most of the extra help was let go; with the help of my guardian angels, Candice and Barbara, I was able to work at Gimbels for a few extra months, even though the activity at the personal property window was almost non-existent.

When my job at Gimbel's finally did end, in the spring of my senior year at Central, I heard that Gadiel's, a drugstore within walking distance of the school, was looking for a delivery boy and soda jerk. In those days, every drugstore had a soda fountain of polished granite with stationary stools on pedestals in front of the counter. Cokes were prepared by mixing Coca Cola syrup with carbonated water. A selection of ice cream was available, and there were appliances to prepare milk shakes and combinations of sodas and ice cream.

Mr. Gadiel, the owner and pharmacist, was also a German refugee, which probably had something to do with my selection for the job. Little did I know then that applying for that job would have monumental consequences for the direction of my life.

On my second day at the job, I was still somewhat unsure of the intricacies of mixing exotic soda fountain drinks when the corner door of the drugstore opened and in bounced a girl several years younger than I. She looked around the store, headed straight for the soda fountain, and climbed onto the middle stool. "Hi, my name's Betty. What's yours?" she asked with a combination of a grin and giggle. "Could I have a cup of water, please?" Somewhat puzzled, I placed the paper cone in the metal holder, filled it with water, and slid it in front of her. She did not seem interested in the water, but told me she lived in the house on the other side of the apartment building that was right next to the drug store, was attending Wagner Junior High School, and would be going to high school after the summer. Mr. Gadiel, watching this interchange from the pharmacy at the rear of the store, did not look pleased.

Betty left her stool, went down the aisles of merchandise, picked up a few items, and went to the back of the store to have Mr. Gadiel charge them to the Kaplan account. Betty looked back at me periodically, smiled, and giggled. When she got to the front door, she turned, waved at me, and said, "So long, Peter, pleased to meet you. See you soon." She bounced out the door, giggling, in the same way she had entered. I noticed she had not touched her water. "Now, that was fun," I thought.

I looked forward to her daily visits and her family's telephone orders requesting delivery to her home, only two doors from the store. Mr. Gadiel was less than enthusiastic about the romance blossoming in his drug store. His marginal business made him careful to avoid offending a family member of any customer, so he never spoke to Betty or her family. He did express his displeasure to me, however, as each delivery trip took longer and longer, because Betty's parents were not home during the day. They worked at her father's advertising agency downtown, returning home no earlier than six thirty in the evening.

I finished my workday after the drug store closed, having cleaned up the fountain and straightened out all the shelves by five thirty. Just as Betty never missed a daily visit to the drug store, I always stopped by her house on my way to the subway for my ride home, always leaving before her parents arrived.

Our protracted daily farewells became a ritual. Betty's house had an enclosed porch with one step up leading into the living room. Since I was almost a foot taller than she, I stood on the lower level as we hugged and kissed our farewells. One afternoon, while saying our traditional farewell on the step, I was teasing her when she responded, intending to call me a jerk, with, "You ... you quirk!"

I burst into laughter, grabbed her around the waist, and swung her around. She did not realize what she had just said, so I proudly told her that the word "quirk" perfectly described us: peculiar, strange, or unique. Immediately, "Quirk" became our name for each other.

I had started to smoke while at Gillespie, and thought it only fair to teach Betty that sophisticated habit; however, she had learned before I met her. Barely five feet tall, she certainly looked like a sophisticated thirteen-year-old with a cigarette dangling from her mouth.

For several months, until Betty left for summer camp, we saw each other almost daily. To me, her strongest attribute was her wonderful sense of humor, since she laughed and giggled at every one of my attempts to amuse.

One of the highlights of my repertoire was the fishing line. I would hold a pocket comb in one hand and run my thumb over its teeth, while using the other hand to mimic the reeling in of a big fish. Betty acted as if she thought this was a show business masterpiece. Many of the boys who walked with us slinked away from such great performances. We regularly used "Quirk" for our names sometimes shortened to *Q*. We created our own reality, excluding the rest of the world.

At the end of the summer, on the date of her expected return from camp, I called her house several times to speak to her, but each time her sister Sylvia said that Betty was not home. On my third try, I was told that Betty had called. She had asked Sylvia to tell me she had called, that she would be home at four, and I could come over then, if I wanted.

When I arrived at four, Betty was not home. Sylvia and Betty's mother fed me chocolates, and for many awkward minutes—which felt like an eternity—I unsuccessfully attempted to carry on a conversation. Finally, Betty arrived with a boy who, I found out, had co-starred with her in their camp production of *The Mikado*. He left quickly. Betty and I took a long walk while I told her about my latest holy grail: Ayn

Rand's *The Fountainhead*, which I had read during the summer, certain it contained the secret of life.

Ayn Rand celebrated the worth of the individual, based on the premise that self-interest was a virtue that promoted the progress of civilization and altruism was a vice leading to the destruction of civilization. My self-perception, as a perpetual outsider at the age of sixteen, primed me to enthusiastically accept this philosophy. No book before or since has had such a profound effect on my life. From the time of that long walk, after Betty's return from camp, and for many years thereafter, I explained myself to her as the alter ego of Howard Roark, the protagonist of *The Fountainhead*.

In September, Betty had her fourteenth birthday. I gave her an inexpensive watch that hung from her belt and drew a cartoon birthday card, which she thought was hilarious. That started the routine of my weekly cartoons of us, which I gave her each Friday. Even if the *New Yorker* did not want my cartoons, I had found a very appreciative audience.

Betty and I often made spectacles of ourselves on the sidewalk in front of her house, dancing to imaginary music. I would swing Betty from one knee to another, and then between my legs, acting out what we thought were hilarious facial and body movements. Betty's best friend Marilyn, who seemed to appreciate our eccentricities, was sometimes our admiring audience.

With high school graduation approaching, I felt a great deal of pressure to select a field of study for a future career. Although I was interested in science, my schoolwork followed its usual pattern: mediocre performance in mathematics and science, fairly good grades in English, history, and art. I reminded myself of my former conclusion that not having any talent for math or science definitely limits one's career choices.

The son of one of our distant American relatives was just completing a course in the emerging profession of industrial design at the Philadelphia Museum School of Art. We met, and his drawings and models of automobiles, locomotives, kitchenware, appliances, and packaging fascinated me. Here was a profession, related to science and engineering, that did not have mathematics and science as primary prerequisites; and, best of all, it was related to architecture—Howard Roark's profession.

My parents were delighted that I had become enthusiastic about a real profession. Within a week, I applied for admission to the Industrial Design Department of PMSA and was advised that my admission would depend on the quality of a portfolio of my work that was to be submitted by the middle of the summer. This created a problem. I knew that my Saturday morning charcoal drawings, high school art projects, cartoons, and pencil copies of lingerie advertisements would not impress the admissions committee. I would have to get busy.

Since Betty was now fourteen, certainly old enough to go on a regular date, I took her on our first night on the town. I had learned to drive after enduring the shame of having to take the test three times. I did not have the required foot coordination to get a manual transmission car moving from a dead stop on a hill without stalling. Although I had finally obtained my license, my father would not permit me to drive unless he was in the car. So, Betty and I made our trip downtown on the subway.

I sensed that Betty was as excited about this first real date as I was. We saw a first-run movie in one of the largest movie palaces in Philadelphia. I had a special surprise for Betty: Maurice's, a fancy delicatessen in the old part of the city, where classical music was played continuously. We spent more than an hour there, then took our time walking to the subway, which ran infrequently after midnight. It was after one AM when we walked up the steps at Betty's subway stop at the end of the line, where we were greeted by Betty's mother, father, sister, sister's fiancée, and several Philadelphia cops. Betty had neglected to tell me that she was to be home by eleven.

I asked Betty to my senior prom. After I convinced my father that it would be totally inappropriate to take a girl to a prom by public transportation or have a parent supervising the driving, he agreed to let me have the car for the first time.

After I picked up Betty and pinned the orchid corsage on her gown, we drove to my apartment house so I could introduce her to my parents. I was ashamed of where we lived and told my parents that when I blew my horn they were to come down to the street to meet Betty so I could avoid bringing her into the apartment house.

As expected, we had a wonderful time. I had befriended some of my classmates, and we asked another couple to join us in my car. I explained to Betty that the balding man sitting on the sidelines of the dance floor was my chemistry teacher, who stood between my graduation and failure, so she should be very nice to him. She must have charmed him, because I passed.

Shortly after the prom, my parents bought a typical Philadelphia row home. This was a big step up for us—three bedrooms and bath on the second floor, and living room, dining room, and kitchen on the first. I was delighted to have the back bedroom, which was large enough for me to have people over. I had my parents' Bauhaus sofa, which converted to a bed when the four bolsters were removed and the three cushions were turned over. I kept it as a bed, and made it into a sofa only when friends came over.

We now had a spare bedroom, which soon was occupied by my cousin Hannah, who came from the newly established nation of Israel. She was a striking beauty who had been sent by her father, my mother's brother, to get a business education in America. Her courses, at a private school, emphasized English, typing, and bookkeeping; she was only sixteen.

My social life at Central improved considerably because of Hannah's beauty. Although Betty at first considered her a rival, they soon became friends and corresponded once Hannah returned home after a year. Hannah and I got along very well, primarily because she could not do enough for me. No romance ever developed. She was my first cousin, a fact that alone would not have stopped me, but my infatuation with Betty prevented any serious relationship.

In June, I graduated from Central High School; Betty and my parents attended the ceremony. Afterward, when the four of us were standing across the street from the school, my father showed his disappointment by saying, "Peter, did I miss the honors you were awarded?"

– 8 –

Art School

The building, then the Philadelphia Museum School of Art, now the University of the Arts, resembled a cartoonist's version of the famous Philadelphia Art Museum. A poor imitation of a small Greek temple with plaster walls and four columns holding up a triangular peaked roof, sat at the top of some twenty wide steps. It may have been prophetic that it once was an institution for the insane. I never knew, until graduation, that the school had an administrative relationship with the museum. The museum's director presided over my graduation and signed my degree, which had the seal of the museum with its griffin emblazoned on it.

The previous summer, I had prepared a portfolio—a prerequisite for admission—filling it with examples of my work: a watercolor of a gnarled tree; an oil painting of Hamlet holding a skull, with Shakespeare's lines lettered in the upper left-hand corner to help the viewer, who undoubtedly needed all the hints available to recognize the scene; assorted pencil and charcoal nudes copied from drawing textbooks; and several of my Saturday morning efforts. Surprisingly, I was admitted.

Soon, it became apparent that I probably was the only student entering PMSA that year whose only previous art training had consisted of Saturday morning classes at a community center in lieu of formal art lessons.

On the day of registration, representative work from each department was displayed in the school's main lobby. The Theater Department had the most impressive display: models of scenery and costumes on mannequins. Since I had always been a rabid theater fan, going as often as my meager funds would permit, I was tempted to enroll in the theater design program. However, my parents and I had agreed that industrial design was a practical career for someone who had displayed limited academic aptitude. When I was told that the theater design program was being discontinued, I was saved from betraying my parents' trust and registered for the industrial design program.

The first year at PMSA consisted of a core art program, which was the same for all students, regardless of their intended majors. Attending classes with students of painting, illustration, fashion, and art education, I immediately began to sense that familiar feeling of impending failure. My charcoal drawings of classic plaster casts appeared somewhat twisted—eyes on different levels gazed in different directions. More than fifty years later, I still remember struggling with a drawing of an upturned stool, trying over and over to get its four legs to appear the same length.

My pain was not just for myself but also for my parents, who had made a great financial sacrifice to send me to college and now would be faced with a son headed for total failure. My only hope was to survive this first year. I could then begin anew in my second year, competing only with industrial design students, who I assumed would not be as well trained or talented in the disciplines of traditional art.

Not all drawing and painting classes were a lost cause—there were life classes. After getting over the initial discomfort of being in a crowd and staring at nude women while faking a professional attitude, I attempted to draw these beauties, who, I fantasized, had a reciprocal interest in this skinny, awkward, eighteen-year-old. These classes became the highlight of my first year. When there was a ten-minute model break, the other students rushed out or gathered to socialize, but I stayed at my easel while the robed model circulated around the room viewing the students' work. I hoped against hope that the model would engage me in some conversation; who knew what that could lead to?

During one hot, humid, Philadelphia June afternoon near the end of my first year, I was attempting to draw a young nude woman while concentrating on the path of a bead of sweat running from under her arm, around the side of her breast, proceeding downward ever so slowly, and leaving a silvery reflective trail. I prayed that the impending model break would hold off until that bead reached its final resting place. *Please, God, if you have any mercy on this undeserving clod, just another 10 minutes, PLEASE!!* My faith in the power of prayer was renewed as the drop hung under her breast for a full five minutes.

PMSA had just been accredited to grant bachelor of fine arts degrees in addition to the certificates it had traditionally bestowed. To receive the degree, a student was required to take two academic courses each semester, extending the school day by two hours. Rejecting my argument that my time would be better spent devoted exclusively to my art training, my father insisted that I pursue the degree program. He prophetically pointed out, based on his own experience, that you never can tell what life has in store for you and the more options the better. How right he was. Where would my life have taken me without that degree? As pedestrian as it was, that BFA got me into law school ten years later.

Miraculously, I made it through that frustrating first year, hoping my limitations in drawing and painting would somehow be overlooked since my future courses would now be in industrial design. I had done well in art history, design, color theory, and composition, but barely passed drawing and painting. My only As were in my two academic courses: English and psychology.

During that first year, my artistic taste developed quickly. I could creatively conceptualize art, but my limited ability to execute it resulted in work that was disappointingly mediocre at best. My frustration was agonizing. The talented art students, if they noticed me at all, could affirm their own talent by comparing themselves to me. I was, without doubt, the lowest common denominator. Two girls, one of whom lived on the street across the driveway from my house, were the only students to recognize my presence and meet with me. The other students must have assumed that association with me could, like a leech, suck their talent from their bodies.

Although I needed all the money I could earn, jobs were not plentiful. I looked for summer employment related to industrial design, regardless of pay. I must have telegraphed my belief that experience was more important than money, as potential employers promised me real design experience for minimum wages.

My first job during the three summer months was with an embroidery factory that had contracts with the large department stores to personalize off-the-rack clothing by adding embroidered monograms and custom designs. As a designer, I created several designs, but most of my time was spent on my feet, ironing appliqués on sheets and pillowcases.

In late June of the summer between my first and second years in art school, the Korean War began, and the military draft was reactivated. Deferments were routinely granted to all college students, postponing military service until after graduation. Having no opinion on the merits of the war, I believed that, if I were called up, serving would probably be the least I could do for the country that had given me sanctuary and an environment of freedom to choose a profession, even if I demonstrated very little ability.

Assumptions that the powerful United States would defeat the primitive North Koreans in short order were proven wrong—the war dragged on for three years. I secretly thought that being called up would postpone my exposure as an untalented failure in my chosen profession.

Between my second and third years, I was a draftsman with a power equipment manufacturer. My creative effort was to lay out the placement of dials and switches, with equal spacing, on the front of large metal cabinets. Not a very creative summer. During my last summer in art school, I had a real design job at a plastics manufacturing company that made advertising gimmicks for the liquor industry. Although the products were kitsch, I was delighted with my experiences: sketching a design the client approved; making the working drawings the die makers used to create the molds for the injection molding machines; and, finally, holding the finished product in my hands. I enjoyed visiting bars, not to drink, but to see my creations displayed in their intended setting.

Betty and I saw each other daily. We interrupted our subway rides, which were in opposite directions, to meet on subway platforms. Every Friday, I gave her a cartoon I had created just for her.

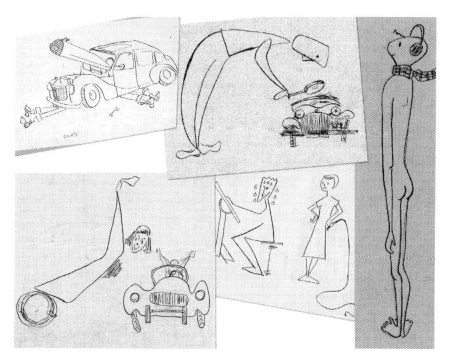

Several projects were assigned to all the students in the industrial design program each year. In my sophomore year, my first in industrial design, we had some instruction in the techniques for presenting our creations. The most basic was mechanical drawing: the use of a T-square and triangle. I mastered the presentation of all views of an object in the convention of top, front, and side views.

The program introduced me to the beauty and truth of geometric forms. I had felt incompetent in the math classroom, so it was incredible that I should become an enthusiast of conic sections and golden rectangles. I could visualize a mobile composed of conic sections. Conceptually, it is impossible to create a non-elegant conic section. However, my crude execution, in three-dimensions with jagged edges, destroyed the effect of what should have been an elegant artistic truth, but was like all my artwork—unprofessional.

The principles of perspective were an insurmountable challenge for me. My classmates seemed to comprehend the lectures and demonstrations, putting perspective into practice. I, on the other hand, read books on the subject and painfully struggled, attempting to create a three-dimensional illusion on a two-dimensional surface. The use of pastels and an airbrush to illustrate highly polished car bodies, wooden furniture, or ceramic pottery, remained a mystery.

We were required to present our projects as three-dimensional models, but I could not cut cardboard with a razor blade to create a straight edge or use a jigsaw to cut a piece of wood to a desired shape. It became painfully clear to me that I could conceive creative designs but was unable to render them in a professional manner. I worked as hard as I ever had in my life with very little success.

Many of our projects were assigned with the cooperation of local manufacturers, who gave us access to their engineering and marketing resources and described for us their business objectives and obstacles.

Our first project, sponsored by a local tubular steel manufacturer, was to design a public-school student desk. I thought I had created a very good solution: a bent metal frame, made of one piece of tubing, with a plywood work surface, hinged in front so it could be raised at varying angles for art projects.

My sketches were surprisingly recognizable and were well received by our "client." I believed that if I worked harder than any of my classmates,

I really could be a designer; however, there were many distractions. Not insignificantly, there was Betty; but there also were other girls, because Betty and I had agreed we would not limit ourselves to each other's company, due to our ages. Betty and her parents moved within walking distance of the school, and I saw her every day, sometimes twice a day, leaving little time for my design project and the extra effort which I had hoped would make up for my lack of talent.

I certainly could not confess my failure to my parents, who were making their utmost financial sacrifice to send me to college. I had chosen the design career because of my lack of ability in math and science and had no alternative career path.

I made some friends among my industrial design classmates. This was a new experience for me. Previously, my few companions had been the children of my parents' refugee friends. Now, my friends were real Americans, not refugees.

I met Charley O'Donnell in Central High School. Upon discovering, in our senior year, that we both were headed to PMSA, we became close friends, probably as a defensive strategy to avoid entering college without a friend. The friendship lasted throughout our PMSA days, and although we rarely see each other now, we still consider ourselves friends.

The second-year industrial design class had fewer than twenty students, all male; half were returning veterans using the GI Bill. Charley, Phil Beaston, Harold Yoos, and I, all recent high school graduates, became a close-knit group that supported each other through those emotional, destructive, art school days. Art and design became our creed; although, looking back, none of us were world-changing talents, with me at the bottom of the list. We certainly talked a good game, though, and passionately felt the purity of the principles of good design: the honest use of materials and the precept that form follows function. The veterans, of course, were experienced in the ways of the world and looked at us as naïve kid brothers. Two of the married veterans, Ray Finkleston and Dick Toland, peripherally became part of our group.

Gordon Sylvester, whose home was in the New York area, was one of the few out-of-town students. Betty arranged for blind dates with some of her friends for Gordon. To reciprocate, he invited me to spend a weekend at his parents' home. He arranged a blind date for me, and we went to the movies in Gordon's parents' car. Not only was my date very attractive, smart, and funny; most important of all, by touching my arm and holding my hand, she showed her interest in me. I anticipated a wonderful evening.

During the movie, with my arm around her shoulders, I planned a strategy for the upcoming car ride. After the movie, Gordon and his date were in the front seat; my date and I were in the back. The evening looked promising as I put my arm around her shoulder and she placed her head on my chest. As the radio warmed up, an announcer reported that Arnold Shuster, the young man who had identified Willy Sutton, the legendary bank robber and jail escapee, a few months earlier on a New York street, had just been found shot to death. As the radio story developed, my date stiffened up and started to sob—Arnold Shuster had been her good friend. That ended a promising blind date.

Pop Renzetti, the creative design instructor for all three of our industrial design years, became somewhat of a hero to the entire class. As part of a very popular exercise, demonstrating that natural forces create beautiful forms, we filled condoms with liquid plaster. They would shape themselves into graceful three-dimensional forms. His classes produced hundreds of these beautiful sculptures. When I, a skinny nineteen-year-old, asked the pharmacist for three dozen Trojans—at that time they were kept behind the counter—seeing his face, with its expression of disbelief, followed by admiration, was almost worth the frustration and lack of self-image that dominated my art-school years.

Although none of us knew how, we were convinced we would take contemporary design to its next, as yet unknown, level. We were certain that cars designed by the American automobile industry, with their tailfins and splashes of chrome, were dishonest, bastardized abominations; we condemned them as representative of the evils in society, swearing never to drive them. We were drawn to European designs: MGs, Aston Martins, and VWs, for what we considered their purity of design. Paraphrasing Einstein, we decided that nature is pleased with simplicity.

Our group discovered a creed, which we embraced as a religion, and I felt the same emotional stirrings of religious fervor that I had experienced when reading *The Fountainhead*. My classmates and I became fervent disciples of the masters of contemporary design: Frank Lloyd Wright, Le Corbusier, Mies van der Rohe, Walter Gropius, Philip Johnson, Henry Dreyfus, and Raymond Lowey. At that time, Dreyfus and Lowey had successful industrial design offices and might someday become our employers. In our senior year, Lowey introduced the Studebaker coupe, which we recognized as the possible redemption of the American auto industry. Unfortunately, the public preferred the fins and chrome, and the Studebaker Company went bankrupt within five years.

My classmate Gordon Sylvester invited Betty and me to spend New Year's at his parents' home in New York. When Betty told her parents about our plans, all hell broke loose. I remember the phrase, "Over my dead body!" being bandied about.

Betty and I took the train to New York on a very snowy day. The subway car from Penn station had the malodorous smell of wet wool. It was so crowded that Betty was raised off her feet by the pressing bodies around her, still holding onto a pole. As the train slowed and pulled into a station, a large man wearing a black leather jacket pushed through the crowd, squeezing us even tighter, and headed for the opening door. I grabbed his shoulder, spun him around, and landed a full punch on his nose. I saw the incredulous expression on his face as he fell backwards out the door.

Fortunately, the doors hissed shut before my adversary recovered his senses. The train pulled out of the station, carrying me to safety. Betty was wide-eyed at what she had just witnessed, but the other passengers did not seem to notice.

I had other adventures during my art-school years. PMSA was located in the cultural center of Philadelphia, now known as the Avenue of the Arts, within two blocks of the theaters and the Academy of Music. Young people were hired, at $1.00 a performance, as supernumeraries for crowd scenes in opera productions. I played a soldier in *Carmen* and *Aida,* and a sinner in *Nabuko.* Of course, it was not the money that attracted me; like sweeping up after the elephants in the circus, it was show business and had the added benefit of meeting attractive dancers.

I met Rosemarie, a dancer from one of the operas, and we hit it off immediately. She must have thought our relationship had promise, for the next day she excitedly told her friend at high school about this guy she had met at the previous night's performance. Betty just happened to be standing behind her. I never saw Rosemarie again and started to believe in fate.

I desperately clung to my Fountainhead principles. I refused to admit to Betty or myself that all my bravado could not make up for my lack of ability. A mediocre artist's realization of his limited ability is probably one of the most agonizing epiphanies one can experience.

The returning veterans, many of them married, who made up half the class became, in some sense, like older brothers whose world experiences and goals became our aspirations. None of us had great financial ambitions. We looked forward to nothing more than owning a small suburban home, with a small plot of ground separating ourselves from our neighbors, and having a car, preferably foreign-made. The GI Bill provided the veterans with housing and educational benefits plus a small living allowance.

I had a real touch of envy watching an upperclassman park his pre-war MG on Broad Street each day, right in front of the school. "Now, there is a man who has it made!" I thought. When I found out that, upon graduation, he would be a designer for Maidenform, the bra company, I realized that some people had all the luck.

In the beginning of my senior year, I noticed Louise as she was hanging a freshman student exhibition. Her back was turned to me. She was wearing very tight jeans and a black turtleneck sweater. Her long black hair completed what I thought was a dramatic sight. She lived near my home, and for several months we had a serious, although rocky, relationship. Every day, I saw Betty in the morning before school, and Louise later, at school; sometimes after school I was with one or the other. I don't know how I ever got any schoolwork done.

After a few months, Louise issued an ultimatum, demanding that I choose. I explained that I could not—or more likely, would not. As that relationship ended, I sensed this was the cue to the stage manager: lower the intensity of the red, yellow, and orange overhead stage lights as the blue and green come up just a little. The lights dimmed a little more.

It became obvious that Betty and I were committed to each other; however, I believed that marriage was an artificial social institution that got in the way of a truly loving relationship. Betty and I frequently discussed the topic, and agreed that we would not be conformists but that we would live together as soon as I was financially able, in lieu of getting married. That lifestyle was not generally accepted in 1953, but I think we both believed that by defying society we would strengthen our bond.

In my senior year, when I became certain that I would graduate, three issues became my primary concerns: finding a job as a designer, validating my four years in art school; getting drafted by the army, at some unknown time; and dealing with the pressure that Betty's parents, primarily her mother, Eva, were putting on us to get married.

The army would not permit me to live off-base with Betty unless we were married. We considered marriage, then, so I could avoid living in the barracks with more than fifty men rather than with Betty.

In addition, Betty's grandmother was dying, and Eva saw this as an opportunity to achieve her goal of uniting Betty and me in a conventional marriage. Without any forewarning, Eva suggested that Betty and I go upstairs to tell her grandmother that we were engaged. "It would make this old dying woman so happy," she said.

As a twenty-year-old, I did not know how to respond, and after a few painful minutes, we went upstairs and announced our engagement to the dying woman. That manipulation by Betty's mother destroyed any possibility of my having a positive relationship with her.

In March 1953, two months before my graduation, Betty and I met in the drugstore across from the Academy of Music. That was our routine, but this time when we met, I teasingly threw a ring box into the air several times, catching it and telling her she would see what was in the box that evening when we saw the pre-Broadway premiere of Cole Porter's Can-Can. The following Monday, my cartoon to her was a scene from Can-Can with high-kicking dancers on stage and a woman in the audience with outstretched arms and a diamond ring on her left hand. I had designed the ring using two diamonds from my mother's jewelry and asked the jewelry instructor at school to make it.

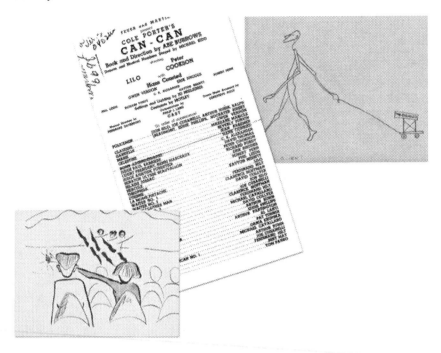

To the relief of my parents, Betty, and myself, I did graduate and become an industrial designer. In spite of my pedestrian talent, I was the first in my class to secure employment in my field. Just before graduation, Philco Corporation hired me as a designer of home entertainment products. When I got the job commitment, I bought a used Austin A40. Six months later, I was drafted.

I drove the Austin, with Betty at my side, to my graduation. After the ceremony, I was driving Betty to her parents' home, going south on Broad Street. At a traffic light, my father, who was driving north, spotted a couple in the opposite lane kissing passionately while waiting for the light to change. My parents, still clinging to their German standards, found public displays of affection inappropriate. He pointed out to my mother what he thought was a totally irresponsible couple. When the light changed and the cars passed, he recognized the culprit in the driver's seat as his son. I heard my father's distraught voice drifting across Broad Street "Oh, my God, it's Peter!"

I had always resented the Jewish high holidays of Rosh Hashanah and Yom Kippur that my parents insisted that I observe by not going to school or work, but instead spending some time in religious services.

They believed it was important that we all acknowledge our Judaism to this minimal extent. I frequently had other plans, but always complied.

In 1953, at the time of the Jewish holidays, my mother was in Israel attending my cousin's wedding. I had started working at Philco and was spending most of my free time with Betty, so my father did not know how I was recognizing Yom Kippur.

Shortly after our graduation, Harold Yoos had bought a sailboat. He invited Charley, his girlfriend Joye, Betty, and me on its maiden voyage, which was set for Yom Kippur. I drove my friends, in my newly acquired Austin, to the Jersey shore to try out Harold's boat.

As we struggled to keep the boat righted in the inlet, on our way to the open sea, it became apparent that no one on the boat knew much more about sailing than I did. Many of our classmates had discussed the intricacies of sailing in class. I never participated in these discussions because I had never been on a sailboat in my life and did not even understand the vocabulary. Now I was beginning to wonder if these sailing discussions had been based on experience or fantasy.

The wind got stronger by the minute. The flags on the shore, which I learned later were storm signals, were whipping and straining at their ropes. The small boat sped up as we headed out to sea. All of us, except Betty, were on one side of the boat, using our weight and leaning far out in a vain attempt to keep the boat righted. Then, just as we leaned back so far that we were almost standing, the edge of the boat on Betty's side touched the water. The boat tipped and all of us tumbled into the water. Betty was underneath the sail as it hit the water!

Fortunately, Betty was a good swimmer, and after a few terrifying minutes, she appeared on the surface. All five of us hung onto the hull, unable to see the shore. Because it had been a chilly fall day, we all were wearing heavy jackets that were now waterlogged. Everyone shed their outer clothing but me—I had pinned the Austin's keys in the pocket of my field jacket and knew we would need the car to get us home if we got out of this alive.

We debated our alternatives: abandon the boat and swim to shore, or stay with the boat and try to kick our way to shore. Each alternative had the same basic flaw: we didn't know which way shore was.

We became increasingly cold. After about half an hour that seemed like an eternity, we heard the welcome putt-putt of an engine. In a few minutes, we were lifted like drowned rats onto the deck of a fishing boat. The fishing crew towed Harold's pride and joy to shore.

To cap off the day, the Austin broke down on the way back to Philadelphia. Perhaps God does punish sinners who play rather than worship on Yom Kippur.

In September, I received a notice to report for army service on December 15, so we made hurried plans for an October 2 wedding. When my mother returned from Israel, she was greeted by the news that Betty and I would be getting married the next weekend.

We were married in Betty's parents' apartment. There was a wedding lunch for about twenty-five guests at Longchamp's Restaurant, on the street level of the apartment building. Betty and I left immediately after lunch for our two-day weekend honeymoon at the Hotel Statler in New York. The hotel bill was $26.45 for the two nights, including $1.25 for two long-distance calls.

Driven by the desire to get my designs finished before I left for the army, so they could be manufactured and introduced at the following Miss America Pageant in September, I believed I could not spare time away from my job at Philco. My design group thought that I was crazy and that my marriage was destined to be a very short one. While in New York, we saw a memorable production of Porgy and Bess with Cab Calloway as Sporting Life and Leontyne Price as Bess.

In short order, my classmates Phil and Charley each got married. Phil turned out to be the most stable of the group, working for the same engineering company from the day he graduated to the time of his retirement. Charley stayed in design his entire professional life but with many different employers, including some of the large design firms. Harold was in the design department of RCA until his retirement. Dick opened one of the first VW agencies in this country. Ray had various engineering and design positions related to pharmaceutical packaging. Gordon, who had not attended our wedding, sent a telegram, "Congratulations to both on the unanimous choice." He was with the Henry Dreyfus design firm until his death at a young age.

I, on the other hand, had multiple careers, in vastly different fields, depending upon how they are counted.

During my art school days, Senator Joe McCarthy was rising to prominence with his anticommunist witch-hunts. My friends and I paid practically no attention to the political change and damage he caused our country. My apathy at that time is hard to reconcile with my activism twenty years later.

– 9 –

US 52336239

The Reluctant Warrior

December 15 arrived. My mother, Betty, and I took the subway to the Beurey Building where my draft notice had directed me to report. A soldier holding a clipboard was in the hallway on the eighth floor. He checked off my name and said that I, alone, was to go into the office marked "Selective Service Board 146." He was totally unresponsive to our questions relating to where I would be stationed. There were quick good-byes and a promise that I would call as soon as I could, to let my family know my destination.

I was ushered into a room filled with recruits. After a long wait, which I spent wondering why I could not have waited outside with my mother and Betty, I had a short interview dealing with sexually transmitted diseases and criminal activity, and a cursory medical exam. After we pulled up our pants and zipped our flies, we recruits stood in three rows and raised our right hands. I became a member of the U.S. Army in about two hours from the time I arrived at the Beurey Building, with most of that time spent waiting. In my usual does-not-play-well-with-others mode, I had not spoken to any of my fellow draftees.

I took the oath seriously, feeling immense gratitude to this country for granting me admittance; if all the United States wanted in return was my military service, I would give it gladly, without reservation.

We draftees, each carrying a buff folder, lined up in a column of twos and marched out to the elevator under the supervision of two sergeants. We rode to the first floor and were marched over to a lieutenant who was standing in front of a bus. We carried overnight bags with toiletries and a change of underwear, and we were in varying modes of dress. All questions about our destination got the shouted answer, "Shut up! You're in the army! You don't speak unless spoken to. Get on the bus, look at the file you are carrying, and memorize your serial number! You have lost your parents, girlfriends, wives, and your names—your number has become your name!" I memorized US 52336239.

Most of us were anxious to know where we were headed. *Would our final destination be a short bus ride away, where our families could visit, or would we be taking a cross-country train trip?*

I found a window seat and considered it my good fortune that no one sat next to me. My fellow recruits appeared to be younger than I, which I attributed to the three-year deferment I had been granted to complete college.

The bus went south, past the North Philadelphia station and out of the city, indicating that perhaps this would not lead to a cross-country train ride. I wondered if the guy in charge of us was an aberrant asshole or if he was typical of those who would be guiding my military service. My first doubts about military service challenged the good feeling I had experienced earlier, when taking the oath, about giving back to this country. *What logical reason could there be for keeping our destination secret, when revealing it could reduce the anxiety felt by the recruits and their families?*

The bus pulled into the parking lot of a roadside restaurant. Lt. Asshole stood in the front of the bus, announcing, "You worthless excuses for recruits have twenty minutes to eat and use the latrine. Any of you not on the bus in twenty minutes will be considered AWOL, and will face a court martial."

By the time I made my way off the bus, a line of three had already formed at the pay phone mounted on the outside wall of the restaurant. I knew the first order of business was to go to the bathroom—"latrine" in Lt. Asshole's language. It did not seem like a good choice to wait the whole allotted twenty minutes to place a phone call while I had no information for my family, particularly when I had no idea when I would have another chance to use a latrine.

After a five-minute wait for a urinal, I had ten minutes to get two hot dogs. As advertised, this indeed, was the best-fed army in the world. I saw Lt. Asshole and the sergeant eating a steak and baked potato at a corner table. Figuring that the twenty-minute deadline was just a harassment tactic, I went outside and waited in line to use the phone. I was able to tell Betty I loved her, did not know where I was going, and would call when I got there. After forty-five minutes, I was back on the bus waiting for the lieutenant and sergeant. I was learning more about the army than the word for bathroom.

I looked out the window and determined from the highway markings that we were in Virginia. At dusk, the bus turned off the four-lane highway and passed a large sign proclaiming that we were entering Fort Meade. We stopped at a guard post and were quickly waved on. All the buildings we passed looked identical: two-story, white, wooden structures. The bus stopped in front of one of these.

Lt. Asshole ordered us off the bus and the sergeant lined us up, marching us to the front of the building. We stood facing the barracks, as the asshole droned on about our asses belonging to the army and how we were to forget any attachment to wives, sweethearts, or families because we now had only one loyalty: the United States Army. *That's what you may think, lieutenant,* I mused.

Another sergeant came out of the barracks, referring to us as pieces of crap. Once again we were told whom our asses belonged to. He blew his whistle and told us that every time we heard that whistle we were to line up in front of the barracks in two rows in less than a minute. When we were dismissed, we were to go into the barracks, pick out a bunk, unroll the mattress, and place our belongings on the mattress. "*Dismissed*!!" he screamed, and we all ran into the barracks. I picked out a lower bunk from the two double-decked rows, and then the whistle blew. We all ran outside and were marched to the mess hall.

Lining up in the food line, we each picked up a stainless steel, compartmentalized tray and proceeded down the line as the servers of the best-fed army ladled food randomly onto our trays. We could take what we wanted, but had to finish what we took because, when we returned our trays, someone would be checking to make sure we were not wasting food. Dreaded consequences, such as KP, would befall any violator.

On the way over to the mess hall, I spotted a pay phone on the side of one of the buildings, and after we had returned to the barracks, I snuck out and called Betty. I told her I was at Fort Meade, Virginia, but that I had no idea how long I would be here. I also told her how impressed I was with the efficiency of the U.S. Army that had managed, in less than one day, to turn an eager draftee who believed it his patriotic duty to serve into a belligerent opponent.

The whistle woke me. It was still dark outside, but the barracks' bulbs were on. The sergeant from the previous night, standing in front of the two rows of beds, shouted, "You worthless pieces of crap have ten minutes to use the latrine, get dressed, washed, shaved, and assembled in two rows in front of the barracks! The last ones out there will be sorry! Step on it!" There was a flurry of activity, with shoving toward the sinks and toilets. I shaved without water, assuming I would regret being either unshaven or late.

The last six to arrive were pulled out of line. The last two were assigned to clean the latrine; the others were assigned to clean the barracks. "I want the floors, crappers, sinks, and plumbing to shine, you worthless excuses for soldiers!" the sergeant hollered.

"The rest of you, *left face*!" After a few seconds of confusion, we were, once again, marching in two columns, if you could call our shuffling "marching." The sergeant called out, "Left! Right! Left! Right!" Our response showed little unity. Ending in front of a one-story building, we received the command, "*Halt*!" After a ragged stop, with the end of the columns crashing into the middle, we once again were in two rows.

As the sergeant read our names from his clipboard, we were supposed to respond loudly and then enter the building eight at a time. Three minutes later, each group emerged with very little hair.

Our columns were then marched to the mess hall, where we lined up for breakfast and again were reminded, "This is the best-fed army in the world," and "take what you want, but eat what you take." The oatmeal and scrambled eggs ran together on my tray because the server had placed both items in the same compartment.

Again, we assembled outside and marched to another one-story building. We lined up and were issued a duffel bag, underwear, socks, khaki shirts and pants, a webbed belt with brass buckle, and two sets of dark green shirts and pants with matching jacket, cap, and overcoat. The only items requiring consideration of size were two pairs of boots and one pair of brown dress shoes. The procedure was so hurried that I did not have time to put the clothing into my duffel bag, so I carried the bundle in my arms all the way back to the barracks.

"When I dismiss you worthless pansies, I want each of you to take a shower and wash off all remnants of civilian life!" the sergeant barked. "The next time I see you, I expect you to be trying, at least, to look something like soldiers! Look at the drawing on the wall. Now, arrange your uniforms on the bar next to your bed and put your toiletries, underwear, and socks in your footlocker, just like the drawing shows. Your civilian clothing should be placed in the laundry bag and sent home. Inspection will be in one hour, just before lunch. *Dismissed!*"

The communal shower was unpleasant, with many naked bodies crowded into large shower rooms. A greater challenge, however, was getting dressed in my recently issued uniform, complying with the pattern of hanging them up, and arranging my footlocker. I surely did not want to have to clean the latrine or be put on KP duty, which I now knew meant working in the kitchen.

The boots were tight, but I managed to get them on and laced, just before the sergeant's damned whistle blew. We all rushed out to stand in the usual two rows. My favorite spot was in the second row, right in the middle, where I could be as inconspicuous as possible. We now looked dramatically changed, more like the other men I had seen walking and marching around the post.

We marched to a medical unit, where we were given the large file folders that we had brought with us from the draft board and turned over to Lt. Asshole when we got on the bus. I remembered learning in my high-school history class that General Meade was a mediocre Union general during the Civil War. It seemed fitting that this camp should bear his name.

We gave blood samples, were injected with various drugs, and were given physical exams; then we lined up again outside the building for more marching, this time in columns of four. Our marching was always punctuated by our sergeant's screaming. His screaming was so agitated that the unfortunate target of his anger was sprayed with spit. Fortunately, I had planned ahead to always be on an inside column.

By now, I had concluded that this was an irrational system, run by madmen, and that my planning would not be enough to protect me in all situations. While we waited outside a building for our sheets and pillowcases, my name, along with four others, was called. We marched into the building, received our bedclothes, and were ordered back to the barracks to make our beds in military fashion, whatever that meant, and then report to the mess hall for KP—all within ten minutes.

The cooks outdid the sergeant in sadism. I was assigned to the tray-cleaning detail that consisted of scrubbing used trays with scalding water; as the steam rose around me, I realized I had been fortunate—two of my compatriots had been assigned to clean the grease pit. Although the army had been officially racially integrated for more than five years, I never served with an African-American in any capacity except KP. When the noon meal ended, I was exhausted and soaked from head to foot. No sooner had I finished the trays than we were ordered to clean the pots.

As soon as the floor was cleaned, it was time to start preparations for the evening meal: chopping vegetables, peeling potatoes, washing lettuce, and forming meat into hamburger patties. The food was prepared in such large quantities I thought I was in a chemical plant rather than a kitchen.

After midnight, we finished cleaning up from the evening meal, and I was anxious to get out of the sweltering, steam-swirled kitchen. For an instant, the December air was welcome, but as I walked back to my barracks soaking wet, the freezing air started to stiffen my fatigues. I wanted to get out of the cold, but upon seeing a phone on the side of a building, I decided I wanted, even more, to talk to Betty.

"How are things going?" I heard her cheerful voice, still rough with sleep.

"Terrible," I responded, and although I had resolved not to worry her, I involuntarily burst out, "You've got to get me out of here! I don't care what you have to do! These people are crazy! I'll try calling tomorrow." I continued, "I love you. Now, I have to get out of the cold and back to my barracks. Love you." I hung up and rushed off to the barracks.

As I lay on my bunk, staring at the steel frame of the bunk above me, I calculated that I had 709 days left in this fucking army. Oh, shit, 1954 was a leap year. I had another 710 days.

The dammed whistle blew. We jumped out of bed and stood at attention in front of the footlockers at the foot of our beds. "When I came back from your policing the parade ground, I saw your feeble attempts at bed-making," Sgt. Asshole announced. "You will now see a demonstration of what a military bed looks like. Pay close attention. A bed that is not perfect will get you to KP." Although I resented every word, I paid close attention to the demonstration, as I never wanted to get back to that kitchen again.

The next day became the best I had at Fort Meade, because it seemed that some rationality directed its activities. My group of recruits was given tests similar to the IQ tests I had taken throughout high school. We then were individually interviewed regarding our past work experience and training. When my interviewer learned that I had some familiarity with German, he ordered me to a special bench. I then took a language test that consisted of listening to recordings of German aircraft crews speaking to one another over heavy static. I then was asked questions about the dialogues.

At the conclusion of these tests, I was ushered into the office of a captain who interviewed me from behind a desk. He ended the meeting by telling me that after basic training I would be sent to the Army Language School in California. This sounded rational. The army was going to use whatever talent I had.

One rainy evening, as we assembled in front of the barracks and the sergeant brought us to attention, a lieutenant read out a list of names that included mine. Those on the list were ordered to remain. The others were dismissed to return to the barracks. The officer informed us that we had qualified for Officer Training School. We stood in the rain while he told us the advantages of being an officer. He also told us we would be in the army for an additional two years, if we became officers, and then asked if we had any questions. I raised my hand and asked, "Do these five days since my induction count?"

He was not pleased. I left the group and returned out of the rain to the barracks.

Polishing our boots seemed to be one of the most important activities in the army. My boots had become a special problem after the grease and steam from KP duty had dulled their surface.

The next few days were spent marching from one parade field to another and policing them—which meant walking in single file across the field picking up trash.

Eventually, my assignment for basic training appeared on the bulletin board. I was assigned to Company G at Aberdeen Proving Grounds, which was much closer to Philadelphia. I was delighted.

Company G was commanded by a pompous strutting asshole, Lt. Olynzack. He delighted in telling us that he expected perfection from our motley crew, so we would have inspection twice a week. If anyone earned any demerits, the company would be restricted to the post that weekend. We worked every evening polishing our boots, placing our toiletries perfectly in the top tray of our footlockers, and cleaning and oiling our rifles; however, week after week the company was denied weekend passes.

Betty had discovered that my friend from art school, Charley O'Donnell, was also doing his basic training at Aberdeen. Every weekend, Betty and Charley's wife, Joye, took the train from Philadelphia to Aberdeen to visit us.

The second week of basic training, was intended for us to bond a close relationship with our M-1 rifles, a relationship that was to last throughout our army careers. Since I had a problem bonding with my fellow recruits, I found it even more difficult to build a relationship with a rifle. I had never had any mechanical talents, so my attempts to dismantle and reassemble this weapon within a limited time period, sometimes blindfolded, were a failure.

Basic training is a physically exhaustive outdoor activity, which works up a good appetite. I noticed that, week after week, the quantity of food available to each recruit at each meal declined noticeably, until about the fourth week when each of us was served one hot dog for the evening meal. A rumor circulated that the lieutenant had been selling our food to restaurants in town. Betty could not understand why I had developed such a voracious appetite, and she brought large cream-filled pastries on her weekend visits in a vain attempt to satisfy my hunger.

In our fifth week, after failing inspection again—this time because one mess kit had a trace of grease—we were given a particularly galling lecture. The lieutenant explained this was for our own good and related the story of one of his basic training buddies who had a dirty mess kit and was killed in Korea. *You stupid fool, are you telling us that the North Koreans examined Americans' mess kits before they decided whom to kill?* I thought. The CO left us standing as he strutted to his car.

One of the recruits ran into the barracks and appeared on the second-floor balcony with tears streaming down his face and his rifle on his shoulder, screaming for bullets to kill Olynzack. Fortunately, no ammunition was available. Olynzack never returned; rumor was that he was in the military prison at Ft. Leavenworth. With the arrival of a new CO, we had weekend passes for the last two weeks of basic training.

By the middle of the sixth week, it became obvious that there were two types of trainees. My type, whose serial number began with the designation *US*, would, at best, do what was asked, stay out of trouble, and serve our time. The other group, who had *RA* regular army designation serial numbers, was enthusiastic about the training program but managed to get into trouble more frequently than the draftees.

Our map-reading exercise became a failure when we draftees, doing the best we could, got hopelessly lost as night closed in. We started laughing uncontrollably, assuming that since we were on a military installation we would be found sooner or later. An RA, who took the situation as a personal failure, started screaming, "You just don't care! That's what pisses me off! You just don't care!" The other RAs joined in, and an obvious schism developed between us. Our unified front against the army was forever destroyed.

During that same week, we were double-timing four abreast down a paved road with forests of pine trees on each side. I saw a flash of movement on my left an instant before a deer struck me on the left hip, and I went down as the deer disappeared into the woods across the road. Because I had stopped so quickly, the column behind me fell on top of me, with a clatter of rifles. I had used the butt of my rifle to break my fall, and as I looked down, I saw my rifle butt had split on the paving.

After we were dismissed, I had to go into the supply tent to request a new rifle butt, "Because Private Ney was struck by a deer, which broke my butt."

The supply sergeant responded, "You think you're funny, don't you, you worthless recruit? I'll show you how funny this is when you get the cost of the butt withheld from your pay." Since I needed all of my earnings to pay for Betty's visits, this was not an insignificant threat. The replacement cost was never withheld.

I started to become skeptical about the various penalties that were threatened: the guard having to serve the remainder of an escaped prisoner's term; or a tardy arrival to a formation resulting in a court-martial, with a prison term and an extended enlistment period. It became clear that I could be punished for no infraction; on the other hand, never be punished for serious violations. The best defense, clearly, was never to get caught.

I looked forward to my promised orders to language school, but while members of my basic company received orders to various schools, mine did not arrive. I was not concerned; since I knew the language school was special, so I was not surprised that it was left for last.

I finally received my orders—not to California but to remain in Aberdeen and attend optical fire-control instrument repair school. I never found out if the change was intentional or one of the many army screw-ups I had learned to expect.

I had no knowledge of optics to prepare me for my army specialty, so under twisted army logic, my being trained as an optical instrument repairman made sense. I was grateful not to be assigned to the infantry. I lived in barracks with students of bomb and explosive disarmament. They were an enthusiastic group that I diagnosed as crazy. They talked nonstop about the explosives they had detonated that day. I was concerned that anyone could be so enamored of explosives.

I finished my twelve weeks of training in June and was transferred to Ft. Kilmer, New Jersey, to await assignment to my permanent unit. My main fear was getting an assignment overseas, where Betty could not join me. I called Betty twice a day for three days, to let her know my name had not yet appeared on the bulletin board. On July 3, the fourth day of waiting, I was ordered to Watertown, New York to join the 86th Ordnance Company at Camp Drum. I called Betty and told her to pack and meet me as soon as possible at the information desk in New York City's Grand Central Station.

We rode the train all night, happy and excited to begin our independent life together and relieved at my not having been ordered overseas, which would have resulted in our separation. My mother had loaded Betty up with food for our trip, so I saved the army-issued food coupons for future use.

We arrived in Watertown at dawn on Sunday, July 4, and had to find a place to live. At the train station, I bought a newspaper for the classified ads, which Betty and I scoured in the square at the center of town. The streets were deserted so early in the morning on a national holiday. There was only one ad for an apartment that we could afford with my $165.00 per month income—which included base pay, marriage premium, and off-base living allotment, assuming I would be granted permission to live off base. I had learned not to take anything for granted.

We waited until nine thirty to ring the bell at 146 Union Avenue to inquire about the advertised apartment. A grumpy landlady took us to the second floor of the converted white wood, two-story house. The apartment turned out to be one room, with a Murphy bed that swung out of the wall leaving barely two feet on each side, and a closet that had two electric hotplates on a small shelf. The bathroom, which we shared with all the other tenants on the floor, was down the hall. We had no other choice, so we took it and unpacked Betty's suitcase and my duffel bag. As modest as our first home was, we were truly happy it was all ours; we could shut the door and lock out the rest of the world. I particularly appreciated not having to sleep in the barracks with fifty GIs.

The streets were almost deserted that late, sunny Sunday afternoon, as we walked to downtown Watertown. I had been ordered to report to the 86th Ordnance Company on July 6; evidently, the army was recognizing Monday as Independence Day, giving us another free day to enjoy each other.

We sat in the town square, again looking through the classified section of the Watertown newspaper. My army pay would not be sufficient for our living expenses, so Betty planned to look for a job. We had no idea what she would qualify for, having spent two years at Temple University studying primary education. Perhaps she could be a teacher's aide, but this was summer and the schools were closed. Betty intended to apply at the schools for the fall, but needed something now.

I had some savings from my six months at Philco and the sale of my beloved Austin A40, but that would probably have to be used for another car. As dusk arrived, we had dinner at one of the economical cafes, using my army meal ticket for both meals. We returned to our apartment and negotiated the Murphy bed. Having not slept for over twenty-four hours, we had no trouble falling asleep in what felt like luxurious surroundings.

Sightseeing in Watertown did not take long, and we soon ended up at the town square, just like the previous day. I sat on a park bench while Betty wandered in and out of the surrounding stores looking for a job. She returned, smiling, in less than an hour. She would launch a new career in shoe sales.

Bus service to Camp Drum was infrequent. The forty-five-minute bus ride was scheduled only for 6:00 AM, noon, and 5:00 PM. Now that we were financially secure, we thought about buying a car.

My heart sank the first day I saw the 86th Ordnance waiting for morning formation. Based on my six months of military experience, I was sure I would not be seeing Betty that evening. There stood a motley crew: some with fatigue pants over their boots, others with pants in their boots, fatigue shirts in, fatigue shirts out; all with boots un-shined and covered with grease.

I reported to the company headquarters and handed my file to the First Sergeant. I noticed that he, too, had un-shined, grease-covered boots and was wearing a dirty field jacket. He became my hero when he signed the authorization for me to live off-post. He pointed out the instrument repair squad, and told me to get in formation with that group. I stood in the last row, not wanting to bring attention to my highly polished boots and neatly pressed fatigues. Was it possible I was the most military-looking soldier in the company?

The instrument repair group spent its days in a large enclosed truck, which had a workbench on each side. I learned that the 86th

Ord. Co. was at Camp Drum for the summer to support the army reserve units in their two-week training exercises. It was expected that we would be transferred to an unknown location in about two months. The workload was almost non-existent.

Interruptions for meals and the periodic arrival of tank range finders requiring adjustment were the only breaks in the monotony of waiting in the truck, day after day. The older tanks, which the reserve units used for training, had optical range finders that used a fixed length between prisms located in steel bubbles on each side of the turret. As the gunner adjusted the prisms to create a triangle at the target, the gun's elevation was adjusted for the appropriate distance. The optical system was connected to the gun by mechanical linkages that sometimes loosened and had to be adjusted.

So, about once a week, I crawled into a tank turret to adjust the linkages. We spent the rest of the time in our truck bullshitting, looking at girlie magazines, or, perhaps, reading books. Our truck had been issued one gallon of 199-octane alcohol, to be used for cleaning lenses and prisms. I don't recall cleaning lenses or prisms, but we regularly mixed the alcohol with orange juice for our afternoon screwdrivers, served to the select few from the rear door of the truck.

One night, Betty woke me suddenly, in the middle of the night. "There is something or someone in the apartment," she whispered.

"Impossible, there is no room for anyone else to be in the room with the Murphy bed down," I replied. I switched on the light and saw a gray, furry mouse run into its hole. Now, Betty was even more frightened, and demanded we move that instant. When we realized the absurdity of that request, we sat in bed laughing hysterically.

Betty made a friend in the house: a prostitute on our floor with whom we exchanged pleasantries on our way to and from the bathroom at the end of the hall. Betty would tell me about the times she spent with our neighbor when neither of them was working.

One day, as Betty was walking in the town square, she saw a familiar face from high school: Aileen. Both were in Watertown for the same reason. Aileen had married Bobby Rosenberg, the son of a clothing manufacturer in Milwaukee. Bobby had been drafted and assigned to Finance. He was awaiting his discharge in the spring, when he was planning to go to law school. The four of us became a social circle.

On weekends, we explored the northern New York countryside and the newly constructed St. Lawrence Seaway. During the week, we spent many evenings together talking about our plans after the army and playing games.

One evening, Bobby was assigned to guard the payroll for the whole army post. At that time, every GI was paid in cash, so there was an extremely large amount of money in the safe. Bobby had asked Aileen to bring us over for a game of Scrabble so we could help him kill time on his guard duty.

Bobby had placed his carbine on the desk, halfway across the room, while we all sat around a table, engrossed in our game. There was a knock at the window, and two MPs asked if everything was okay. We all waved and the girls giggled, assuring them that everything was fine. That scene was repeated every half-hour, until the MPs came in and took Aileen, Betty, and me into custody. We spent the night in cells in the brig, awaiting investigation. All the money was found in the safe, so none of us was charged.

Betty and I bought a maroon 1949 Studebaker sedan. A model that I had always admired for its unique design. On weekends, we drove to the St. Lawrence Seaway, and once crossed into Canada, visiting Montreal. Betty found a teaching job that would begin immediately after Labor Day. We seemed to be on easy street. In the middle of August, Bobby and Aileen were transferred to Fort Devens, Massachusetts.

By the end of August, all the reservists had left Camp Drum, and our company was assigned to various cleanup details. At a morning formation, the First Sergeant announced that our unit would move, in two weeks, to Fort Totten, on a New York peninsula jutting into the East River at Bayside, Queens.

After studying a road map, I volunteered to be on the advance party, to relieve Betty's anxiety at having to travel separately to New York.

Through the efforts of my cousin Ruth, who lived in Queens, we found an apartment—no small feat in metropolitan New York.

The advance party's duty was to prepare the barracks and command post, including telephone and mail service, for the arrival of the entire company a week later. At Fort Totten, we cleaned windows and washed floors in the brick buildings assigned to our company. As soon as the phone was hooked up, it rang. We had been sent to Ft. Totten by mistake, and were to contact our unit to redirect them to Fort Devens, Massachusetts.

The officer in charge of our advance party told me he had seen orders that I would be reassigned to Korea. That news was devastating, as I had begun taking it for granted that I would remain stateside until I had less than one year remaining, when I no longer would qualify for overseas duty.

Before driving to Massachusetts, we detoured to Philadelphia to see our parents. I told my parents that I would soon be going overseas, so Betty's parents and relatives visited to say goodbye to me. I spent the weekend plugging the rust holes and painting the maroon Studebaker yellow to hide its rust spots. My mother was less than delighted with the yellow overspray on the walls of their garage. We left Philadelphia, with heavy hearts, in the middle of the night.

We arrived in Littleton, Massachusetts at dawn and, as had become our habit, purchased the local newspaper in the town square to look at the classified ads. Bobby and Aileen had arrived in Massachusetts about a month previously.

Since our time together seemed short, with a probable one-year separation, Betty and I decided to splurge. We rented a small, unfurnished house around the corner from Bobby and Aileen.

Betty got two jobs: teaching at a pre-school in the neighboring town of Harvard in the morning and at the Ft. Devens day-care center in the afternoon. This worked out well. Betty would take me to Ft. Devens in the morning, drive to her pre-school job, return to the post to teach, and then pick me up for our drive home together.

About two weeks later, I learned that my military occupational specialty, MOS, had been designated as obsolete. All fire control was now electronic. This meant that I would not be going to Korea. We were so relieved that we decided to replace the now-yellow Studebaker, which had developed serious mechanical problems.

I considered our new 1953 Studebaker Starlight coupe the most beautiful car ever mass-produced in the United States. The Studebakers might have been the best-looking cars in America, but they were also the worst running. After all, I was a designer, not a mechanic.

Betty and I were at Aileen and Bobby's home for Christmas Eve. We had decided we were not going to spend money on presents, so we were surprised when they brought out a shoe box and handed it to us. Inside, there was a small black and white ball of fur. This week-old Border collie mix puppy became the center of our life. There was, of course, only one name possible: Quirky.

Bobby had made friends with another married draftee in Finance. Howard Rubin was from Philadelphia and had completed law school before he was drafted. Howard and his wife joined our social circle. Because Bobby was planning to go to law school and Howard had finished, much of their conversation, which I found very interesting, dealt with law. I wished that a law career would be an option for me, but thought it was out of the question.

Betty's mother came to visit, so we drove to Boston's Logan Airport to pick her up in our beautiful Studebaker. It was snowing and I was driving at a relatively slow rate of speed. Suddenly, I could not see the road. The long, sloping hood had come loose and flown over the windshield, bending over the roof. I pulled over and securely tied down the hood. I had owned the car for only six weeks. How would I get this fixed? I certainly did not have the money; and even if the thirty-day warranty had covered the hood latch, it had already expired.

Bobby and Howard now had a real case to discuss. After much research, they framed an argument for me to use when I went to the dealer in Boston the next Saturday. It worked, and the car was repaired at no cost to me. My interest in law increased. Perhaps, some time in the future, I could go to law school.

Now that I had no job in the army, my time was spent either totally idle or occupied with army make-work duties: whitewashing rocks that marked paths and roadsides; policing grounds; or counting and stacking blankets, mess kits, and sheets.

I knew if I spent my remaining year in the army without any productive activity, I certainly would get into trouble. I investigated the possibility of getting an early out for educational reasons, although I had no logical continuing path from art school. I considered an engineering program, but knew that would be certain disaster. Going back to Philco, my previous employer, would not be considered essential to the national interest.

I learned about the Army's stage production of *Finnian's Rainbow* and convinced the director that I could put my design education to good use as scenery designer. On January 11, 1955, by order of the Chief of Staff, I was assigned to the Army's production of *Finnian's Rainbow*. The initial temporary assignment was for only twenty-nine days, but I was confident that I could and did get it extended. My First Sergeant and CO were not pleased. Although they had no productive work for me, I had successfully gone over their heads and found something productive to do.

In March, my company was ordered to participate in two-week maneuvers on Cape Cod. My sergeant made it his project to get me reassigned to the Company for these maneuvers. He won that round. The score was now tied at one to one.

Operation Shoelace was held in below-freezing weather, with over a foot of snow on the ground. Each enlisted man supplied one half of a pup tent, sharing the resulting two-man tent. The poor soldier who was assigned to me will not forget that first night when I awoke having to piss in the worst way. The cold weather only increased the urgency of my need. I struggled to get my boots on in the cramped quarters, and then succeeded in unbuttoning one end of the tent. However, crawling out of the tent with one arm on each side of the supporting pole, I broke the three-part pole, causing one end of the tent to collapse.

There was no way to repair the damaged pole, so I stuck my companion's rifle in the ground, barrel up, as a substitute pole. When I finally got out of the tent, it was snowing and pitch black. I stumbled over some ropes from the walled tents, and decided to relieve myself next to one of them. A light went on inside the tent, and I could see the silhouette of a figure rising from a cot. "What the fuck is going on out there?" rang out, obviously referring to my stream striking the tent. In my best military manner, I responded, "Private Ney urinating, sir." I retreated to my tent, confident that he would not catch the name or recognize my voice.

As I looked out of the tent the next morning, I saw several soldiers taking down their pup tents, obviously to move to a new location. While they were in the mess line, I substituted the three parts of our broken pole for their intact pole; then, I switched my prize for my buddy's rifle. Everything was fine, except for the rifle's barrel, which now, most likely, was a rusty mess. Thank God for sound sleepers.

I was assigned to a machine gun squad where I met Sgt. Radotsky, one of the many non-commissioned officers left over from the Second World War who now had no real leadership position. He had the experience to keep us fed and out of the cold, most of the time, but more importantly, he kept us out of trouble.

While I wanted to get out of the army as soon as possible, Radotsky had the opposite problem. The army was re-qualifying men who had served honorably in the war and the following ten years, had no training for civilian life, and were planning to retire after twenty years of service. Now, they were being retested under the guise of the army raising its standards, but the result was to selectively throw these men out of the army, depriving them of their retirement.

No matter what problems I had with the present army, my heroes were those who served and won the Second World War. Radotsky, who had joined the army immediately after graduating from high school, was petrified by the qualification exam that was scheduled, throughout the army, in three weeks.

Our machine gun emplacement was on the high ground around the area of the command post. I noticed a circling helicopter that landed in front of the CP tent. The pilot ran into the tent, and immediately the First Sergeant ran out screaming, "Ney! Where the fuck is Ney?" I panicked. How could they have found out, with a helicopter, about my urinating episode? I walked down the hill to face the music.

There was no escape. When I faced the sergeant, who was trembling with rage, he handed me an envelope with Betty's familiar handwriting on the outside. I opened Betty's letter: "Take care of yourself. Darling, I love you always. Quirky." The sergeant screamed for me to return to my position, and what the hell was I waiting for? The score: at least two or three to one, depending on how you calculated the urinating episode.

I found out later that Betty, through her job at the day-care center, had become friendly with the general's wife, who told Betty that her husband was on *Operation Shoelace* maneuvers. Betty volunteered that her husband also was there. The general's wife offered to have a letter sent to me from Betty, as she was just sending one to her husband in the general's helicopter.

As the maneuvers ended, we were packing our gear with the continual screaming of the CO urging us to move faster. Being fairly far away, I yelled, "You may chew my ass as long as you want, but you'll never digest it, you fucking asshole!"

The CO screamed, "Who said that?" Fortunately, no one responded, and he never discovered the source. Score: four to one.

When I got back to Fort Devens, I again found refuge in Finnian's Rainbow.

The day of the NCO qualification test arrived. As Radotsky and I had planned, I put on his field jacket, with his sergeant's stripes on the sleeve and his ID card in its pocket. I walked into the mess hall with all the NCOs who had been ordered to take the test. No one seemed to notice that I was more than ten years younger than any of the NCOs who were there or that the field jacket I was wearing was much too large for me. The fear left me as I filled out the space at the top of the page while referring to Radotsky's ID card to make sure I had his serial number correct: "S/Sgt Radotsky, Albert, RA 23756374." Six weeks later, Radotsky was informed that he had passed with a high score.

In April, Bobby was discharged and gave Betty a great deal of clothing manufactured by his father's company. Betty was now better dressed than she had ever been. We frequently remembered the Rosenbergs with great affection, because Quirky—who grew by leaps and bounds—lived with us for many years, giving us much joy.

We had been happy in our house in Littleton, but eventually were notified that my company would be returning to Camp Drum, New York. I produced some drawings of Betty, in anticipation of our return to civilian life in eight months.

Sgt. Radotsky made sure I was assigned to the advance party so Betty, Quirky, and I could travel to Watertown together. As we were driving through the Berkshires in our beautiful new Studebaker, negotiating a hairpin turn, a tire blew out. I was able to come to a stop on the inside of the turn. We were in a blind spot, so Betty had to walk up the road with a flashlight, to warn traffic. I managed to get the tire changed and called for Betty to get back in the car. She opened the door as I was replacing the tools, and Quirky jumped out, heading down the hill in the pitch-black darkness.

I clambered down the hill, with Betty standing on the roadside, again warning traffic. After about forty-five minutes, just as we were thinking of giving up, out of the darkness a black and white tail-wagging dog appeared next to me. I grabbed his collar and looked up the craggy hill, figuring it probably was about two hundred feet back to the road. Using my belt as a leash, I made it back to the car with Quirky. It must have been after midnight when we resumed our journey without a spare tire.

It was around 2:00 AM when we drove into Albany, New York. "Where would we get a tire at this time?" I wondered, doubting I'd find an open service station. I turned a corner and could not believe my eyes: straight ahead, I saw there, on the dimly lit street, some tough-looking guys selling automobile parts, hubcaps, and tires. They even had a compressor, and mounted the replacement tire for an extra two dollars.

Driving through the night, we arrived in Watertown about ten in the morning and immediately began searching for a place to live. We were hoping for something better than the previous year, but realized our search would be more difficult now that we had a medium-sized dog accompanying us. In the last four months, Quirky had grown rapidly from his shoebox size.

We found a real apartment that was suitable and at the right price. The landlady was very skeptical about Quirky, but we exaggerated her good qualities: "Oh, no, she never barks, is perfectly housebroken, and will never disturb your landscaping." She agreed to rent us the apartment with the condition that if Quirky were to cause any problems, the dog, or all of us, would have to go.

Betty found a job as a saleslady in an upscale dress shop. Watertown was relatively close to the Canadian border. The military, and Canadians who crossed the border to take advantage of the favorable exchange rate, supported its economy.

One late afternoon, I got home from my window washing and floor sweeping duties as part of the advance party, to find Betty crying hysterically. During our second week on Colorado Street, Quirky had dug up a tulip. The landlady could not be moved—Quirky had to go.

We stayed up all night hugging Quirky. Two weeks earlier, we had searched the town for an apartment, to no avail; now, there were fewer vacancies, as the town was filling up for the summer. It was the army's fault, forcing me to stay for another seven months even though there was nothing productive for me to do. I even considered deserting, but fortunately, came to my senses.

As dawn broke, we had rationalized that Quirky would be happy on one of the farms in the surrounding rural countryside, where he would have room to run. Betty had not yet started working, so it was her job to take Quirky to the animal shelter. She told me that the woman at the shelter assured her that Quirky would be placed on a farm—a perfect place for a border collie.

The complete company arrived from Ft. Devens, with the full complement of asshole officers and NCOs. I was happy to see Radotsky again. He told me his wife had driven to Watertown by herself and found an abandoned chicken farm for the two of them to rent. Explaining why I was so surly, I told him what had happened with Quirky. He asked Betty and me to have dinner with him and his wife that weekend.

Radotsky had met his wife at a displaced persons camp after the war. She was French, about twenty years younger than he, a flaming redhead with a personality to match.

On Monday, Betty received a phone call from an elderly woman who told her that she had adopted Quirky, but couldn't handle the dog because she lived in an upstairs room. She asked if we would like to have her back, perhaps to find him a more suitable home.

Betty rushed over, and as she climbed the stairs she heard Quirky's familiar bark. When she saw Quirky, she was straining against an electric cable bolted to the floor. The cable broke at the bolt, and Quirky was in Betty's arms. Betty spent the day in the park with Quirky, sneaking her into our apartment.

"Sarge, we got the dog back. Would you let us keep her at your farm?" I asked. "Betty and I will take total care of her. If we don't work this out, I think I'll desert, as I can't put the dog or Betty through this again." He agreed, and right after work, Betty and I took Quirky to her new home. I told Radotsky I never again wanted to hear how thankful he was to me for taking his test. We were more than even.

Every evening, we played with Quirky at Radotsky's until September, when we were again assigned to Ft. Devens. In those five months, Radotsky had become our good friend.

When the time for transfer to Massachusetts arrived, I had less than ninety days left in the army, so we decided that I would take a thirty-day leave and live at my parents' home in Philadelphia with Quirky. This was tough on my parents, but they put up with it. All of us were excited that I was getting out of the army.

I had always planned to return to Philco, and when I visited them, they seemed delighted to have me return. We found a new, three-bedroom house under construction in Horsham, outside of Philadelphia. The house was $10,900 and was to be completed by December; I committed to the purchase and applied for a mortgage. On November 28, I received my orders to transfer to a separation company, getting me out of the First Sergeant's clutches. I am sure each of us thought we had won. I received my good conduct medal, which meant, I suppose, that I had listened to the mandatory reenlistment lecture and not been court-martialed. I found Radotsky. We shook hands, exchanged best wishes, and sent regards to our respective wives. I lifted my duffel bag onto my shoulder, turned, and walked to the separation company.

I had been inducted on December 15, 1953. The army kept me until the very last day of my two-year obligation. What a waste! I took the train from Boston to Philadelphia; and during the six-hour train trip, I mentally reviewed the past two years.

After my discharge on December 14, 1955, I never communicated with any of the people I had met in the army.

– 10 –

The Designer

On November 28, 1955, three weeks before my scheduled discharge, Betty and I had paid the down payment on our first home, at 33 Maple Avenue, Horsham, Pennsylvania. The new three-bedroom house had a living room, separate dining room, kitchen, and bath, but no basement. Closing was set for December 16, two days after I was to be discharged from the army. To commemorate this solemn occasion, we planted a cherry tree on the front lawn of our one-third acre mud lot.

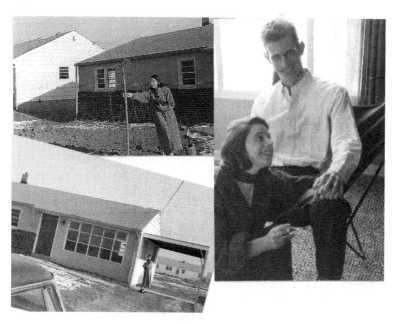

I believed that we could manage the $48.17 monthly payments, as Betty and I both had job commitments. I had been told, on my visit to Philco, that they eagerly awaited my return; Betty would be teaching at a preschool. The bank holding the mortgage was the Philadelphia Saving Fund Society—the same bank my father had used long ago to make the point that you should buy a car only if you had the cash to pay for it.

While our small, basic bungalow was far from an architectural masterpiece, I was determined to use thought and good taste to design each feature. We decided that the color of the living room walls should reflect my profession as a designer. The result was terracotta red on one wall and beige on the other two. The wall facing the street was almost floor-to-ceiling glass.

In our absence, while I was in Massachusetts completing the discharge process, the neighbors looked at our house while it was being finished. They might have wondered about the strange people who would be living next door and who had selected such an unusual color scheme.

Immediately after my discharge from the army, we moved into our home and picked up our lives where we had left off two years earlier. Our move was easy, as our only possessions were several boxes of wedding gifts.

Before our wedding, we had made a statement of who we were by rejecting conventional sterling silver tableware and carefully selecting contemporary dinnerware and stainless steel flatware. Our only living room furniture was the contemporary *Bauhaus* sofa that had been my bed since my parents gave up the boarding house. Our bed was an oversized six-by-seven-foot metal frame with two box springs topped by a foam rubber mattress.

To furnish our dining room, we bought a contemporary Formica-topped, surfboard-shaped table with matching metal-framed chairs from Betty's cousin's kitchen furniture store. Over the next few months, we completed furnishing our house: red and black butterfly chairs for the living room; a Paul McCobb buffet—our pride and joy—for our dining room; and a matching walnut bureau and chest of drawers for the bedroom.

We had now spent years' worth of savings, including money I had earned delivering newspapers and magazines, saved from bar mitzvah gifts, and saved during the six months I'd worked at Philco before being drafted. We were not in debt—and were deliriously happy, in our less-than-modest home, without a worry in the world.

On the first Monday after my discharge, I returned to work at Philco, sitting at the same drawing table I had left two years before, next to very large windows just above the marquee of the Philco headquarters building. I was one of four designers in the radio division who were responsible for the design of all table, console, and portable radios plus all record-playing devices. I had waited for this moment—dreaming of emulating my hero, Howard Roark—designing products as unique and artistic as my 1953 Studebaker Starlight coupe, which was designed by the Raymond Lowey studios.

However, product design was not left to the unfettered inspiration of designers, but rather was the result of marketing strategies that rightly or wrongly targeted specific groups of consumers. Philco used data compiled using the previous year's product sales, sales of competitors' products, demographics, and my old nemesis from junior-high days—social scientists.

This marketing strategy determined which products would be assigned to the design group and how many models of table radios, portables, and record players would be produced and marketed to which targeted consumer groups. Targeted groups were identified by characteristics such as age, education, occupation, recreational activities, and income. This information was formed into assignments, which the designers translated into products. For example, a product-and-target-audience pairing in a particular year might be a portable radio for the younger, college-bound consumer.

It seemed to me that, although the process sounded scientific, it was probably closer to witchcraft than science. One problem was that the design process was always based on data almost two years behind the market we were targeting; second, it used data based on the social sciences—in which I had no faith.

Prior to my army service, I had designed two radios that went into production. A corporation had enough faith in my design to actually invest in the manufacture of my creations. When I saw them in a store window during the Christmas season, I felt I had arrived.

On my return to Philco, I worked with Ross Gilbert, a very decent human being and talented designer who was about fifteen years older than I was. Ross was the senior designer. He had been a furniture designer before coming to Philco and was a natural for designing cabinets to house large combination radio and record players. Another designer in the group had gone to PMSA but had already graduated when I entered the school. Another designer, who had a wide range of design experience, including work in the auto industry, completed the group.

Ross gave me my first two assignments: a table radio and a table clock radio. I enthusiastically started sketching when the idea struck me that a single design for a plastic cabinet could be used for three radio models: a table radio, an economy clock radio, and a deluxe clock radio with a full clock face. My rather simple idea was to design a plastic cabinet with crisp corners and a picture-frame front. A plastic molded grille, with a metal Philco insignia, would fit into the picture frame. This would be the table radio. An opening in the front of the cabinet could permit the production of two styles of clock radio, since it would take either a small-faced clock or a clock with a face extending to the picture frame front.

This idea eliminated the tooling required to manufacture two separate plastic bodies and gave the company the flexibility to manufacture the same radio body for three models that could be manufactured as the market demanded. Ross gave me full credit for the idea, and management liked my idea and way of thinking.

I had enjoyed the exercise of logic needed to design the picture-frame radio, but I still struggled with the sketches required to communicate my ideas. After Ross gave preliminary approval for a concept, the designer would prepare a mechanical drawing from which a very talented model group would make a wooden prototype—an exact representation of the finished product that was presented to management for approval.

At that time, some radio features identified with higher priced products had very little to do with performance. For example, on less expensive models, customers selected a radio station by rotating a knob that had a pointer; either the numbered frequency scale was printed on the cabinet or the numbers were on the knob and the pointer was on the cabinet. But on higher-priced units, the pointer moved behind a transparent horizontal window with frequencies printed on it. Additional labor costs were incurred by using a string-and-pulley system to move the pointer horizontally. I designed a knob with only an edge outside the cabinet. A shape was printed on the knob; as the knob was turned, the shape passed behind a horizontal rectangular opening, creating the illusion that a horizontal pointer was moving to indicate the selected frequencies. This design eliminated those extra labor costs.

In the mid-fifties, the transistor radically changed the radio industry by making it possible to design much smaller radios. The first hand-held, portable transistor radio I designed used my printed knob / horizontal slot method of station selection. This set off my design from those of Philco's competitors, who were all producing hand-held portable radios. Management liked the novelty because it could be priced at a premium without costing more to manufacture than a design using a simple knob.

After about two years, I established a reputation at Philco for designing creative solutions to merchandising problems. Although I felt a great deal of satisfaction when my creations became real products, some of my early designs were already being replaced by my more recent designs, and I started to become restless. I wanted the satisfaction of doing more important things than participating in the show business excitement of seeing a new line of radios introduced annually.

I knew that Philco had treated me well, but the yearning to do more meaningful work frustrated me.

Henry Kaiser was a legendary industrialist whose company had built cargo ships at the rate of one per month during World War II—and once completing a ship in four days. In addition, Kaiser established an automobile company and created a health-care program that still exists.

I learned that he was interested in using mass-production techniques in the housing industry to fill the post-war need. The concept of factory-produced housing was not new, but it had always resulted in inferior products. Kaiser was considering installing factory-produced kitchens and bathrooms in houses that were built on site.

Shortly after reading about Kaiser's interest in prefabricated bathrooms and kitchens, I saw a job advertisement for a designer for the Kaiser kitchen company. The company manufactured steel kitchen cabinets. I naively assumed that the kitchen cabinet company's need for a designer was related to Henry Kaiser's interest in prefabricated kitchens and bathrooms. I applied and was hired with a generous pay increase. The design group at Philco threw me a fabulous farewell party and wished me well in my future career.

Within days at my new job, I realized I had made a terrible mistake. I had been hired to design steel kitchen cabinets—nothing but cabinets—at that Kaiser facility. What a fool I had been, trading an interesting design position for this dull, dead-end job designing steel kitchen cabinets. My challenge was limited to defining the radius of the corners and deciding what handles or finger grips would complete my masterpiece. Worst of all, I knew that it entirely was my fault and I had no one else to blame. Besides, Betty was pregnant.

In the middle of my second week at Kaiser, I took a late lunch and called Ross Gilbert at Philco to explain my predicament. Without hesitation, he invited me back to Philco, joking about the farewell party and gifts I had received two weeks earlier. My parents believed that making a mistake in an important life decision would have serious, irreparable consequences. I believe this philosophy was based on their European education and experience, paralyzing their actions in America. This experience taught me to think differently.

I learned an important lesson from my Kaiser experience. In addition to my general recognition that the United States is a land of unlimited opportunities, I adopted the belief that this also is the land of second, third, or even more chances. The possibility to start over, I believed was, unique to America and of greater importance than its being the land of opportunity. I certainly have taken full advantage of my right to third and fourth chances to begin anew.

Around that time, a do-it-yourself craze was sweeping suburban communities, placing a tremendous burden on males like me who had absolutely no handyman talents. When a faucet leaked, rather than call a handyman, I disassembled it, and, by using successively larger wrenches, I managed to ruin the entire faucet, thus requiring the services of a real plumber, which ended up costing many times what the original repair job would have cost. I constructed a dog pen with a doghouse for Quirky that became the eyesore of the neighborhood. But the high point of my do-it-yourself career was the construction of a tool shed that enclosed one end of the carport. *What could be hard about that?* I thought. After several false starts, and with the help of ever-increasing numbers of neighbors, the shed was finished, but the shingles never did line up. Fortunately, it was never noticeable from the street—or to the building inspector, who would have ordered the abomination torn down. My manhood was severely challenged whenever I had to hire professionals to correct my mistakes or when undertaking future projects.

On October 4, 1957, the Soviet Union launched Sputnik, the first satellite to circumnavigate the earth. Sputnik did nothing in space but send a radio signal to earth. It did, however, have enormous consequences for the entire world. In the United States, the launch of Sputnik had a spectacular effect on education, on the defense industry, and on national pride. The United States set for itself the task of catching up with the Soviets in space exploration. My imagination, as well as that of the entire country, was captured by the Soviet feat. Using plans in a popular science magazine, I built a radio that permitted me to hear the ping, ping, ping of Sputnik.

Day after day, I spent hours in the yellow bedroom that soon would become our first-born child's room. We had painted the room yellow, because it was not possible, at that time, to determine the gender of the baby prior to birth. Two weeks after the launch of Sputnik, our daughter Linda was born. The night before we brought her home from Rolling Hills Hospital, I assembled her crib to the accompaniment of the sounds of Sputnik—"ping ... ping ... ping ..."

My late assembly of the crib was not due to procrastination but to old Jewish folklore that advised against getting ready for a baby before the successful birth. I, of course, did not believe in the superstition that bad things would happen to Linda if I had the crib assembled before her healthy birth—but why take a chance? So, after several false starts and an attempt to read the instructions, there I was in the early morning hours, still putting the finishing touches on the crib without having parts left over. "Ping ... ping ... ping ..."

Fortunately, Linda and Betty had a healthy delivery and we were delighted to be parents for the first time. Betty had miscarried her first pregnancy, so we had some concerns. I displayed the same misguided values that I had shown on our two-day honeymoon—while Betty was in delivery, I spent all the time on the phone in the waiting room, worrying about the progress of a radio in the model shop rather than the progress in the delivery room.

Like most first-time parents, we were overly protective of our first-born. Betty's father had to leave the house once he lit his ever-present cigar, and we worried about maintaining the exact right temperature in the house. Linda was born prior to the advent of infant car seats; our concern, after a snowstorm disrupted the electricity in our house, was how to take Linda to my parent's home in our new VW Beetle with its inadequate heating system.

The purchase of the VW had caused some conflict within myself and between my parents and me. I had tremendous antipathy toward all things German, and my parents, of course, remembered that Hitler had used the development of "the people's car" as a significant issue in his political campaign. But in the end, my admiration for the car's minimalist design had won.

Shortly after Linda's birth, I was invited to IBM in White Plains, New York, to interview for a job in their design department. IBM was then considered one of the leaders in industrial design; a design position there would clearly advance my career.

The review of my portfolio by the head of the design team went very well, and I began to imagine our family moving to White Plains. The final step in the interview process was a meeting with human resources.

The human resources professional took personal information that was not included in my resume. I was told I would receive a formal offer of employment within two weeks. The conversation then turned to the company's health and retirement benefits, along with their vacation policy, all of which was given to me in writing.

Then, the interviewer changed the subject ever so subtly by stating, "We, of course, expect all IBM employees to comport themselves honorably at all times on and off the job."

What the hell does that mean? I thought. As I sat there, somewhat in disbelief, the interviewer explained that all IBM employees were expected to wear white shirts and appropriate neckties. It also was expected that my wife and I would participate in the company's social events, which included local country-club membership—all expenses to be paid by the company.

My head was swimming as I drove back to Philadelphia on the New Jersey turnpike. Working as a designer for IBM would be prestigious and include a substantial salary increase; however, there was the control over my dress, social behavior, and country-club membership to consider. *Could I tolerate working under such conditions?* I knew what Howard Roark would do.

I pulled into the next turnpike rest stop and called Betty. I blurted out that I would probably be getting a job offer with a substantial salary increase; then I repeated the latter part of the interview—the white shirt and tie, the social life, and the damned country-club membership.

"You don't feel comfortable with this, do you, Quirk? We have survived on your present salary, so if you don't have a good feeling about this, don't take it. I'm with you all the way; just do what makes you happy," Betty said. That's how our marriage has lasted more than fifty-five years.

Linda, a blonde, blue-eyed doll, was developing quickly and we were convinced we had an obligation to give her every educational advantage. So, when a door-to-door salesman demonstrated an overpriced child's three-in-one activity table, we felt compelled to have it. The table surrounded the child: one top was Formica, for feeding; another had holes in it, for hammering pegs; a third transformed the table into an easel. One day, while hammering, Linda missed the peg, struck her finger, and said her first word: "Shit!" We were very proud that she spoke so early, but where could she have learned that word?

Again, I was becoming increasingly restless at Philco, as year by year, just like before, my previous year's designs were being replaced by my new designs and management was ordering more superficial, decorative additions to my designs.

As the transistor became cheaper, it was incorporated into more and more models. The engineers had designed a radio that could be encased in a cabinet no larger than a pack of cigarettes. Although the radio had no speaker and could only play through an earpiece, management believed its novelty would sell it.

My assignment was to design the appearance. I designed a very clean, crisp case with no decoration except a frame around the word

Philco. It had no speaker, so needed no grille. Management liked the design but directed some "minor" changes: a lip around the entire front, with the front edge flashed with gold; the framed *Philco* on a gold appliqué glued into the frame; and a molded faux grille in the front.

As I read about the space program, which had accelerated after Sputnik, I thought that design work in the space industry must be more honest because it was based on science, not merchandising. Although the early rocket tests were a series of dismal failures, many scientists spoke about human space travel. I believed I could be useful in that effort.

In 1959, NASA began a selection process for the first astronauts; I wanted to be part of that project. I read the few books that had been published on ergonomics and human engineering and sent my resume to all the space industry companies that advertised for engineers. Many of these companies were in California, in cities with beautiful sounding names: San Diego, San Jose, Monterey. I was ready to leave Philadelphia and start a new adventure. Betty was agreeable, as usual.

I made my resume sound as applicable to the space program as I could with only a bachelor of fine arts. My readings had given me some of the vocabulary of human engineering, phrases like "the man-machine interface."

The only positive response I received from my mass mailing was from the Glenn L. Martin Company in Baltimore. Steve McDonald, the head of a small human engineering group, invited me to Baltimore for an interview. Though Baltimore was not one of the beautifully named cities in California or the Southwest that I fantasized about, Martin had been very successful during World War II designing and producing a series of seaplanes. After the war, the company had switched to building commercial aircraft. Steve, who had an industrial design background, had been with Martin since its aircraft days.

Most of the activity in the Baltimore division involved the testing and production of the Seamaster seaplane. This would have been the first jet-powered seaplane. The aerospace division was in the process of moving to Denver, where a new facility was being built.

The interview went well, but on the drive back to Philadelphia, I worried about the reality of making a career change after a relatively successful four years as an industrial designer. This time, if I made a mistake, it would take much more than a phone call to get me back to a place where I had been comfortable, but restless.

Although Steve McDonald had been positive about how my background would fit into human engineering, I knew that the traditional degree for a human engineer was a doctorate in experimental psychology. I certainly would not be able to scientifically validate my designs as promoting efficiencies in operation, training, and maintenance by the human operator. Designing for "the man-machine interface" not only sounded impressive, it sounded as if it was related to math and science, fields in which it had been clearly established that I had no ability.

I stopped at a gas station diner, just as I had when driving back from my IBM interview, and used the pay telephone to call Betty to tell her I would probably be getting an offer. The job sounded exciting, but I had concerns about whether I had the education to be successful at it. As always, Betty had utmost confidence in my ability to do anything. On the way out of the diner, I bought a copy of *The Baltimore Sun* for its real estate classified ads.

The Saturday after my interview, Betty, Linda, and I spent a very discouraging day in Baltimore looking at houses. The houses we saw were more expensive than comparable ones in the Philadelphia suburbs, and we had heard that Baltimore was a very segregated city where Jews were expected to live in specific suburbs. Betty and I would not have felt comfortable living in an all-Jewish area, and we certainly would have felt resentful if forced into a particular neighborhood because of our religion. In Horsham, we were the only Jews on our street, as far as we knew, but never gave it a second thought. The houses we saw in Baltimore were unattractive and seemed damp and musty since they were all built on slabs.

In spite of my concerns about the job and our unhappiness with the homes we saw, I spent all my free time reading about human engineering and ergonomics. My excitement with the concept that I would have some part, albeit a small one, in the space program pushed all the negatives to the background.

When the formal offer came, about ten days after our Baltimore trip, I accepted and we put our house up for sale. We decided that

Betty, Linda, and Quirky would stay in the house until it sold; I would rent a room in Baltimore, while continuing to look for housing after work. I would come home each weekend.

– 11 –

Space Program

I sat in the light blue VW beetle outside the rooming house, on a modest Baltimore street. I had driven from our home in Horsham and arrived here in the late afternoon. The last thing I wanted to do was enter the house with its worn rugs and furniture and its dusty disinfectant smell. *What have I gotten myself and my family into?* I thought.

I had read a few thin books about human engineering. Would that, along with my industrial design education and four years of experience designing consumer products qualify me for the job I was starting the next day?

I retrieved one of my human engineering books from the backseat like a schoolboy cramming for the next day's exam. Even if I was not qualified to be a human engineer, I could sound as though I were by learning the vocabulary and using key expressions like my favorite, "the man-machine interface."

I had sold myself to the Martin Company with my belief that industrial design had a relationship with ergonomics and that I, therefore, had a contribution to make to the space program. After all, my industrial design education was an era that believed "form follows function." The design of a chair, desk, radio, or automobile started with the capabilities and limitations of human beings. A good design for a pitcher, cup, or pen was directly related to the human hand. The dimensions of a room bore a relationship to the range of human body dimensions and movements. Was this not human engineering: design for humans at the man-machine interface where the equipment or product interacts with the operator? Anyway, that was my pitch when I attempted to convince the aerospace companies that I had a place in the space program.

I had convinced at least one company to take a chance, probably largely due to my eagerness to be part of the industry that would define the present era. Now, I would have to perform. After a restless night in my boarding house bed, I reported for work in my new career in the aerospace industry. As I walked from the parking lot to the human resources department, a Seamaster flew overhead. I wondered if, as a human engineer, I would ever be a passenger in one of these state-of-the-art, jet-powered seaplanes.

I carried a thick package of forms. I had spent many evenings gathering the required information, including every address I had ever resided at during the twenty-six years of my life. The forms warned that there could be no gaps and any falsification would be a federal crime punishable by a fine and incarceration.

I arrived, as instructed, at the human resources office, but I was an hour early. I went through several interviews, some related to security, where I was relieved of many of my papers. The requirement for security clearance for my job only added to the mystique of this new career.

Human resources personnel explained the company's health insurance and retirement benefits and gave me booklets explaining other company policies, replacing the paperwork I had just given up. I left the office with a larger package of paper than when I had arrived. After lunch in one of the company cafeterias, I reported to Steve McDonald.

Steve explained that his group was designing information displays for space vehicles that would not be built for years. I learned that, as vehicle speed increased, information could no longer be displayed to the pilot and crew with traditional pointers moving around a circular dial; and that, although weapons systems were becoming more sophisticated and more complex, they were still operated by military enlisted men with limited training. My challenge would be to design equipment that would accommodate the limitations of humans.

I was certain that I could meet that challenge. I convinced myself, as I obviously had convinced Steve, that although I had no academic background in experimental psychology, my design background and my ability to solve problems logically made me capable of contributing to the design of this equipment.

It became clear to Betty and me that our living arrangement was untenable. We also decided, since we had not found a house to our liking, that we would rent a house in Baltimore. So, after I had been working at the Martin Company for less than two weeks, we moved into a two-story corner duplex on Pioneer Drive. The house was across the street from a park—an accommodation for Linda and Quirky, since the house had a very small backyard.

I found the work enjoyable even though the other members of the human engineering group had a much stronger academic background for this work than I had. I wondered: *Was I a great imposter?*

After a few months, I became restless again. It seemed to me that the most interesting work was going to the newly constructed facility in Denver. After a one-day trip to Denver to discuss the design of a launch console for the Titan Intercontinental Ballistic Missile System, I knew that was where I wanted to live. We had some flexibility to make another move, as we had sold our house in Horsham in November.

Shortly after our move to Baltimore, Betty realized that she was pregnant again. She needed to see an obstetrician quickly because she had lost a baby before she was able to carry Linda to full term and also had miscarried just before our move. We promptly arranged for an appointment after I received a recommendation from a co-worker.

Since we had only one car, which I drove to work, Betty took a cab to the doctor. Everything appeared fine but, because of Betty's history with miscarriages, the doctor recommended that she avoid strenuous activity until delivery. This would be difficult while taking care of a two-year-old.

The most disturbing part of the doctor visit was Betty's report of her cab ride. After a few minutes, the black driver, whom she had engaged in conversation, asked her if she was Jewish. Betty, somewhat taken aback, said she was. But why was he asking? He told her that Jews all lived in another part of the city and were the only ones who would talk to him. Then he asked what she was doing in the part of town where she did not belong. After that, we were determined that I would try to get a transfer to Denver, but we put everything on hold until the baby, due in late May, was born.

The human engineering group grew quickly with the addition of more PhD psychologists; designers became a minority in the group as more of the activity tended toward scientific experimentation.

In January 1960, Frank Lee, a friend of mine in our group, came back from an interview in Denver with a glowing description of the city and its semi-rural suburbs. I listened intently and enviously. As a favor, Frank had taken copies of my resume to Denver, and he had given them to supervisors who might be interested in hiring me.

In early spring, I had an interview with the Denver human engineering group. The trip was a smashing success, and I believed I would be offered a position. I had planned the interview for a Friday so I would have extra time to see the area. The Martin facility was about twenty miles south of the city. Driving to and from the plant took me past many properties with horses, and I saw foals playing. After my interview, I looked at houses being built—part of a housing boom generated by the Martin Company's arrival. The houses and neighborhoods were attractive and reasonably priced. I could hardy contain my enthusiasm as I described Denver to Betty.

I accepted the transfer to Denver on the condition that my start date be delayed until the end of July, when the expected baby would be about two months old. We planned to drive cross-country.

During the last month of Betty's pregnancy, she spent as much time in bed as Linda permitted. Diane was born on May 31, with average height and weight; her delivery was normal. It seemed to take forever before I was able to see Betty and Diane. Diane, with her dark hair and round face, resembled Betty. My mother came to stay with us to help with Diane and Linda during the first week after the birth.

When I brought Betty and Diane home from the hospital, I discovered I had acquired a staph infection, most likely during my visits to the hospital. My mother was meticulous in cleaning the house with disinfectant and keeping Linda and Diane away from me. Staph infections seem to be easy to acquire but difficult to get rid of. My mother stayed with us an additional week, until I was free of the infection.

Six weeks later, we loaded up Betty's father's five-year-old Oldsmobile. Our VW was too small for the trip, so we had sold it. The Martin Company paid for all moving costs, including transportation, meals, and temporary housing for one month.

We set up a portable crib on the backseat for the two girls and installed a roof carrier for a large trunk. All the space in the Oldsmobile's trunk and around the crib in the backseat was filled. We purchased one luxury—an evaporative water-filled cooler for the non air-conditioned Oldsmobile. When we pulled a string on the cooler, which was installed on the front passenger window, a felt-like pad would rotate into a water reservoir; then, the airflow from the moving automobile would pass through the saturated pad and enter the car.

After we left Baltimore, we made a detour to Philadelphia, where we stayed with my parents for two days to say farewell to our families and friends on the East Coast. At dawn, in a very overloaded car, we waved good-bye to my parents and headed to the Pennsylvania Turnpike. As we turned west to begin our new adventure, I was surprised to see Betty wiping tears from her eyes.

We soon discovered that, when we traveled at the speed limit over the expansion spaces in the concrete highway, the overloaded car swayed in ever-increasing rhythm. I exited the turnpike and looked at the AAA map for an alternate route to Colorado. We took Route 40 due west, stopping overnight in Ohio—the furthest west Betty had ever been.

The August sun turned the car into an oven, so Betty, who was nursing Diane, pulled the string on our cooler every few minutes, resulting in a constant spray of water on both of them.

We took a break on our drive to see some Mark Twain memorabilia when we reached Hannibal, Missouri. As we crossed the Mississippi, Betty laughingly compared our trip to the expedition of the pioneers who had preceded us in covered wagons.

The car needed its 1000-mile maintenance by the time we reached Kansas; we wanted to forestall a breakdown. Linda fell asleep in the crib just as we drove into the service station. We decided not to awaken her and hoped she would not wake up in a panic while the car was being hoisted on the lift. We paced nervously until the car once again was on the ground with Linda still asleep in the crib. When she awoke, she had a much-needed run around the gas station.

We spent the last night of the trip in Garden City, on the western edge of Kansas. The next morning, we got an early start for our final dash to Denver. The motel in Garden City was in a desolate area. As we looked across the highway, we saw so much space around us; the only evidence of human activity was a group of grain silos next to several railroad tracks. To us, lifelong big-city residents, the scene seemed surreal.

Before dawn, after breakfast at the motel coffee shop, we four modern-day pioneers took our accustomed positions in the Oldsmobile. As dawn started to break, we searched the horizon for signs of the promised mountains. Since leaving the banks of the Mississippi, we had been climbing so gradually that it seemed we had been driving over absolutely flat land. Nearing the Mile High City, would we now see a dramatic rise in elevation? Dawn broke, and the jagged silhouette of the mountainous horizon loomed before us. The display, illuminated by the rising sun behind us, was breathtakingly beautiful. As we approached, we could see the outline of buildings. We had arrived!

Route 40 led right into East Colfax Avenue, the main east-west thoroughfare of Denver. The street was lined on both sides with run-down hotels, bars, strip clubs, and pawnshops. Betty silently surveyed the scene, wondering where was the beauty of the city I had so enthusiastically described to her.

The scenery improved considerably, with the noon sun shining on the mountains, as we rounded the State Capitol and headed south on Broadway. We had a room waiting for us at the Lucky U Motel on South Broadway, just north of Littleton. It was not exactly a palace, but was relatively clean. In addition, the motel had a swimming pool, which Linda had anticipated, and a pizza place down the street.

We hired a realtor and started looking for a permanent place to live. Betty and the girls accompanied the realtor on the search. We had decided that, if at all possible, we would buy a new, contemporary-style house. After almost making a mistake and buying house that was totally wrong for us, we found our home located at 5939 South Steele Street in Littleton. The timing was perfect: my relocation support was just running out and the house we decided on was just about finished. We could still pick out the interior colors. We moved in over the Labor Day weekend.

The house was ideal. It had two bathrooms, a separate dining room, and a full finished basement that had a family room with a built-in bar and a fourth bedroom. There was a large yard, which we fenced in for Quirky. It was about twice the price of our first house; fortunately, I was earning about twice the salary I had when I started at Philco.

Our application for the mortgage was the second and last time in our lives that we entered a financial institution to borrow money. My father's long-ago lecture had had its desired effect. In fact, my avoidance of debt was so strong that, years later, when my children married and purchased homes of their own, I provided the funds necessary to enable them to pay cash rather than borrow for a mortgage.

I escaped being laid off in the periodic cutbacks that continually plagued the aerospace industry. My job was interesting and satisfying. We were again sitting on top of the world.

We noticed that Diane was not progressing as fast as Linda had, but were not overly concerned. We reasoned that they were different individuals, so why should they not develop differently? Our concerns became more acute when she was not walking at fourteen months. Out of an abundance of caution, we sought professional counsel. We did not know a pediatrician in Denver, so we made an appointment with the general practitioner who had given us our insurance exams—not exactly a high recommendation.

The physician gave Diane a roughly ten-minute check-up, and recommended a developmental exam at Children's Hospital. The exam took about an hour; then we were told that we would hear from the referring physician.

Sitting in the doctor's office, we heard the devastating news that our daughter Diane had developmental issues that would keep her from attending public school. His parting message to us was that he hoped we would not fall into the trap that so many parents did by going from professional to professional hoping for better news. He strongly recommended that we unquestioningly accept the news and make plans accordingly.

Fortunately, we did not take the doctor's advice, and we sought a second opinion with Don Schiff, a pediatrician who expressed anger at the general practitioner's advice—particularly his suggestion that we not seek another opinion. Don, who with his wife Rosalie later became our close friends, suggested further testing and training, and opined that Diane would probably mature within normal limits. He was a lifesaver whose prediction proved correct over the next few years.

Diane's maturation and success progressed steadily over the years. Even before she entered school, she wanted to do everything on her own. When she experienced difficulty in achieving results, she would use anger to express her frustration and fought anyone who tried to help her.

The low point came one day at an amusement park when my mother, who was visiting, was riding with the two girls in a *Three Men in a Tub* ride. As the ride ended, Linda jumped out. Diane was having some difficulty negotiating herself out of the unsteady floating tub, so my mother tried to help her. Diane, trying to indicate that she wanted to do it herself, bit my mother's arm. After that incident, though, Diane's frustrations and displays of anger subsided.

Our initial assessment also proved correct: Diane was a different person than Linda; using one individual's traits as a standard for the other was not only unfair but also meaningless. As the years passed, it became obvious that each of the girls had developed a unique personality. Diane was a diligent worker and complied with all prescribed rules to achieve perfection. Linda, on the other hand, challenged formal rules, discerning what invisible ones governed success.

Successful, well-educated persons, who uniformly expressed a very conservative philosophy, populated the Martin Company. The political line was "Pull yourself up by your bootstraps." Many of my coworkers were resentful of John Kennedy's social programs, and later, Lyndon Johnson's. My Ayn Rand philosophy fit right in.

But after our visit to the incompetent doctor's office, my view dramatically changed. *What if you had no bootstraps?* I asked myself. With that charlatan's diagnosis, Diane taught me more than I could ever teach her. My faith in Ayn Rand's philosophy started to wane.

During my first few years with Martin-Denver, most of my design assignments centered on the Titan Intercontinental Missile System, which had just begun to demonstrate some reliability in its test program. The Titan I was a two-stage rocket designed to carry a nuclear warhead five thousand miles with one-mile accuracy. The Titan was deployed in underground silos that were protected by massive concrete and steel walls and doors that opened when an elevator brought the missile up to ground level for launch.

Our group designed the launch console and its placement in the underground control center. One of the primary concerns with the missile system was avoiding an unintended launch while also being able to respond quickly to an intended launch order. The policy required that two Air Force officers respond simultaneously to effect a launch. The consoles we designed would be placed in the control center, out of sight of one another, to avoid any threat from one officer toward another. We designed the displays showing fuel status, targeting information, and the progress of the elevator using easy to read clearly labeled lights to minimize human error.

About the time I joined Martin, the company was awarded a contract for the development of the Titan II system, a much-improved system permitting launch from within the silo. Again, I was involved in the design of consoles and training devices.

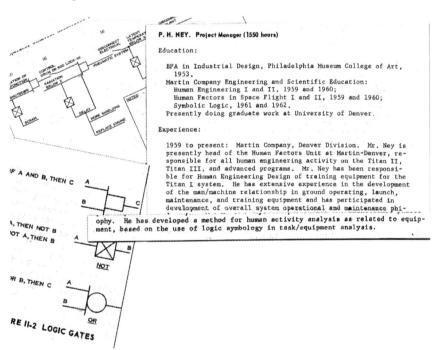

P. H. NEY. Project Manager (1550 hours)

Education:

    BFA in Industrial Design, Philadelphia Museum College of Art, 1953.
    Martin Company Engineering and Scientific Education:
        Human Engineering I and II, 1959 and 1960;
        Human Factors in Space Flight I and II, 1959 and 1960;
        Symbolic Logic, 1961 and 1962.
    Presently doing graduate work at University of Denver.

Experience:

    1959 to present: Martin Company, Denver Division. Mr. Ney is presently head of the Human Factors Unit at Martin-Denver, responsible for all human engineering activity on the Titan II, Titan III, and advanced programs. Mr. Ney has been responsible for Human Engineering Design of training equipment for the Titan I system. He has extensive experience in the development of the man/machine relationship in ground operating, launch, maintenance, and training equipment and has participated in development of overall system operational and maintenance philosophy. He has developed a method for human activity analysis as related to equipment, based on the use of logic symbology in task/equipment analysis.

I developed training devices using logic symbols to represent human tasks that I incorporated into the design of successful training devices. I was pleasantly surprised but somewhat perplexed at the enthusiasm with which both Martin's management and the Air Force received my graphic description of human activity using logic symbology. Martin actually presented the graphic display system in proposals as proprietary, to give them a competitive edge for the award of future contracts, and gave me full credit as the developer.

The increased power of the Titan II made it a likely candidate as the launch vehicle for manned space flight. That, of course, was the area that interested me the most. To my delight, my work at Martin slowly shifted from weapon systems to manned space projects.

Our group continued to design experiments for potential space travelers. Some were useful, some were very naïve and useless but funny. For instance, subjects could experience a sensation similar to weightlessness when submerged in a swimming pool, wearing weights to equalize their weight with the weight of the displaced water.

One of the extravehicular human tasks anticipated in a manned space project was the deployment of the critical, beach-umbrella sized antenna in the event of a failure of the mechanical deployment system. To simulate the mechanics of opening the antenna outside the space station, management suggested that we have a properly weighted subject float in apparent weightlessness while attempting to open a beach umbrella under water.

The beach umbrella was lowered into the water as cameras whirled behind glass windows in the wall of the swimming pool. The subject attempted to open it. We had not accounted for the great weight of the water on the beach umbrella, which we realized as the subject struggled with clenched teeth to open the umbrella against the water's massive resistance. The framework bent back, the fabric tore, and the movie cameras there to record the manual opening of a beach umbrella in a simulated state of weightlessness filmed, instead, the subject struggling with the impossible task of opening a beach umbrella under water. This must have been one of the funniest films in the space program.

Everything was considered secret. We used a colony of mice to gain some knowledge of the long-term effects of 100 percent oxygen on humans. Because these experiments were considered secret, they were housed in a building surrounded by a fence topped with barbed wire. One weekend, I took the girls to see the mice and gained entry to the building by retrieving the keys from under the mat in front of the door. The incongruity did not hit me until I had unlocked the door.

There were innumerable problems, real or imagined, related to humans spending months in space. We had no way to duplicate extended weightlessness on earth. The experiments that most closely duplicated true weightlessness were limited to flights that would expose subjects to several minutes of parabolic flight. The long-term effects of a pure oxygen environment for humans were also unknown.

Since there was so little knowledge of human capabilities in space, the human engineering group developed our own problems to address, based on our imagination and crude experimentation. For example—an untethered, weightless man attempting to tighten a screw would likely spin himself rather than the screw. Or, we wondered, in a weightless environment, could a switch be activated without bracing the operator?

We also considered personal hygiene issues. The parabolic flights demonstrated the hazards of uncontained liquids in a weightless environment. We designed toilets, urinals, and shavers to be used by astronauts. In the mid-sixties, no one imagined females in the space station. Although, as a joke, cartoons of weightless male-female copulation, with the aid of large elastic bands, circulated among the group, never to be proposed to NASA.

In 1962, I went to a party, hosted by a member of the human engineering group, which literally changed my life. At the party, I met Dick Fields, who was working at Martin and going to law school in the evenings.

During my time in the army, through my association with Bobby Rosenberg, I had developed some interest in law, but I had always believed that career path was no longer open to me. I spent the evening peppering Dick with questions that showed how naïve I was: "What are the requirements to attend law school? Could some of my academic credits from art school be accepted at law school? How many years would it take to become a lawyer?"

Within a week of that prophetic conversation, I visited the University of Denver Law School. The assistant to the dean of admissions was very helpful and explained the admission process with the required Law School Admission Test. I was concerned because my undergraduate degree was from an art school—certainly not a traditional background for admission to law school. She said she was not sure, but would see if the dean had time to see me.

Dean Lynn was extremely friendly. He explained that the academic requirement for entry into law school was a bachelor's degree in any field—undergraduate colleges had abandoned the pre-law studies I had heard about. He concluded the conversation by acknowledging that my background for admission was unusual, but not unheard of; in fact, his undergraduate degree also was in fine arts.

He wished me luck in the LSAT and explained that the admissions committee sought students of diverse backgrounds. I thought of my father's insistence that I pursue the degree program in art school—that I thought so useless at the time. Perhaps, after all, he did get it.

The Martin Company had a payroll deduction program that assisted employees with their tuition in pursuit of advanced degrees. I confirmed that I would be eligible for this program even though law had no relationship to my duties at Martin. Even if I never became a lawyer, I was excited about the prospect of going to law school.

I spent every available hour studying for the LSAT, believing that admission to law school would be another new beginning. That summer, my parents came for their semi-annual visit. As we walked across the parking lot at the old Stapleton Airport, my father stopped, placed his hand on his hip, and asked me, "What is all this about going to law school?" I tried to reassure my father that I was not planning another change of career, but rather increasing my education. My father never appreciated what I felt was the greatest gift of America: the freedom of second, third, or more chances to begin life anew.

Betty's studies to complete her bachelor's degree had been interrupted when she joined me while I was in the army. She now took evening classes when I was home to take care of the girls, and sometimes, after Diane started kindergarten, she attended afternoon classes.

Also during those first years at Martin, I unsuccessfully pursued my first career choice: freelance cartooning and some furniture design. This was not the result of unhappiness with my work at Martin, but of my perpetual restlessness when doing only one thing. I wanted to pursue various interests, not knowing where they would lead.

My LSAT score must have been good, as it generated a quick response from the law school informing me of my admission to the evening division, commencing September 1963. This time I would do everything and more to excel. I knew there would be an enormous amount of reading required, so I enrolled in the Evelyn Woods Reading Dynamics course, which taught techniques to increase reading speed and comprehension. I was very motivated and practiced the techniques continually.

Because of my proficiency, I became one of Evelyn Woods' demonstrators, appearing at sales sessions and on the radio, where I read unpublished books in less than twenty minutes and then was tested by the author and the audience.

Orientation for first-year law students in the day and night divisions was held in the auditorium. As I found a seat in an empty row, I was reminded of my orientation at Central High School. There were about one hundred and fifty students in the audience when the program began. We were told about the majesty of the English Common Law and the Constitution, and the importance of ethics in the practice of law. I was already lost. Although this was just an orientation and I was taking good notes, I understood very little. I did understand one part of the presentation, however: half of the audience would not finish law school; one-third of those who did graduate would never see the inside of a courtroom, or practice law, choosing business and political careers instead; the remainder would practice law; and ten of us would be future judges. Well, that last prediction certainly didn't apply to me, I thought. Although I was having trouble with the orientation, I had no doubt that I would finish law school.

The orientation included some practical advice on surviving the highly competitive environment of law school. One suggestion was to organize study groups to meet regularly and discuss the class material. This would give us an advantage, through exposure to diverse viewpoints, leading to better understanding of the class material. It sounded like a good idea, but recognizing my tendency to avoid group activities, was this for me?

On my first day of torts class, I took a seat in the third row of a large amphitheater. Remembering the drastic prediction at orientation of the shrinking numbers of students, I thought this probably was a classroom reserved for first–year students. Soon, a student sat to my left. He introduced himself, "Hi, I'm Earl Hauck." He told me he was a claims adjuster for an insurance company and negotiated with tort lawyers all the time. I concluded he was way ahead of me; I was not even sure what a tort was. Lou Parkinson sat to my right. He was selling pipe for U.S. Steel.

The three of us sat in the same pattern all the way through law school. We organized a study group that met regularly for the first year and invited several other students to join us. As we sat in Dan Sparr's home, studying the intricacies of tort, contracts, and civil procedure, we never imagined where we would be thirty years later: Dan Sparr became a federal judge; Dave Erickson authored the leading Colorado corporate treatise and wrote several articles and a book on the history of the practice of law in early Colorado.

Ray Connell, our torts professor, was a practicing lawyer with one of the largest insurance defense firms. He had a great sense of humor and often went out for a drink after class with our study group. We were all married, most with young children, so it was natural that we became friends.

I enjoyed my work at Martin and found it very interesting, but after completing the first semester of law school, I knew I wanted to change professions once again and become a lawyer. I calculated that I could complete law school in three years if I took a full load every semester, including summers, plus one or two day classes.

My schedule was intense: I would arrive home from work at Martin about 5:20 in the afternoon. Betty would have dinner ready, and by 5:45 I would be on my way to law school. Four days a week, three semesters a year, I maintained that schedule for three years.

As I saw and heard about the role of lawyers in many of the victories of the civil rights and anti-Vietnam War movements, I became more and more impatient to become a lawyer.

I decided that, after completing law school and being admitted to practice, I would open my own law office—a reckless plan for a lawyer with two young children and no ties to the community. As usual, Betty enthusiastically supported the program.

In 1964, Betty was completing class work for her degree. However, she had to have one semester of student teaching to get a teacher's certificate. This obviously could not be accomplished at night or on a part-time basis, so my parents came out and stayed with us for that period.

Betty was set to graduate in June 1965. Since both of our girls would be in school when I graduated in 1966, our plan was for Betty to teach, filling the financial gap until my law practice provided an income.

Although I had only an art degree, Martin promoted me to head the Human Engineering Unit, which had over a dozen PhDs. This was proof of the aptly named Peter Principal. "In a hierarchy, every employee tends to rise to his level of incompetence." The only rational reasons I could find for my promotion were my reasonably good writing ability, thanks to my Central High School education; and my development of the logic graphics presentations used in our Titan trainers.

At the time of my promotion, though, I had irrevocably decided that I would leave Martin when I graduated from law school, study for the bar exam, and open my own law office.

I had two years of law school remaining when Martin was in one of its down cycles and many of its employees were being laid off. To save their jobs, many employees authored proposals that might result in the award of a contract to Martin. I found a NASA request for a proposal for a relatively small one-year study: "Human Engineering Criteria and Concepts for Handling Advanced Nuclear Weapon Systems in Space."

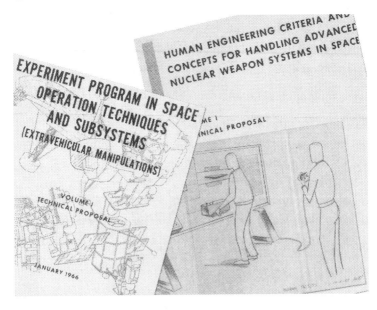

I wrote a proposal for this study, making its centerpiece the system of symbols representing the decision-making process that I had developed for the Titan systems' trainers. I was designated project manager. Some members of my human engineering group, who were fearful of getting laid off, were listed as the other members of the study team. The proposal was submitted in May 1964. We were awarded the one-year contract in the fall, which brought me within six months of completion of law school.

Fate intervened again, forcing another change of plans: Our plan for Betty to teach while the law office became self-sustaining became unworkable because Betty graduated very pregnant. Our son Richard was born in August, nine months before my graduation. Despite the forced change in plans, I was still determined to open my own law office.

In the summer of 1965, Ved Nanda had just joined the faculty of the law school and was giving a seminar on International Organizations. I gave up lunchtime to take this class because I needed three additional credits. Ved Nanda was, without doubt, the most brilliant individual I had ever met. Classes were held sporadically which fit my need to leave work during the day. The class requirement was an academic paper.

I was totally overloaded: working full-time at Martin, taking a full load of courses at night school, and writing a quality academic paper for a professor I greatly admired. Not being sure what the requirements were for an academic paper was my first problem. My time constraints were unsolvable, so my submission was not of the quality I wanted. I was delighted with a B, although that prevented me from graduating *cum laude.* When Ved found out, he apologized for the B, even though I thought of it as a gift.

At the time of my graduation, Linda was nine, Diane was six, and Richard was nine months old. I wrote Martin a letter of resignation thanking them for the opportunities they had given me. I felt driven to open my law office in October, and would use the summer to study for the Bar Examination.

During that summer, I worked for a lawyer. We had an understanding that I would be taking time off for the Bar Refresher and would not commit to any continuing employment after I passed the bar. I learned some practical points in the practice of law in the four months with him.

The bar exam, given in the State Capitol legislative chambers, took four days. The test was grueling and felt more like a fraternity hazing than a tool to measure competence for the practice of a profession. When the test was finally concluded, I left the building and collapsed on the lawn. Betty had come down to join me, along with some of my classmates and their wives, for a celebratory dinner at a restaurant on the top floor of a downtown high-rise. Each student had left a self-addressed, stamped envelope at the test site; now began the agonizing four-week wait for results.

I returned to work for the lawyer, Around this time, I became uncomfortable with a senior housing plan developed by one of the office's clients, a minister of a large fundamentalist church. The basic plan was for the clients to contribute their life savings up front, receiving housing for the rest of their lives, funded by the earnings of their contributions. When I asked what would happen if the earnings were insufficient to keep the project afloat, everyone looked at me and reminded me that this was God's work and, therefore, could not fail. Several years later, the minister was convicted of fraud. The project was never completed and the seniors lost their money.

I left the lawyer's office one week before I would receive my grades for the bar exam.

I found office space and entered into a lease, then ordered a phone and stationery. I started to worry: *What would I do if I did not pass? Unemployed … tied to a lease … Betty and three kids … I could not have been more irresponsible if I had tried.*

Finally, one Saturday, I heard the mailman at our front door and the metallic sound of the mailbox lid closing. I rushed to the door and pulled out the envelope I had left at the State Capitol. Tearing it open, I shouted, "Betty, I passed!" We held each other with tears running down our cheeks.

– 12 –

Walter Mitty

The swearing-in ceremony, in the State Capitol's old Supreme Court chambers, marked a sharp turn in our lives. As the speeches of the Chief Justice and prominent members of the bar extolled the majesty of the law and our entry into this honorable profession, I looked at Betty and our three children, ages one to nine, and wondered if my grandiose plans of becoming a successful trial lawyer were overly optimistic and irresponsible. *Was I taking us down the road to disaster?*

After the ceremonies at the state and federal courts were completed, we drove, at Betty's urging, to the shabby offices of the ACLU. She reasoned, quite accurately, that I needed to associate with some organizations to attract clients, since we knew only a handful of people in the area. She, a natural bleeding heart liberal, thought the ACLU would be the perfect organization for me; it also appealed to my libertarian Ayn Rand leanings.

I walked through the hallway, with its dirty, peeling paint and blue nylon carpet, until I reached the sign: American Civil Liberties Union of Colorado. The door was open and a woman, who I later learned was Dorothy Davidson, the director of the Colorado ACLU, was collating papers at a long table. I cleared my throat and told her I had just been sworn into the bar and would like to offer my services if they had a need for an enthusiastic lawyer. She said, "Just leave your card," and pointed to an empty spot on the cluttered table.

It appeared as if she never looked up, but she must have, because Dorothy told me years later that she had noticed my bow tie and assumed I was an FBI agent. I placed the very first of my business cards, which I had picked up from the printer the day before, on the table as directed.

"One West Hampden Avenue" was about as prestigious an address as I could create for my street-level office in the heart of "downtown" Englewood. To my left was an insurance agency that had a conventional number 3 for its address; to my right was a record store that faced Broadway, giving it a four-digit address that was impossible to spell out. I splurged for a dark wooden sign with bright white, three-dimensional letters that proclaimed to the world "Law Office."

I had designed the layout to accommodate two lawyers, with each office about the same size and a slightly larger, shared reception room. The landlord kept his promise to have the office ready at the beginning of October. My metal desk with the Formica top; the secretary's wooden desk; several slightly used chairs for clients; and new bright orange chairs with chrome legs for the reception area were all delivered the first week of October. A metal four-drawer file arrived the next week. There was no rush since the only file I had was for a recently married law school classmate who was going into the hospital and wanted a will.

I paid for the furnishings and the rent out of savings. Since I had to conserve all my remaining assets until income from clients would pay for my office and living expenses, Betty used her high-school typing class experience to serve as my secretary for about two weeks, until we agreed that I needed to hire a secretary—even though there was not much for a secretary to do—to prevent permanent damage to our marriage.

I had heard of a federally funded program, WINNS, that placed unskilled women in on-the-job training positions and subsidized their salary for a year of training. I was exceedingly lucky that Star, a young, very personable Hispanic woman became my trainee. Together, we learned how to run a law office. Star stayed with me for five years, and then moved on to a responsible administrative position with the Social Security Administration.

To keep the office and home afloat, Betty worked part-time as a special education teacher and made periodic trips to the bank to cash Savings Bonds that I had accumulated during my years at Martin. I was determined not to go into debt. As the six-inch stack of bonds shrunk to five inches, though, I started to worry.

After I finished the will for my first client, a Martin colleague hired me to handle a house sale. I, of course, had never learned how to do that in law school, so I researched the process for hours in the law library. Then, fortunately for me, another Martin colleague was getting a divorce.

Slowly, clients with traffic tickets, neighbor problems, and landlord disputes found One West Hampden. Within two months, Betty's trips to the bank became less frequent.

During the first month in my office, several of the business people in Englewood invited me to service club luncheons. This was an obvious opportunity to make client contacts, so I attended. I felt so uncomfortable at the luncheons, with their rituals, singing, and fundraising fines that I had to tell Betty that as much as I needed clients, I was not going to get them from the service clubs.

In November, Betty dragged me to a Howard Johnson hotel for a Democratic political meeting that saved my practice. Martin Miller, the local district attorney and the only Democratic officeholder in staunchly Republican Arapahoe County, gave a speech. Marty was a short man whose sheer energy made up for his speaking voice and lack of height. Over the years, I learned that even if he was wrong, he never was in doubt about the rightness of his cause, whether in politics or law.

As the meeting was breaking up and at Betty's urging, I introduced myself to Marty, explaining that I was a new lawyer in the county, had opened an office in Englewood, and needed work. Did he have any advice? Much to my surprise, he invited me to call his office for an appointment. Out of that meeting, I became a part-time deputy district attorney in January 1967, and Betty no longer had to make any bond-cashing trips to the bank.

On Thanksgiving Day, while we were all at the office, our son Rick, without any prompting, took his first steps, from orange seat to orange seat in the reception area. We all took this as a very good omen: we, like Rick, were now on our feet.

I faced a decision because 1967 was the last year that deputy DAs in the metropolitan Denver counties could serve part time and also have a private practice. Starting in 1968, all deputies would be full time. The elected DA could maintain a private practice until the end of his term. Thereafter, newly elected DAs would also be full time. So, I had one year to get my practice self-supporting or give up my practice and become a full-time deputy.

On my first day Marty asked me to call his secretary when I arrived at my assigned courtroom, to let him know I had found the courthouse in Aurora, which seemed halfway to the Kansas border. He told me he would know I was doing a fine job if he never heard from or about me. During the year, Marty called three staff meetings where I met the other deputies. I was responsible for all criminal cases that came through my assigned court. These were set for hearing for two or three days each week. Civil cases were heard the remaining days.

I was authorized to make all disposition decisions. The judge, who unfortunately was a lazy, alcoholic bigot, was primarily interested in completing the day's docket as quickly as possible so he could leave.

Some days, he would show up late; others, not at all. Sometimes, he would arrive after lunch, obviously under the influence. With the help of the court's staff, we covered the judge's problems as best we could. Complying with Marty's subtle parting admonition, I did not call him but instead used my independent judgment.

During that year, Marty called me only once. A trial lawyer with a fantastic reputation for his courtroom skills was representing a defendant in a "driving under the influence" case in my courtroom. There had been an established policy that a plea to a lesser charge would dispose of a case, depending on the defendant's prior record.

Because I wanted to try the case against this celebrated lawyer, I had not agreed to the standard disposition, hoping to force the case to trial. The lawyer complained to Marty about the unreasonable deputy he had in Aurora. Marty called, and the case was disposed of, consistent with all other cases.

The job gave me invaluable trial experience, courtroom presence, and the financial cushion to make it possible for me to survive the first year of my somewhat improbable dream.

One of the clerks in my court was getting a divorce. She hoped that she and her husband could work out the details and requested that I represent her. We were able to resolve all issues, and I drafted a comprehensive stipulation to present to the court after asking her the mandatory legal questions to establish jurisdiction, venue, and grounds, which I had received from an experienced lawyer.

To my shock and disappointment, the judge refused to grant the divorce until the parties attempted to reconcile with the help of a marriage counselor. Though I found out later that this judge had personal objections to divorce in general, losing a non-contested divorce shattered my confidence. My client, less disappointed than I, told me to cheer up. "What's another month or two?" she asked.

During my first year of practice one of my divorce clients, a hospital nurse, was attending a Native American patient who had been burned over 30 percent of his body as a result of a work-related accident. He had been using a propane-fueled torch to thaw railroad tracks when a gas leak caused a ball of flames to envelop him.

The nurse was present when the Union Pacific lawyers attempted to settle the claim with the patient, who was in and out of consciousness and spoke very little English. Concerned that her patient would not be treated fairly, she suggested to the patient's family, who were staying in the patient's room day and night, that they consult an attorney before they settle.

I was brought in because the family knew no lawyer and the nurse knew only me. Several months later, the case was settled for multiples of the original offer. My fee was the first surplus money that I could invest since I opened my practice.

During that year, my law practice consisted primarily of minor legal services: landlord-tenant disputes, contracts, leases, divorces, and employment claims. I devoted more time and energy to these cases than lawyers who had more successful practices. I also volunteered to provide legal services to the poor.

I explained to Dorothy, at the ACLU, that I could not be associated with any criminal defense cases while I was a deputy DA; however, I was more than willing to volunteer for any legal work on civil matters. She took up my offer and assigned me as an ACLU representative to a massive lawsuit led by a prestigious law firm to establish, on behalf of the retarded citizens of Colorado, their right to a publicly funded education.

I was very eager to participate, based on our experience with Diane, who, by this time had shown the progress that Don Schiff had assured us we would see.

I interviewed many parents who described the frustration and financial devastation they had suffered trying to get appropriate education for their children. The case eventually led to some corrective state legislation. It was not until 1971 that federal law mandated a public education to everyone. Although my part in this litigation was minor, I began to appreciate how the power of the law, if used intelligently, could influence society.

In the spring, Lou Parkinson passed the bar and took the second office as we had previously discussed. Since my practice was not keeping Star busy full time and she had gained proficiency as a legal secretary during the six months she worked for me, Lou and I shared her time and salary in addition to the rent.

Lou had been a longtime resident of Englewood, served on its city council, and was known for his legendary golf prowess—all of which garnered him connections with business and political leaders of the city, an asset I certainly did not have.

Recognizing that golfing skill could be used to attract clients, Lou offered to teach me the game. I told him I had never held a golf club and that my past experience in sports did not make me optimistic about my success.

He persisted, and one sunny afternoon we made it to the course. He had brought an extra set of his clubs and golf shoes for me. After two holes, he said I was right, I would never learn the game, and I would have to rely on my embryonic legal skills to lure clients.

One early afternoon, I returned to the office from my DA duties and saw that Lou had his office door closed, which probably meant he had a new client. That was good news. In a few minutes, Lou came into my office and asked if I had heard about a railroad crossing accident where there were four fatalities. I had not. He asked me to come into his office and meet his client. He thought this case was so big that we both should work on it.

The client told us that a month earlier, his wife had been driving their three kids when a train hit them at a railroad crossing. The police investigation revealed that the crossing barrier, flashing lights, and bells were inoperative at the time. The man's wife and one of the children died at the scene. Two of the children were taken to the hospital, where one died the next day and the other died three days later.

The bereaved father, having decided he needed to talk to a lawyer, was attracted to our convenient, street-level office. He told us that when he sought some compensation for his loss, the representative from Union Pacific had laughed and told him the railroad was not accepting any responsibility. We were willing to take the case on a contingent fee even though we had never even drafted a contingent fee agreement.

We asked the man to return in an hour after we had done some investigation. Lou was to call his contacts at the police department, and I was to draft a contingent fee agreement.

The police had not heard of any recent Englewood railroad accident. Perhaps it was in Sheridan, Littleton, or Denver?

Our client returned as scheduled, asking if he could have a few dollars in change for the meter. We, of course, were more than happy to oblige. As he left, Lou exclaimed, "There are no parking meters in Englewood!"

We never saw our "client" again. I often wondered if he made his living scamming parking meter change from hungry lawyers who had dollar signs in their eyes. Although we didn't tell many people about the incident, Lou and I had quite a few laughs over our big personal injury case against the Union Pacific Railroad.

During the summer, I was visited by a caseworker from the Department of Social Services. She requested help for one of her clients who had been injured in a fall down an outside stairway. The woman's elbow had been chipped in the fall so her lower arm swung too far backward when she straightened it and required permanent immobilization with a brace. As a result, she had lost her factory job; her husband was not employable because of a chronic physical condition.

The social worker had seen other lawyers, all of whom had immediately rejected the claim. Because I agreed to talk to the woman and examine the premises to see if a claim against the landlord would be possible, she believed that I was the best lawyer in town and made several referrals to me over the next few years.

My investigation resulted in a mixed bag. I found an iron boot scraper set in the concrete apron at the top of the stairs. I also noticed that there was no handrail, which I discovered was required by the Englewood building code. On the night of the accident, my client had tripped on the scraper, falling headfirst down the concrete steps. Unfortunately, I also discovered that my client had been drinking prior to her fall. Although my client's case was far from strong, I agreed to take it on. I had the time and ambition to use every opportunity to make a name for myself as a trial lawyer.

I read every trial practice manual I could find, talked to experienced lawyers, and even bought a model of an elbow to use in the jury trial that I had requested and was certain would occur, since the attorney for the insurance company had assured me that under the facts of the case, no offer of settlement would be made. With false bravado, I responded that I was looking forward to the trial because I needed the experience. The trial was set to begin in the spring of 1968.

Near the end of 1967, Marty called a staff meeting to determine which of his staff would remain as full-time deputies until the end of his term. I thanked Marty for the invaluable opportunity he had given me, but declined.

I was looking forward to my personal injury trial, which I was sure would start me on the road to becoming *the* trial lawyer of Colorado. I now had enough business to make a meager living, and leaving the DA's office released me from the prohibition of taking on criminal defense cases.

In the spring of 1968, the broken elbow case went to trial. I tried it as if it were the most important case in the country. Two lawyers were opposing me. In addition to the insurance company's lawyer, there was the landlord's own attorney, one of the best-known personal injury lawyers in the state, since I had requested judgment greater than the insurance policy limits.

I methodically plowed through the evidence with drawings, medical reports, and the testimony of my client, her husband, the doctor, and building inspectors. I knew that the judge, with whom I would serve on the Court of Appeals twenty years later, could not throw me out of court until I sat down announcing, "the plaintiff rests."

On the third day of trial, counsel for the insurance company approached and asked me for a settlement offer. I was thrilled that my courtroom prowess had intimidated the opposition.

After consulting my clients, I gave him my demand—about twice the amount that my client had told me would make her deliriously happy. We advised the judge that we were in settlement negotiations and asked if we could be excused for the rest of the afternoon, possibly to conclude the matter. I discovered then that "settlement" is the most welcome word to all trial judges who struggle with impossibly large dockets.

With the time pressure relieved, my opponent confided to me that he was offering to settle, not because of my awesome trial ability but because he had noticed that my client's husband had six fingers on each hand—and the jury could not keep their eyes off his unique deformity.

He thought my offer outrageous but said that he would convey it to his company. I watched him as his arms gestured wildly in the phone booth. He came back with an offer about half of mine. I was very tempted to take it: I was exhausted after three days of trial, the idea of a certain conclusion to the months of uncertainty was tempting, and my client had authorized me to take considerably less than my offer.

I asked her permission to reject it and make a counteroffer close to the midpoint of the two offers. Because I was so nervous, it took all of my remaining energy to convey this to the lawyer in a confident manner.

It was settled. I could hardly believe it. I drove my happy clients to their home, never telling them the role the extra fingers had played in our success and letting them think they had the greatest trial lawyer in the state.

At about the time of my personal injury success, the city of Sheridan was going through a very difficult time. The city council was fending off accusations of corruption that appeared in the daily newspapers.

The city attorney resigned during this turmoil and Marty recommended me to the mayor to fill the part-time office. It paid a modest retainer for attendance at city council meetings and the prosecution of ordinance violations in the municipal court. I would receive additional pay for representing the city in any litigation and would not be limited in my law practice, which had grown substantially in caseload if not income. I could certainly use the retainer—I accepted.

The leaders of the partisans in the city council feud were two strong-willed women: the mayor and the treasurer. The treasurer was a successful businessperson. She owned a large gravel pit that she had converted to a landfill because it was getting deeper and less productive in yielding gravel. She had contracted with the City of Denver to accept its trash. The mayor attempted to use her office to bring reform to this economically depressed town. Both factions attempted to use the city attorney as support for their positions. I attempted to walk a middle course, giving legal opinions when called for but making it clear that political decisions were up to the council.

At the urging of the mayor and her supporters on the council, I drafted a much-needed health code ordinance for the operation of the landfill, and I brought the city ordinances, which had been neglected over the years, into an organized code.

The last feud was settled amicably when the treasurer, after much delay, produced her financial report, which I had opined the council was entitled to.

I was quoted in the newspaper as blaming all past troubles on misunderstandings between the factions. Miraculously, now that these false impressions were settled, the remainder of the year was comparatively peaceful. A new election brought in a reform council that selected a new city attorney.

No lawyer learns how to try cases in law school; he gains experience in the courtroom, and guidance from other lawyers. I was fortunate to get much-needed advice from an unlikely teacher.

In a complex personal injury case, I was having problems questioning a difficult witness. The court had called a mid-afternoon recess after repeatedly sustaining my adversary's objections.

The court reporter came out as I was talking to my client in the hallway and asked if she could speak to me. When we were out of earshot of my client, Carol said, "Pete, we all know what you are trying to get out of this witness, so why not handle it a different way?" She then proceeded to give me the script for my next few questions; things went swimmingly when I went back into the courtroom. I was delighted and grateful to take help from wherever it came.

Some time later, I received a collect call from Calvin, at the Denver County Jail, requesting that I visit him. I made the long drive to the jail, since now I could take criminal cases. Calvin, who was black, told me he and his wife were being accused by their employer, a slum landlord, of pocketing rent payments they had received while acting as apartment house managers. His wife also was in jail based on the same false report of theft. A review of the records with the prosecutor revealed that every penny had been accounted for. The criminal case was dismissed.

I filed a malicious prosecution case against the landlord; however, he died before the case went to trial. The estate's lawyers filed a motion to dismiss, because at that time malicious prosecution claims did not survive a party's death.

The judge saw the equities of the case and suggested that Mr. Ney could amend the pleadings to avoid dismissal. "Why don't both of you go into the jury room," he recommended, "and see if this case can be settled." The defendant's lawyers were extremely unhappy; however, the case was settled for a nominal sum that satisfied my client, who had expected nothing.

Increasing public protest against the war in Viet Nam in 1968 and continued civil rights street demonstrations culminated in the election of Richard Nixon. It was the perfect year for me to begin accepting criminal cases.

In April 1968, Dorothy Davidson telephoned to take me up on my offer to accept volunteer assignments from the ACLU. Would I represent University of Denver students who had been expelled and criminally charged for occupying the registrar's office as a protest to the Viet Nam war? I immediately accepted.

This case embodied the reasons I had become a lawyer: I would be working with Ed Kahn, a well-respected trial lawyer with a large law firm, who also was on the ACLU's volunteer legal panel. My *pro bono* status did not cause any hesitation in my commitment to what certainly would be a long and time-consuming responsibility. The case seemed to be a perfect match for my somewhat quixotic approach to law as well as my personal feelings regarding the war and civil rights.

That evening, I met Ed Kahn and our forty-one clients in a student lounge on the university campus. We interviewed the students and learned that the occupation had been peaceful, no one had been injured, no property had been damaged, and, most important of all, the students were enthusiastic, dedicated to their cause, and interesting.

It immediately became obvious to me why Ed had the reputation as one of the foremost lawyers in the legal community: he recognized the legal issues instantly and set the strategy. Without his leadership, I doubt if the students would have been adequately represented.

The immediate problem was that the chancellor had expelled the students before a disciplinary committee had been convened, under the university rules, to determine the appropriate action to be taken. Our first success was with the disciplinary committee. It revoked the chancellor's order of expulsion after several days of hearings and recommended a period of probation. The chancellor resisted that recommendation, and we were off to federal court.

Our primary and somewhat insurmountable problem was that the University of Denver was a private institution and therefore not required to afford its students the constitutional rights that limited state and federal governmental action.

Our time in federal court did give me the opportunity to cross-examine the chancellor for more than a full day under the less-than-sympathetic eyes of United States District Judge Hatfield Chilson. Ed Kahn complimented me on my give-no-quarter cross-examination, but Bob Yegge, the dean of the law school, in a letter to me, questioned if I had not confused personal involvement with professional zeal to a point where I had forgotten the major objectives of my legal education. Looking back, I see he may have had a point.

The chancellor became an icon for a minority of college administrators who advocated taking a hard line against student protest. In the fall, when the students were acquitted of the criminal charges, he was greatly disappointed and suggested that the laws be rewritten.

In July, Dorothy Davidson set up a volunteer observation group in a small park across the street from the Golden Apple, a hippie hangout, in response to their complaints of police harassment. Betty and I were eager to participate and were assigned the first evening shift. What a colorful sight—feathers, painted bodies, beads, long hair, varying states of dress and undress all immersed in a haze of smoke with the distinctive odor of burning rope.

Betty and I entered the Golden Apple and were easily accepted by the group, although we must have looked like we had come from a foreign land. The members of the band, playing their original music that night, became my friends and clients.

During our two-to three-hour shift, we had a wonderful time but observed no improper police conduct. Dorothy and Frank, another lawyer who was the vice-chair of the ACLU board, arrived to relieve us but we stayed for another hour to enjoy the ambiance.

Just as we arrived back in our suburban house, high from our great adventure, we received a call from Dorothy's teenage daughter who had accompanied her mother on the escapade. "My mother and Frank have just been arrested and are being taken to jail," Linda said, requesting I get them out.

When I arrived at the jail, Ed Kahn was already there. We visited the miscreants, and after a few telephone calls had bond set. They were released to answer a multitude of misdemeanor charges ranging from loitering and disturbance to interference with a police officer.

Never were loiterers so well represented. At least five attorneys, including me, represented the two defendants, who secured separate trials. Dorothy's trial went first and lasted three days, resulting in a not guilty verdict. The city then dropped the charges against the other defendant.

Well, 1968 was certainly shaping up to be a vintage year. Not only was I having a wonderful time giving away my legal services, but I had become recognized as a hotshot criminal lawyer by University of Denver students who were being charged, in droves, for marijuana-related violations.

At that time, these were considered serious felonies that resulted, upon conviction, in penitentiary terms. Most parents were willing to support their kids and pay attorney fees; however, some were not and cut their children off without any support. Some of the students ended up living in our house for short periods of time. Betty and I concluded that our own children benefited from the diverse population in our home.

I was contacted by a family Betty and I had met at the Lucky U Motel when the Martin Company transferred both families from Baltimore to Denver. "I can't believe it!" our friend from our first days in Denver excitedly yelled into the telephone. "My son, a student at Colorado State University, is in jail in Fort Collins charged with cattle rustling! A Jewish cattle rustler! Unbelievable!"

It seems our friends' son and two of his college buddies thought they could put up a year's provision of meat by executing a calf, which they then loaded into the back of a pickup. When they brought the carcass to the freezer locker for butchering, they raised sufficient suspicion for the police to be called; and since the students could not explain their possession of the carcass, they ended up in jail.

The local ranchers took cattle rustling very seriously; we found some humor in the term, not thinking of it as what it was—theft of livestock. The two other young men negotiated pleas to lesser charges, but my client was considered the ringleader and was not offered a plea to a lesser charge. So we had no choice but to go to trial.

This was my first felony case that actually went to trial. The public section of the courtroom was three-quarters full when I arrived. With the exception of my client's family, everyone was dressed in western style clothing.

The court was called to order; the judge took his seat. The first two rows were cleared and the jury panel was brought in. Again, the preferred clothing style was cowboy hats, western shirts, and tight blue jeans. This didn't look good. It was beginning to look like a movie set for *High Noon*.

The DA questioned the jury panel, and then it was my turn. How was I going to make these cowboys like me? When we broke for lunch, my client's parents assured me that my *voir dire* was masterful, especially when I thanked each jury member for a candid answer that indicated not one of them would tolerate any punk kid stealing any of their cattle.

The trial proceeded with the prosecution's case. The owner, a brand inspector, and a person from the freezer locker all testified. An idea came to me just as the brand inspector finished his testimony. The judge asked me if the inspector could be excused. "No objection, your honor," I replied. The inspector had never testified that the brand on the calf belonged to the rancher.

When the prosecution rested, it was late in the afternoon of the second day. The judge asked if I was prepared to proceed with my case the next morning. I responded that I would, but first, I had a motion. Did the court wish to hear it now or tomorrow?

"Let's take it up in chambers after a fifteen minute recess," the judge responded. "Bailiff, please clear the courtroom and lock up."

After we reconvened in the judge's chambers, I moved to dismiss all charges against my client because the state had not proven who owned the calf. Neither the brand inspector nor the owner had tied up the evidence of ownership.

The judge looked at me as if he didn't understand what I was saying. The DA responded as best he could, but seemed to know he had a problem. After I repeated my whole argument again, the judge granted my motion and dismissed the case.

He turned to me and said, "Young man, the courthouse is emptying out rapidly now. I suggest you wait another half-hour, and then get in your car and drive directly back to Denver. Your case is dismissed, so there is no need for you to be here in the morning."

I wondered, as I drove back, what those ranchers would have done to my client and me after they found out that the charges against my client had been dismissed.

As a direct result of the cattle rustling case, I was retained in my first murder case—a young Fort Collins mother who was accused of drowning her five-week-old infant in his bath. When she appeared in court, it was clear to everyone who observed her that she was confused, depressed, and disturbed. Initially, she was held without bond, but at the urging of her family, I successfully argued for the setting of bond. Shortly after she was released, she drowned herself in the local reservoir.

Lou and I agreed to an office sharing arrangement with Joyce Steinhardt and Earl Hauck, who had gone to law school with us. This, of course, required larger quarters. On July 1, we moved the firm to a space in a newly constructed office building. We had offices for four lawyers, a conference room, space for two secretaries, and a waiting area.

In August 1968, a newspaper warned, "White suburbia is target of militants." Twenty-six youths, all from white, middle-class families, had come to Littleton to educate suburbia about inner-city problems from which the students believed suburbia was insulated.

The group was the reverse of VISTA, a government-sponsored war-on-poverty program that sent students to the inner city to fight poverty, so they took the name ATSIV. We and other Littleton families took in the students. ATSIV achieved its purpose over the summer, giving talks at churches, service clubs, and business associations. Arapahoe Community College hosted community talks, and our backyard, not surprisingly, became their headquarters.

Our kids—Linda, not quite eleven; Diane, eight; and Rick, three—mingled with these activists. We were certain that the contact with them was having a positive influence on our kids, while our neighbors believed we were permanently damaging them.

June, one of the ATSIV students, made jail reform her summer project, having based her claim that the treatment of women prisoners was inhumane solely on interviews with previously incarcerated women. She decided that her allegations would be more credible if she relied not only on interviews but also on personal experience as a prisoner inside the Denver jail, and requested that I stand by to secure her release in case her stay was totally intolerable.

One evening, she jumped into a center city fountain and proceeded to splash pedestrians. Eventually, the police arrived and received a thorough soaking. June got her wish and spent a day in jail. She found the conditions so appalling and degrading that after one day she called me and I secured her release. She did not wish to defend the misdemeanor charges, but pled guilty instead, making a prepared statement in which she described what she had experienced in jail. Her statement was reported in the media and sent to the mayor, manager of safety, and the chief of police.

June spent the rest of the summer speaking at public forums describing her experiences in jail and was sought for interviews by newspaper and television reporters. I believe that conditions in the women's section of the jail improved as a result of her efforts. She received the John F. Kennedy Award from Loretta Heights College as the woman who had done the most for the underprivileged in the Denver area.

During this time, probably inspired by the young activists around us, Betty herself became a demonstrator, marching against the war and picketing the carnation growers for better working conditions for migrant workers.

She also set up and manned petition-signing tables for gun regulation, much to the annoyance of shopping center management. Our three kids were usually with her on these projects. I assured her and the other suburban housewives with her that they would not have to worry if they were arrested, as recent Supreme Court decisions were on their side. Although the women were frequently warned, they were never arrested.

Betty organized "Let's See," an interracial summer day camp for fifty children, in Denver's black community. To racially integrate the program, she transported our kids and other suburban white kids to the camp. We hope it helped our kids; I am positive it did not hurt them.

On New Year's Eve of 1969, Harry Gilmer and his wife came to Denver for the holidays to meet two Denver friends whom they had not seen for several years. They were to celebrate the New Year at the

Denver Playboy Club and reminisce about old times. After ordering drinks, they were asked to be quiet, or leave, because they were speaking too loudly. The group agreed to leave.

When Gilmer asked for his party's overcoats, the manager of the club told the coatroom attendant not to return their coats to them because they had not paid for their drinks. Gilmer explained that they had never been served any drinks.

An argument ensued, resulting in Gilmer being forced onto an elevator by the club's security guard, an off-duty Denver police officer. The versions of what occurred on the elevator ride to the street level varied wildly between the two occupants. However, it appeared that the officer's uniform had been torn and his hat was missing. A physical altercation occurred on the first floor between Gilmer and the officer, resulting in Gilmer's incarceration on charges of intoxication in a public place, resisting arrest, disturbance, and destruction of public property.

Gilmer retained me to represent him on the criminal charges. A jury acquitted him of all charges. As we left the court, Gilmer turned to me, a proud, hotshot criminal lawyer, and asked, "What do we do now?"

"I don't know what you mean, Harry," I replied. "You've been acquitted. You can return home to North Carolina." Harry replied, in all seriousness, "You're not going to let them get away with this, are you?" I did not have the slightest idea what I could do to satisfy Harry's quest for revenge, but I knew that I would not let any client of mine think I was a wimp. "Let me think about it," I stalled. "Meet me in the office tomorrow."

The next morning, after a sleepless night, I announced to Harry that we would sue the Playboy Club on a claim of false imprisonment. My theory was not based on the evening he spent in jail, because that was the action of the police, but rather on the Playboy Club's manager's refusal to return Gilmer's overcoat, which made it unreasonable for Gilmer to leave on a cold winter night, thereby imprisoning him.

After the Playboy Club had been served, my law school tort instructor called and told me he was representing the defendants. He asked if I, by filing such a wacko lawsuit, had possibly lost my mind, or had I learned nothing about torts in his class. I asked if he wanted to discuss settlement, and he roared with laughter, telling me he would see me in court.

The jury returned a verdict in my favor, assessing the Playboy Club actual and punitive damages. As my former teacher left the courtroom he said, "It's all my fault; I must have over-trained you."

He appealed. The actual damage award was sustained, but the punitive award was reversed.

My practice grew rapidly during the first two years in areas of personal injury and divorce; however, after I no longer was a deputy DA, most of the growth was in criminal defense, primarily with drug cases that usually evolved into constitutional search and seizure issues.

I had represented Benny while I was still a law student in a student practice program. I had argued a statute that made the status of being a drug addict a criminal offense was unconstitutional. The trial court agreed. Now Benny was in jail for burglary. He had no funds but asked me to represent him. For old times sake I agreed.

Benny was walking in front of a formal wear clothing store, across the street from the courthouse, when he evidently was so overcome with the urge to possess the shoes on display that he did not notice the police car parked across the street. The police officers seated in the patrol car testified that they saw Benny break the glass and remove the shoes.

I couldn't believe it, but as in Fort Collins, the DA was so sure he could not lose the case that he forgot to prove the ownership of the stolen property. This time, I was very assured of my argument and kept raising my voice for emphasis. The elderly, retired judge assured me he could hear perfectly well and understood my argument.

"Let's adjourn for lunch and give Mr. Fielder an opportunity to research the issues raised by your motion to dismiss," the judge ordered. I spent the lunch hour with Benny in the holding cell.

After lunch, the case was dismissed. Benny and I walked into a late afternoon snowstorm. He was still in the summer clothes he had worn at the time of his arrest.

I filed suit on behalf of the hippies of Denver against the mayor, chief of police, and others, to protect the hippies' civil liberties against police harassment.

Hispanic students who were suspended from public school for wearing black berets as a sign of protest also became my clients.

A disabled African-American veteran who had purchased a new home to be constructed near the entry to a new housing development contacted me in the fall. He had found himself reassigned to a lot in the rear of the development.

The success of that suit brought me to the attention of Metro Denver Fair Housing Inc., a non-profit corporation organized to eliminate housing discrimination and provide planning and financing for low-cost housing. I became its attorney in 1969.

My activism gave me a public image that brought me a great deal of new business—only half of it paying. I was now working seven days a week.

To give me time with my growing children, I arranged visits to my jailed clients for Sundays when the whole family would picnic on the lawns of the various metropolitan jails. Denver County Jail was a favorite because it was located just behind Stapleton Airport, where the kids could watch the planes landing and taking off.

The police had determined, without any legal authority, that they would harass and make life miserable for homosexuals in Denver. I received complaints that the police would park near known gay bars and cite patrons for offenses such as loitering, jaywalking, and lewd acts.

The police also verbally abused and threatened them. I agreed to represent those who wished to contest the citations, investigate their allegations, and file a complaint against the city, if warranted.

One evening, several police officers entered a lesbian bar and charged all patrons they observed holding hands, kissing, hugging, and dancing, with the offense of lewd act. Five of the women wished to fight the charges, but there was a serious problem: one woman was a flight attendant; another, a nurse; still another, a probation officer; the fourth, a hair stylist; and the fifth, an accountant. They were certain their careers would be destroyed if their employers discovered their sexual orientation.

The defense was quite simple: all the acts complained of, if committed by a man and a woman at high noon on the front steps of the courthouse where the case was being tried would never be considered lewd. Therefore, I argued, how could their activity be unlawful merely because the participants were all women? The case was dismissed.

I recognized two newspaper reporters in the courtroom and explained the situation: if they printed the women's names, the police would win in spite of the acquittals. No story ever appeared.

Betty and I invited all the defendants to our house for a celebration. We had a great party, which started a tradition of victory celebrations for special clients. Linda, our worldly thirteen-year-old, said to Betty, "This evening, instead of flirting with the women, Dad's got to look out for our guests making passes at you."

Four years earlier, when I had decided to open my own law office, I entertained what seemed like an impossible dream that I could make a difference, using whatever talents I had for law, to expand individual liberties and constitutional rights. I had no ambition to earn a great deal of money, however, I was well aware of my responsibilities to provide our family with some financial security.

The practice had grown sufficiently so that when we heard about a house with a walkout basement for sale, Betty immediately looked at it. In the house we then had, we were always concerned about letting one of our children sleep in the basement bedroom, which had no exit. Betty was so excited when she called me at the office that I knew we had to see it together right after work.

Seeing the house at sunset, I was as enthusiastic as Betty. It had a spectacular view of the mountains. Without looking at much of the practical features such as closets, kitchen, and bathrooms we made a written offer. The offer was accepted the next day because the present owners were going through a divorce and wanted a quick sale.

Since the new house would require an additional $50 each month for the mortgage that we were assuming, I had many sleepless nights worrying if I had bitten off more than we could chew.

Thirty-eight years later, we are still enjoying the view and have never considered any major changes to the house, as we fortunately, though belatedly, discovered that it had all the practical considerations we needed.

Rather than financial success, I fantasized a trial practice specializing in constitutional law—a contest between David, the individual, versus Goliath, the government.

When I opened the practice one month before my thirty-fifth birthday—somewhat too old to embrace unrealistic career fantasies more appropriate for a teenager—I had already discarded two solid, unrelated careers in which I had achieved sufficient success to comfortably support my family. But, I believed that in this country anything is possible, and anyone can dream, even if the dream is unrealistic, I became a contemporary *Walter Mitty;* James Thurber would have approved.

– 13 –

Don Quixote

The tall, attractive, stylishly dressed woman sitting across from me had been referred to me by the ACLU because she had been ordered by Denver police officers to report to the Venereal Disease Clinic at Denver General Hospital for a vaginal and rectal examination. Roxanne related that police officers had stopped her while she was crossing a hotel parking lot, asked her to identify herself, and handed her a document that looked like a traffic ticket. The ticket ordered her to report to the VD clinic on a certain date and warned that failure to appear would result in her arrest. She had twice previously responded to these tickets and had complied with vaginal and rectal examinations conducted without her consent.

"Do they think I'm an idiot and don't know how to take care of myself?" she asked in a trembling rage. "I see my own physician on a regular basis and don't want to be touched by a doctor or nurse at an unsanitary public hospital—it's degrading, humiliating, and dangerous. Can you help me avoid this?" she asked.

"We will certainly try," I responded, trying to sound confident when I didn't have the foggiest idea what I would do next. But I, Don Quixote, did know that this Dulcinea was not going to be subjected to the humiliation and degradation ordered by the summons.

Roxanne and I appeared at the VD center at the designated time. I told the woman behind the desk that I was there with Roxanne and asked her to call the doctor because I wanted to see him. The receptionist told us to sit down and said that Roxanne would be called in due course.

I handed her my card, and told her in a voice loud enough to get her attention, "No, you obviously do not understand. I am here as Ms. Reynolds' lawyer. Now, you mark her present on your clipboard and call the physician in charge and tell him that I want to see him." Gritting her teeth, she placed a telephone call.

In a few minutes, a very young man in a white lab coat with a stethoscope hanging from his neck came from the back. I introduced myself and said, "Doctor, I can see you have not been a physician for very long. It would certainly be a pity for you to lose your medical license so early in your career. I want to make it absolutely clear that Ms. Reynolds is here pursuant to this ticket, and I want you to understand most importantly that she is not consenting to your touching her in any manner whatsoever. You, of course, do as you wish. However, I assume that you have been taught the consequences of touching a patient without consent."

The doctor assured me he would never touch someone without consent and that my client's appearance in response to the ticket would be recorded. The women waiting to be called watched the drama in front of them. Since Roxanne and I left quickly, I never did find out if any of the women took my lead by explaining their lack of consent.

That solved Roxanne's immediate problem, but she wanted to take steps to stop the degrading procedure. So, we were off to federal court, suing Denver's mayor, manager of safety, police chief, and manager of health and hospitals.

During depositions, the attorney for the city repeatedly referred to Roxanne as a whore. Each time, she corrected him, asking him to use "prostitute" when referring to her admitted profession. I knew the attorney was just waiting to embarrass Roxanne in court, so we prepared a trap.

Roxanne moved away from Denver but returned for the trial. I drove her to court with Betty and my daughter, Linda, in the backseat. Roxanne turned and inquired of my thirteen-year-old, "Well, Linda, what do you want to do when you grow up?" We all laughed, getting in the mood for the trial.

When it came time for Roxanne's cross-examination, the city's lawyer did not disappoint. He continued to refer to Roxanne as a whore, and she consistently corrected him, stating that she was a prostitute. After repeated exchanges, the lawyer said, "Ms. Reynolds, I have called you a whore because you are a whore. You have been correcting me by using the term 'prostitute.' Please explain the difference."

Roxanne straightened up her beautiful body in the witness chair, swung her hair with a twist of her head, and, looking straight into the lawyer's eyes, responded, "It's precisely the same as if I called you a lawyer or a shyster."

The courtroom, including the judge, burst into laughter. U.S. District Judge Winner frequently referred to that sequence in his speeches. We never got the injunction, but Denver and its hospital stopped the procedure and were careful to secure a voluntary consent prior to physical examinations.

In 1969 Grove Press, the United States distributor of the Swedish motion picture *I Am Curious (Yellow)* retained me to represent them in Colorado if, as they expected, there might be legal problems with the film's showing, as there had been in other sections of the country. After much fanfare, the movie opened. I received a call from the owner of the movie house on the second day of its showing. He asked me to come to the theater because he had heard the police were coming to seize the movie, and he was unable to locate the theater's lawyer.

I sat in the back of the theater watching the controversial movie and thinking that subtitles did not add anything to erotica. There was some frontal nudity, but the audience was certainly going to be disappointed if they expected to see any obscenity.

As expected, the film went dark and the house lights went up. I was surprised to see that about three-quarters of the seats were filled. Uniformed police came down both aisles announcing that the film had been seized, the show was over, and everyone was to leave the theater. I went to the crowded lobby where I saw Ed Sherman, the lawyer for the theater. We started to speak at the same time. He said, "This film is going to be very difficult to defend. I've never seen anything that meets the definition of obscenity more closely."

Simultaneously, I said, "This film is so mild I don't see how we can lose." Perhaps the twenty-year age difference explained the disparate reactions, or obscenity is all in the eye of the beholder.

I went to federal court on behalf of the film's distributor, asking for an injunction restraining the district attorney from interfering with the showing of the film, attacking the constitutionality of Colorado's obscenity statute, and challenging the validity of the search warrant and film seizure. Ed sought relief in state court on the same issues on behalf of the theater.

The city returned the film voluntarily to counter our argument that our clients, deprived of the film during emergency hearings, were being irreparably damaged. Within two days of the seizure, the film was showing again but now to full houses.

The litigation in federal and state courts spanned more than two months. There was an article in the paper almost every day reporting on the court activities, along with front-page pictures of the state judge going into the theater to evaluate the obscenity of the film. Editorial cartoons lampooned the DA for his crusade against smut while dangerous criminals were robbing and raping the citizenry.

The three months I spent representing Grove Press were the most financially rewarding of my young practice. I called my client to apologize for the size of the bills, explaining that it was impossible for me to devote any time to other cases because I had to be in one court or another every day.

My contact at Grove Press laughed and told me not to worry about my fees—they had been reading the Denver papers and were allocating my fees to their advertising budget rather than legal costs. That deflated my pride in my legal prowess somewhat, but the final unconditional victory was sweet indeed.

The court never determined if *I am Curious (Yellow)* was obscene, as charged, because the Colorado obscenity statute was found to be unconstitutional. The court also found that the procedures used to seize the film were invalid. All criminal charges were dismissed, and the film continued to enjoy a very successful run in Denver.

Not long afterward, an eagle-eyed Denver police officer, apparently appointing himself an arbiter of fashion and decency, arrested a twenty-two-year-old woman who was wearing a see-through blouse and charged her with public indecency. Placing her in jail for ten hours, he claimed he had been able to see her nipples. Of course, this was just the sort of story the media relished, and they described the blouse as "a transparent green bolero-type garment with a bare midriff and white lace trimming." They went on to say, "The lace trimming on the long collar obscured what Ney dubbed 'the critical area.'"

On the day of trial, the case was dismissed at the request of the city and I secured my reputation as Denver's defender of salacious conduct. Exactly what *Walter Mitty* and *Don Quixote* had inspired.

Soon, I became the attorney for an adult bookstore, The San Francisco Book Exchange. Over the years, many obscenity charges were filed against this cultural center. We prevailed in almost all criminal cases and, as a bonus, succeeded in having several obscenity statutes and ordinances declared unconstitutional. I represented the Exchange until 1988, when I left private practice.

In the middle of one night in 1973, the owner of the Exchange telephoned me, requesting that I come to the store as soon as possible, as there had been a shooting! I arrived at about two thirty in the morning to see a brightly lit, surrealistic scene at the Colfax Avenue store. A tall magazine rack with over a hundred sex-related magazines had been upended, and magazines were scattered all over a bloodstained carpet. Several young women in abbreviated clothing were clustered around police officers in the main room of the store.

Shortly after I entered, a hysterical man rushed into the store screaming biblical passages about sinners. Before the police could restrain him, he lunged at a display case, breaking the glass while the contents, "Rubber Goods and Marital Aids" according to its sign came bouncing out, covering the floor with rubber products.

It seems that a group of youths had entered the store at about midnight and attempted to talk to the girls. The manager, Tiny, who could be mistaken for a large refrigerator, warned the boys that if they wanted to socialize with the girls, they would have to buy a "session," which would entitle them to take their selection to a back room. The boys pooled their money and one of them took one of the girls to the back room. A few minutes later, Tiny heard the girl scream, "Keep your hands off me! What do you think this is, a *hoore* house?" Tiny grabbed a large revolver from under the counter and ran down the back hallway, where he shot the boy in the neck. The youth staggered into the front room, where he pulled down the magazine rack as he collapsed to the floor and bled to death.

I would have been a hero to my clients even if the jury had returned a verdict convicting Tiny of manslaughter, or better yet criminally negligent homicide, rather than the charge of murder. I was amazed when the jury acquitted him of all charges, but for my clients' benefit I acted nonchalant: What else would you expect when you hire Peter Ney?

The San Francisco Book Exchange gave a formal dinner in my honor at a fine Chinese restaurant. Betty and I were seated at the head table with Tiny and the owners of the bookstore. The other tables were occupied by drug dealers, prostitutes, persons of varying sexual persuasions, and street people who made their living in various, mostly illegal, ways on notorious Colfax Avenue. All were dressed most colorfully.

This was an evening that neither Betty nor I will ever forget. Betty likes to tell that the high point of her evening, literally, was when gigantic Tiny, in his uncontrollable enthusiasm, threw his arms around her and lifted her off her feet.

My practice became so busy that I hired a young lawyer, explaining that he would be working just for his salary, with no chance of becoming a partner. I was adamant about being the only one to make decisions in the practice. Since there was no office available, he had to use the conference room. My increased business caused tensions in the office, as my workload used more of the secretarial resources and space than my one-fourth contribution to the overhead expenses equitably entitled me to. I did not want to negotiate. Instead, I paid to have a wall built to divide the office in half. My side had a separate entrance with my office, the conference room, and a secretarial/reception space for Star.

I incorporated the practice, which required new stationery and business cards. I chose buff paper with dark red printing and appropriated a Picasso image of Don Quixote seated on his trusty steed, Rocinante, with his squire, Sancho Panza, in the background.

In 1971, The Little Photographer opened as a photography studio where a customer could rent a camera and photograph nude models for a fee. It had been open no more than an hour and a half when the police arrived and arrested a model and the two owners, charging them with lewd acts and indecent exposure. There was absolutely no indication that any activity other than photography had been taking place in the studio. Before the court had a chance to hear the first case, the police had raided the business multiple times, arresting models, the owners, and once, a customer.

I argued that criminal offenses based on indecent exposure and lewd acts prohibited acts in public, not in private, for if the law prohibited the acts in private everyone would be violating the statute. The court ruled that the activities at The Little Photographer were legal and all pending cases were dismissed.

The Little Photographer prospered, moved to larger quarters, and hired more models. Judy, one of the models, was, according to the media, the girlfriend of a member of an organized crime family. The racing commission had recently banned her and her boyfriend, Gene Smaldone, from attendance at horse and dog tracks in Colorado.

I became their lawyer and the bans were lifted after much litigation. However, the bans turned out to be the least of Gene's problems, as he now was facing federal drug importation charges. The Smaldone family lawyer had recently been appointed to the Colorado Supreme Court, so they were looking for a replacement. Although Gene's entire family was adamant that no family member ever be involved in drug trafficking, which they strongly believed was beyond their moral tolerance, Gene's parents' anger did not lessen their concern for their son's welfare. I had to admire their support for a son who had severely disappointed them.

The family decided that Jim Shellow, a Milwaukee attorney with a national reputation in drug cases, based in part on a chemistry degree, would be lead attorney and I would be the local attorney.

The government's theory was that Craig, a friend of Gene's, had purchased cocaine in Peru and planned to transport it to Gene in Denver. The plan failed when Craig was apprehended in Peru; he was awaiting trial in the notorious Lurigancho prison.

To defend Gene properly, we sent an investigator to learn what had transpired in Peru, but he was arrested on currency offenses within days of his arrival. Since there was no alternative, Jim and I had to go. We contacted the State Department and asked for their assistance with the Peruvian government in arranging a prison visit with Craig. We were assured that the U.S. Embassy in Lima would make the appropriate arrangements with the Peruvian Department of Interior.

Our flight from Miami to Lima was delayed twelve hours by mechanical problems. This was critical because we had planned to arrive in Lima before dawn, giving us ample time to make contact with the embassy to obtain the appropriate documentation for entry into the Lurigancho. Now, we would be arriving after noon on July 3, and the embassy would be closed the next day—the fourth of July.

After we touched down at the Lima airport, we saw that the runway was flanked by massed troops interspersed with tanks. We knew that the Peruvian government was a military dictatorship, but this seemed a bit overdone. We found out this was an honor guard—not for us, but for the Pope, who was also arriving that day. After getting through the serpentine lines of passport and customs control, we raced to the lines of taxis without taking time to exchange currency. The cabbie seemed delighted to accept our dollars for the ride to the embassy.

We arrived at the embassy before it closed and received the documentation to get into the Lurigancho to see Craig the next day between noon and 4:00 PM. An official cautioned that we must strictly adhere to the schedule and under no circumstances use or exchange U.S. currency in other than official exchanges, like banks. The Peruvian government was a military dictatorship that guarded its currency very seriously and the embassy would not be able to help us if we violated any currency exchange laws. Jim and I looked at each other wondering how much time we had earned in the Lurigancho by paying the cab driver with U.S. dollars. Fortunately, a bank was open down the street, so we legally exchanged some of our money.

Our hotel was in the business district of Lima. It was obvious, as we walked around the city, which had once been beautiful, but the landscaped parks had deteriorated and nothing remained but dried vegetation. Groups of soldiers with heavy weapons were on almost every street corner. We retired early to the apparent safety of our hotel.

The next morning, July 4, we took the long taxi ride to the Lurigancho. As we climbed into the hills around Lima, we passed the city dump; it was teeming with people scavenging the trash. On the heaps of garbage, there were shelters made of wood, corrugated steel, and cardboard.

We pulled up to the top of a desolate, grassless, wind-blown hill at the entrance of the high-walled Lurigancho prison. Along one wall of the prison, waiting patiently in the blazing noonday sun, was an unending line of women carrying large bags.

We were let into the Lurigancho through a normal size door that was set into a massive, swinging, double front gate. Once inside the darkened space, we were confronted by several men in uniform on a raised platform behind a counter. We presented our authorization to one of the guards who grunted and asked for our passports. He placed them in separate pigeonholes behind him and gave us each a brass disk with a number crudely incised into its surface. I had number 1.

Another guard took us into a massive yard where more than a hundred men were sitting or standing, singly or in groups. I looked up at the walls of the buildings surrounding the yard and saw arms reaching out of almost every barred window. Scattered throughout the yard were metal garbage cans containing an orange swill with an oily liquid on its surface—the prisoners' food, unless they were fortunate enough to receive some from the women whom we had seen lined up outside.

We were taken to Craig, who was sitting on a rock. I gave him greetings from his girlfriend. After he realized who we were, he was more than willing to talk to us. We told him we had arranged a meeting with his lawyer that evening to discuss how we could help him.

Craig was certain that both his supposed contact and the courier were drug agents of the Peruvian or American government. Shortly after he made contact with the supplier, he was arrested and tortured, in the presence of American DEA agents. He signed a confession that was written in Spanish, which he could not understand at the time. He had not yet had a trial, nor was one scheduled.

He explained that he would have to subsist on the orange swill I had seen, unless he had money. The situation inside the buildings, with the heat and stagnant air, was intolerable. The strongest men would fight to get near the windows for air. The only way he had been able to survive was with money his girlfriend had gotten to him through his lawyer. He used it for food and bribing guards for minimal privileges. During the months of his confinement, he learned Spanish.

As the time reached three-thirty, not wanting to overstay our welcome, we wound up our discussion by promising to meet with his lawyer that evening and do what we could for him. I promised I would call his girlfriend as soon as I landed in Miami and relay any messages he wished.

As we handed back the brass disks to the guards at the entrance, it was fifteen minutes to the witching hour. We had expected an immediate return of our passports and release from the Lurigancho. It was not to be.

The guard took my disk, turned, and removed my passport from pigeonhole number one, but as he leaned over the counter bringing the passport close to my outstretched hand, he smiled broadly and said something in very rapid Spanish. The only words I could understand were the repeated "Estados Unidos." Each time my fingers reached for the passport, he pulled his hand back and the process was repeated. Jim and I pooled our Spanish, and after about four tries, which seemed like an eternity, we realized he was wishing our country a happy birthday. We thanked him repeatedly—he was reassured that we understood his birthday wishes and gave us our passports. We got through the door and into our waiting taxi.

In the hotel bar, we met Craig's lawyer and a law professor who was there as an interpreter. The discussion was not on any legal theories for Craig's defense but was directed only at money that was needed for bribes.

In the event that any of the patrons of the bar did not understand our discussion about bribes in Spanish, they only had to wait a few seconds to hear it repeated in English. I made several suggestions that we carry on our discussion in a more private location, but the lawyer and law professor assured us that everything was fine. They left at about ten-thirty.

I had to catch a cab to the airport about midnight, as I had promised Betty and the kids I would return in time to go on a long-planned rafting trip. If I spoiled that, the Lurigancho would have looked good.

Jim, who was determined on this trip to buy vicuna cloth for an overcoat, had found out that it was illegal to trade in vicuna textiles in Peru. Not one to be deterred, he pursued his quest in Bolivia.

When the wheels of the plane left the runway, I felt an overwhelming relief. My head spun with images of the past few days. There were no delays and I was able to make my calls in Miami. The family met me at the Denver airport, and we left immediately for our great rafting trip. I was totally exhausted.

Since many of the participants in the drug importation scheme were federal agents, the evidence was overwhelming. Jim, with his chemistry background and brilliant cross-examination skills, almost created reasonable doubt that the seized material was cocaine. However, Gene was convicted.

I represented the Smaldone family for the next fifteen years. There was always at least one case pending. There were gambling, loan sharking, and witness tampering charges to defend, as well as civil matters. I also represented Gene and Judy on several drug cases.

Not once during the time I represented the Smaldone family was I ever asked by any of them to do anything illegal. I could not say the same for the government.

Checkers, Gene's father and the family patriarch, learned that a state grand jury had been convened in Colorado Springs to investigate illegal gambling. I accompanied him there to interview witnesses in preparation for a defense in the event of an indictment. Checkers had earned his nickname when, as a young prisoner, he saved the warden's children by playing checkers with them at their residence within the prison walls during a riot at the Colorado State Penitentiary.

The following day, I returned to my office after lunch and found the telephone ringing. Apparently, my secretary had not returned from lunch, so I reached over her desk, picked up the phone, and heard, "Hello, my name is Sheppard. I understand you are Checkers's lawyer and were in the Springs yesterday asking questions about the grand jury investigation. I have been subpoenaed to appear before the grand jury this evening. I don't have a lawyer and don't want to hurt Checkers. What should I do?"

I explained that I could not give him legal advice because it would constitute a conflict of interest since I was representing Checkers, and that he should hire his own lawyer.

He was concerned that he would not be able to engage a lawyer in time for his subpoenaed appearance that evening. I advised him to honor the subpoena, appear, and ask for time to hire a lawyer. I was confident that he would be granted that request. "But I don't want to hurt Checkers," he repeated. "Suppose I just tell them I don't remember?" Again, I explained that I could not advise him and that he should get his own lawyer.

We danced around the same conversation at least five times. While acknowledging that his goal was an honorable one, I told him that "I don't remember" is a valid answer if he truthfully did not remember, but was a lie if, in fact, he did.

The next morning, I opened the newspaper to a lead article that stated that an agent of the Colorado Bureau of Investigation (CBI) had infiltrated the Smaldone gambling enterprise. The agent, of course, was my caller of the previous day. I broke out in a cold sweat, writing furiously on a yellow legal pad, trying to reconstruct my conversation with Sheppard. Did I say anything that could have been illegal or unethical? My panic turned to rage.

When I arrived at my office, I called the Attorney General's Office and asked to speak with Tom Alfrey, whom I had known for many years and who now headed the organized crime section. Laughing, he picked up and said he expected to hear from me.

"You may think it is funny," I screamed, "but I don't! I want you to have someone bring a copy of the tape to my office right away. Do you understand? Right away!"

Still laughing, he responded, "Don't worry, Pete; you did just fine. We thought it was pretty funny. I'm not even sure we taped the conversation."

I screamed back, "Bullshit! You never would have attempted to frame me without a tape. I don't see anything funny about this. You must realize I could have lost my license, with the possibility of also receiving a sentence, had I made one improper statement. And you know you had no reason to suspect my tampering with a witness."

"Don't worry, Pete," he again responded. "You did fine, and we will get the tape to you."

Several months later, when I had Sheppard on the witness stand, I went over in excruciating detail his attempt to frame me. At one point, the trial judge, who later became Chief Justice of the Colorado Supreme Court, was so upset with the CBI's tactics that he called us into chambers. He told Tom how disgusted he was with the prosecution's methods and asked me what I was going to do about it.

Beyond what happened in court that day, I never came up with an appropriate remedy, but the experience increased my sensitivity to the misuse of governmental power and invigorated my enthusiastic, aggressive fight against this evil.

Concerned that law enforcement had installed listening devices in my office, Checkers and I always went outside when we met to discuss his legal matters. One day, as we were returning to the office from one of our meetings, Checkers, who always wore a porkpie hat and had a thin cigar in his mouth, pointed to the headlines of the newspaper he had just purchased from a machine. With a mischievous grin on his aquiline face, he said, "Look at this, Pete, 'Organized crime this; organized crime that. What the hell do they want, disorganized crime?'"

Starting in 1973, I defended a series of cases where the crimes charged against my clients had been initiated by a very talented CBI agent, Kenny Brown.

At Colorado Mountain College, outside of Glenwood Springs, a rotund, barely five-foot-tall, glib character let it be known that he was a movie producer in search of a cast for a motion picture to be filmed at the college. Not surprisingly, he had overwhelming response from the student body.

After a few weeks of excitement and preparation, the producer had established an inner circle of four students to whom he confided that he had a drug problem. Since, he said, he was a stranger in town, he asked them for assistance in obtaining some drugs. None of them knew a source, but the producer pointed out that this was a college, after all, and that they could find some drugs if they really tried, especially since they had the chance of a lifetime to get into the movies.

After much searching, a source of drugs was found and the students took the producer, who actually was the notorious CBI agent Kenny Brown, and introduced him to a seller of cocaine. The four students were arrested and charged with sale of a controlled substance.

David, one of the defendants, was the son of a highly respected family in Washington, D.C. They were friends of a Supreme Court justice who had contacted his former Colorado law office, where someone recommended me to be David's attorney. David's parents were obviously angry and disappointed in their son's actions, but, like the Smaldones, they did not hesitate to support and protect their son.

I argued that David, acting on behalf of the buyer of the drugs, and never touching either the drugs or the money, could not be guilty of selling the drugs. Eventually, the Colorado Supreme Court agreed and David was acquitted.

Kenny Brown used his talent of deception on behalf of the CBI in other cases I defended. Posing as a recording agent, Kenny Brown promised a glorious future in the recording business to a musician in a dance band. After several contacts, Kenny confessed his problem and asked for help in securing drugs, as he had with the college students. The musician, not wishing to destroy this once-in-a-lifetime opportunity, reluctantly complied and found himself faced with drug charges. Next, carrying a violin case containing a shotgun, Kenny offered his services as an assassin. My client found himself charged with conspiracy to commit murder for hire.

Denver Magazine featured an article, "The CBI's Master of Deception," glorifying Kenny Brown. In it I was referred to as Brown's friend outside the courtroom and adversary in the courtroom. I immediately demanded a retraction, which appeared in the next issue, stating that I was not a friend of Kenny Brown's. *Denver Magazine*, several years later, named me as Colorado's leading constitutional law attorney.

I became even more passionate about the right of free expression. I believed governmental control of content containing "objectionable material" a greater danger than the material itself. In the late sixties and early seventies, I represented civil rights and anti-Vietnam War demonstrators whether they were marching, burning draft cards, resisting the draft, wearing the flag as clothing, or speaking out against the war. Richard Nixon, as president, and his Attorney General, Edwin Meese, promoted policies severely restricting rights of free expression, and local governments followed the lead.

Colorado enacted legislation making flag desecration a crime without specifically defining what constituted flag desecration. This left it for the police to decide whom to charge on a case-by-case basis. The foundation for the charge could be anything from displaying a decal with the flag upside down to showing the flag in conjunction with a peace symbol or wearing it as an article of clothing. I argued that police officers wear flag patches as part of their uniforms, and have flag decals on the bumpers of their police cars where the flag gets splattered with mud; therefore they too must be in violation. The statute was declared unconstitutional.

In 1975, the United States Information Service selected me for a documentary film depicting a lawyer's life in the United States. The film, *One Man Peter Ney*, was shown all over the world, but not domestically. I was not accustomed to being portrayed as a pillar of society. My prior publicity was otherwise and I must confess that I enjoyed that portrayal more. The kids, who never minded the publicity their father brought to their household, were equally enthusiastic about having their lives recorded on film.

In 1978, I spoke in favor of the Nazi party's right to parade, although I vehemently opposed their message and was disgusted by it. I believed that my personal history would give me some credibility in divorcing myself from the message while protecting the right to express any philosophy, no matter how objectionable, without government interference.

While I was battling my windmills, Betty, in addition to raising the kids with little help from me, was also active outside the home. She worked at various schools in Head Start and special education programs and earned a master's degree in special education in 1976. Shortly thereafter, she became a teacher at Havern Center, a highly regarded private school for children with learning disabilities, where she worked until her retirement in 2000.

Betty, who always had difficulty doing just one thing at a time, took up sculpting in various media and regularly entered art shows after she received her master's degree. She designed many sculptures for our children. Our house, filled with many of her pieces, became a unique home.

Betty and I attended an ACLU meeting where Breeze, a prostitute whom I had represented, described incidents in which the police charged her with prostitution while she was simply walking down the street, not working. The ACLU viewed charging a person with a crime based solely on past conduct, without probable cause related to the new charge, a constitutional violation. Betty was intrigued and asked Breeze if she thought the police would contact them if the two of them were to walk down Colfax Avenue together; Breeze thought they would. Betty and Breeze were off to walk the streets.

After dropping them off on Colfax Avenue, I drove around the block and waited ten minutes to give the police enough time to notice them. I drove along the curb behind the women and called when I was next to them; they came over to the car and leaned in the window. We repeated the routine several times, once when a police car was parked directly across the street, but nothing ever happened. No contact from either customers or police . I don't think Betty has ever gotten over the rejection.

During Richard Nixon's second term, his involvement in domestic surveillance programs, including spying on political opponents, inspired me, and many others, to speak and petition for his impeachment.

As passionate as I was about protecting the right of free expression, Joyce Meskis, the owner of the Tattered Cover bookstore, a Denver landmark, was even more adamant. At Joyce's invitation, I proudly became the Tattered Cover's lawyer. This led to my lobbying efforts on behalf of the Colorado Media Coalition, an organization of book dealers and educators supporting freedom of expression. Under their auspices, I lobbied against successive pieces of proposed anti-obscenity legislation.

At each term of the Colorado General Assembly, I explained that obscenity was a narrow, clearly defined, exception to the constitutional prohibition against limitations on free speech. However, each year, the sponsors of the legislation attempted to expand the definition or short-circuit the required procedural safeguards. The legislature's blind enthusiasm made it relatively straightforward for me to successfully challenge the proposed statutes.

I concluded that most of the politicians posturing as being at the forefront of the protection of public morality were actually using the issue to promote their political careers, and never really cared whether their proposed legislation took effect. In 1976, a five-year-old obscenity law was declared unconstitutional. The legislature, within a month, passed a replacement that the Tattered Cover successfully challenged on its effective date. This scenario was repeated in each of the next three years.

The newspapers, beginning to see humor in the legislature's continuing failed attempts to outlaw obscenity, ran headlines such as "Obscenity Law Given 2 Chances: Slim, None" and editorial cartoons showing the legislature on a swayback horse, with a broken lance, charging against smut, and portraying the legislature as a defeated wrestler pleading to his tag team partner, "Your turn; he's not easy."

The next year, I was successful in having both the Denver obscenity ordinance and the state's massage parlor statute declared unconstitutional.

In 1975, I sued the Arapahoe County Sheriff for absolutely abhorrent jail conditions. One of the reported incidents concerned eight prisoners who had been held, naked, for four days in a tiny cell with a small hole in the floor as its only sanitary facility—no ventilation or bedding. The court found the situation inhumane and ordered immediate corrective action. Outside inspectors, including the press, were in disbelief that such conditions could occur in a jail in the United States in the latter half of the twentieth century.

In December 1976, I moved into Marty Miller's office, but only as a tenant, not a member of his firm. I still wanted the independence of my own office. Frequently, Marty asked me to try a case with him that he had anticipated would settle but didn't.

Shortly after moving into Marty's office he and I filed suit on behalf of a woman who was denied admission to the University of Colorado Medical School after her husband, who had inferior academic credentials, had been admitted. We discovered that, under the present standards for admission, it was almost impossible for a woman to be admitted.

The judge assigned to the case called us into chambers on the day of trial and told us he saw no merit in it. "But since we have open courts," he allowed, "I have no choice but to let you proceed." After a year of litigation, our client was admitted and the medical school changed its admission policy.

In 1977, Marty came into my office and asked if I could free up the next two weeks. He had a couple in the waiting room that he felt we should help if we could. As I crossed the waiting room, I saw a young couple slouching on a sofa—they looked totally exhausted. The woman appeared Vietnamese. The Vietnam War had been over for about two years, but images of the chaotic evacuation of Saigon were still etched in my mind.

The woman told us she had three sons. On the day before Saigon fell, rumors were rampant in Saigon, as well as in the United States, that if the Viet Cong were victorious, all children of racially mixed parentage would either be killed or sent to re-education centers.

Representatives of American adoption centers were circulating through the streets of Saigon, offering to secure safe passage to the United States for mixed-race children. In panic and desperation, she gave her three boys to one of these agencies. The newscasts in the United States showed constant images of large transport planes loaded with Vietnamese so-called orphans being evacuated.

Unexpectedly, the mother was able to get on one of the last flights out of Saigon, with the assistance of a Flying Tigers pilot who now is her husband.

For two years, the couple had attempted to secure custody of her three boys. One child, adopted by a loving family, was in rural Colorado. The other two had been adopted in Connecticut, where the court had ruled against the mother. They had lost confidence in their previous lawyer, and a hearing was coming up within a week. Would we take the matter?

I immediately thought of the parallel with my own life, when, forty years earlier, I had been placed on the *Kindertransport*. There was no question that I was on board.

We worked long hours to prepare the case for hearing in a week. A continuance was out of the question. The longer the boy remained with the Colorado couple, the less likely a court would be to change custody. The basis of our argument was that the natural mother had not relinquished or abandoned the child; therefore, the child was never eligible for adoption.

The representatives of the Department of Social Services had determined that the child should remain with the adoptive parents. They lied consistently about his condition at the time of his arrival, attempting to prove neglect and child abuse in order to terminate the mother's parental rights, thereby making him eligible for adoption. We were easily able to prove their testimony was false by cross-examining them on the written reports they had filed at the time of the child's arrival. After two weeks of trial and a vehement dressing-down of the Department of Social Services by the court, the child was returned to his mother.

That was not my only disappointing contact with Social Services. Another case focused on the department's attempt to gain custody of a newborn infant that was on life support because of multiple incurable disabilities. The unanimous medical prognosis was that the child would not survive longer than three years and would be on life support the entire time. The parents wished to disconnect the life support, and the department sought custody to continue it indefinitely. The court denied the department's request for custody.

In another case, Social Services brought child neglect and abuse charges against my clients without any evidence whatsoever. I concluded that Social Services used its intuition, more than fact, to make decisions concerning children's best interests.

An interesting case involved three teenagers who were suspected in the murder of a fourth. A task force of detectives from various jurisdictions met with representatives of the district attorney's office. The DA's office had developed a plan to make contact with the suspects and induce them to make incriminating statements. One of the detectives, concerned about the advice he might be receiving, had tape-recorded the entire meeting.

The plan, outlined by the deputy district attorney, was to simultaneously contact the three suspects, separate them from their parents, assure them they were not suspects, question them without advising them of their constitutional rights, and take them into custody—without telling their parents. Each of the three suspects confessed.

The teens' defense attorneys, each armed with a copy of the tape-recording of the meeting, moved to have these confessions suppressed, as they were obtained through illegal interrogation. The trial court denied the motion, ruling that the confessions would be admissible at trial.

My client went to trial and was convicted of first-degree murder. The other two defendants pled guilty to lesser charges. I appealed to the Colorado Supreme Court, which reversed the conviction and ordered a new trial without the confession. My client was released for time served.

At about the same time, a prominent female physician was murdered in the parking lot of her office. The police had located a couple who were in the parking lot at the approximate time of the murder and had seen a young black man get out of his car and walk toward the doctor's office building. The couple left the parking lot before the murder. The police theorized that the murderer was one of the physician's patients and arranged for patients to come to the office, ostensibly to pick up their records, while being observed by the young couple.

My client, who was one of the victim's few black patients, was identified, arrested, and charged. At his court appearance, all the local television stations photographed my client. Within a few days, we were able to prove that he could not possibly have been in that parking lot that evening. That confirmed my lack of faith in eyewitness identification, which I am convinced is not very good in the best of circumstances—and useless when attempted across racial lines.

Just as the murder charges were dismissed, a reporter for one of Denver's newspapers identified my client, from the television reports, as the person who had raped her in the State Capitol. My client was rearrested. Fortunately, he had a time-stamped receipt, with his signature, for payment of his tuition at the University of Colorado in Boulder, more than forty miles away, at the time of the rape. The case was dismissed. However, the rape victim was always certain that my client was her attacker.

Char had been Marty's office receptionist for some time. She was the first person in the office to be seen by all clients and always went out of her way to make them feel comfortable—no small feat when they were there for the unpleasant purpose of seeing a lawyer. Her friendliness, helpfulness, and, not least, her beauty, always impressed me.

"Can I see you for a few minutes?" asked Char one day, standing in the doorway of my office. "I heard your secretary was moving to Alaska and I would like to apply for the job."

At barely twenty years old, her only job experience prior to being a receptionist was as a parts delivery person for an automobile dealer. Since I had a solo trial practice, my secretary would have to work independently much of the time. I asked her about her clerical skills, like typing; she assured me she would become faster over time. I knew she would be a pleasure to work with and would be invaluable in keeping clients happy when I was delayed at court. I decided that typing might not be that important a skill after all, and hired her—the best business decision I ever made. She worked for me until I retired from the court.

Char had a friend who was an agent in the real estate office that occupied the first floor in Marty's building. Shortly after Char started as my secretary, she told me about a house, two doors from our office, that her friend thought would be suitable for a law office and that would be listing shortly.

The Victorian house was used by a non-profit agency as a residence for developmentally challenged adults. Its location on a busy thoroughfare was no longer considered safe for the tenants. I bought the house, and with some imagination and a talented remodeling crew, the house retained much of its historic flavor and became an efficient office building for five lawyers and three secretaries. The building opened as law offices in 1981.

As I moved into the building, I reflected on my unrealistic dream, fifteen years earlier, of becoming an independent trial lawyer, hoping to become successful enough to support my family and serve my clients. I never fantasized that I could also have the time of my life while also having a positive effect on society. What would Ayn Rand, the heroine of my teenage years, think? Although I had abandoned the life of Robert Roark, I appreciated my good fortune in having been a trial lawyer through the dramatic social revolution of the late sixties and throughout the seventies.

I have always been fascinated by technology even though I had no ability in science or mathematics. The computer was becoming available to everyone—by 1982, I owned one. My computer did not have a hard drive. Instead, it had two slots, one that accepted a floppy disk containing the program, the other for the data. The purchase price included fifty hours of training, which Char and I fully utilized.

The unending paperwork was one aspect of law practice I disliked. In the computer, I saw relief from the repetitive creation of documents that essentially duplicated prior drafts with minimal changes. A few years earlier, I had purchased a typewriter that used a punched paper strip to duplicate repetitive work.

Char complained that learning the computer system, which operated with text commands rather than the graphical interfaces in present-day computers, was becoming so overwhelming that computer programs occupied her dreams—not a healthy nightlife for a young woman.

In 1983, I became so intrigued with the capabilities of the computer that I enrolled in a BASIC programming class at the local community college. For my class project, I started to develop a billing program for the office. It was very crude, but I was convinced that, with a real programmer's help, we could develop a marketable lawyers' billing program. There was none at the time. I hired Tim, the instructor of the training program that came with my computer.

At the time I moved into the house, half of my practice was criminal defense and the other half was divided almost equally between family law and personal injury. Now, in my spare time, I established Quixote Business Systems Inc. to develop and market the billing system.

I set Tim up in a windowless office in the basement with a dented metal desk. He kept his job as instructor, working on the billing program in his spare time.

Miraculously, within a year, we had a usable program. Once a month, Char proudly would start the program, leave for lunch, and return to find continuous paper bills covering the floor. We used the system until I left private practice. We also sold several systems to local law offices. Within a year after we started marketing our billing system, though, large software companies developed better systems at less than one-tenth the price.

I have often thought about how a chance event can have a major impact on a person's life. For instance, meeting Dick Fields at the Martin employees' party led to my career as a lawyer. If I had not had that discussion with him, it is doubtful I ever would have gone to law school.

I was reminded of this one day when I was standing at the end of my driveway and a neighbor walked across the street and asked me, out of the blue, "Do you want to learn how photographs are made?" I took him up on his offer and we spent many afternoons in his darkroom.

After my neighbor introduced me to photography, I became an avid photographer. Our house had a darkroom, which we had been using for storage. I returned the darkroom to its intended use. Our three kids also developed an interest in photography and spent time in the darkroom with me. Rick developed it into a career.

Periodically, I entered photographic exhibitions and competitions. I was delighted when I won second prize in a local show. I told Char of my success and brought her to the show. I took her to the wall where my photograph of two nude women lying on a bed had hung on opening night—it was not there! I was told, after much inquiry, that the city manager had removed the picture. As luck would have it, I saw the culprit soon after at a restaurant where we went for lunch.

After a heated exchange, he told me he had removed the picture to protect it from adolescents who were taking it to the bathroom for closer examination. I filed a complaint against the city and demanded that the picture be re-hung in its original place, which it was. The controversy received a great deal of media attention. My mother, who was still living in Philadelphia, opened *The Philadelphia Inquirer* to read about her son. I also received a letter from one of my art school classmates, Harold Yoos, who was still living in New Jersey. I had not heard from him in thirty years. He asked if the photographer was the Peter Ney who was on that ill-fated boat trip.

The Summer of Love signaled the end of an era. The flower children had left the streets. The Vietnam War was over. Society was changing. My practice continued to emphasize criminal defense; primarily obscenity, drug possession and distribution, prostitution, varying stages of dancers' undress, gambling, loan-sharking, and an occasional murder case appointed by the court. I also still took personal injury and divorce cases.

As times changed, so did my practice. The women's revolution had its start about ten years earlier; I belatedly realized the effect that

that movement had on middle-class, middle-aged women. Increasing numbers of women, who were becoming my divorce clients, expressed anger and frustration over career opportunities that had been denied them by a male-dominated society. I found it very difficult to craft legal remedies for these quite valid grievances, which now were based somewhat on time lost. For example, a young woman who had entered a traditional female occupation, such as teaching or nursing—all the while aspiring to be a physician or lawyer—now wanted to make up for lost time.

I might have been able to secure sufficient temporary support for the limited time their education required, but what if these plans did not work out? Would my clients become destitute? My clients did not wish to hear the negative possibilities, particularly from a man—the oppressor.

Those clients of mine who were prostitutes or dancers appeared more satisfied with their lives. Their objectives were simple and direct—make as much money as possible and stay out of jail. They looked at men, Johns, not as oppressors, but as their victims whom they would separate from their money.

I reduced the number of domestic relations cases I accepted and referred many, who I believed, perhaps erroneously, were nurturing unrealistic goals, to other attorneys.

Some of my prostitute clients reported that the police were victimizing them by forcing them to have sex after they had been arrested but before they were taken to jail. Needless to say, proving these accusations in court presented a credibility problem.

In 1980, a prostitute whom I had successfully represented was charged again. She told me that the undercover detective had identified himself and arrested her after they had entered into negotiations. He then proceeded to undress, ordering her to perform a sex act with him. She was frightened and complied with his request, fearing he would make her situation worse if she resisted.

When her case came to trial, I told the prosecuting attorney what my client had told me. "Who do you think the jury will believe?" the prosecutor asked.

I suggested that he discuss my accusations with the detective before we proceed. "While you are at it," I said, "ask him if he has an unusually shaped penis, which my client will describe in detail; if necessary, I will ask him to display it to the jury." The case was dismissed on motion of the prosecution.

I then filed a complaint against the officer. The press followed my accusations in painstaking detail. I saw the city room editor of one of the Denver dailies in a social setting shortly after the police department instituted strict regulations for the conduct of vice-officers. He told me that one of the vice-officers had referred to me as "that whorehouse lawyer." The newspaper's lawyer, believing I would take legal action, had advised against printing that quote. I told him I was somewhat disappointed they did not use it because it was probably accurate and I would not have been offended.

Another bizarre prostitution case occurred in a neighboring county where the undercover detective paid not only for sex but also for the privilege of photographing the act with a camera mounted on a tripod and activated by a trigger he held. The room where this occurred had been wired for sound to permit detectives, including the participating detective's wife, to follow, in the next room, the sound portion of the crime in progress.

The judge found the conduct of the police so outrageous that he dismissed the case. However, the photographs were passed throughout the court building, much to the amusement of the staff and the embarrassment of the detective.

I unsuccessfully campaigned for the decriminalization of victimless crimes like prostitution and marijuana use. The opposition suggested that these were not victimless and that the prostitutes were the victims. I responded to that argument by questioning their logic—should their alleged victims be punished further by exposing them to police harassment, lack of police protection, and criminal penalties?

Then, in1981 the Colorado General Assembly enacted yet another obscenity statute, after a few years' hiatus and over the governor's veto. This attempt took a new approach, outlawing the display of sexually explicit or indecent, non-obscene, material to children. This would have put large areas of bookstores off-limits to children.

Joyce Meskis, of the Tattered Cover bookstore, sponsored the litigation that was filed on the effective date of the statute. A few days later, the statute was declared unconstitutional. The state appealed to the Colorado Supreme Court.

At oral argument, the chief justice said, "Mr. Ney, from the thrust of your argument, I gather you are arguing that the state is powerless to protect children from the display of sexually explicit, non-obscene material."

I responded, "That is exactly what I am arguing. However, is it better to live in a society that welcomes children into bookstores or one that bars them?" The statute was unanimously declared unconstitutional.

Two large men in leather jackets sat across the desk from me. They wished to hire me for a sizable retainer. They passed me an expensive full-color brochure filled with photographs of incredibly beautiful models, explaining their business plan for an international escort service. Wealthy customers would pay an annual membership fee for the privilege of having access to the woman or women of their choice, anywhere in the world.

I explained that pimping in Colorado was a Class 2 felony with very serious penalties. They assured me that they knew this but would be insulated from any criminal exposure by a contract that I would draft, to be executed by the model, who would agree to act only as an escort and not perform any sexual acts.

I asked if they really thought a jury would believe that was a legitimate contract, not signed with a wink and a nod. They expressed confidence that I would be able to draft an enforceable contract if my legal ability was as good as my reputation. They would pay generously, and this would be only the beginning of a long and profitable relationship. A mental image of the closing scene from *Casablanca* flashed across my mind.

I explained that I would be happy to represent them and give them a vigorous defense if they were criminally charged. However, I would not assist them in committing a crime, and therefore would not draft the contract no matter what the fee. That turned out to be a good decision. I found out later that the two pimps were actually FBI agents who visited several lawyers, one of whom accepted the offer, was charged criminally, and lost his license to practice.

In 1985, a gallant man accompanied his girlfriend to traffic court to give her courage in facing a judge who had earned a reputation for severe conduct and imposing harsh sentences. The couple was sitting in the audience when another case was concluding. The defendant had pled guilty to a lesser charge and was asked if he had anything to say before the penalty was imposed. He said, "I have just one question, Judge. The officer who issued the ticket was standing on the sidewalk without radar and cited me with going forty-three miles per hour in a twenty-five mile zone. How could he possibly have determined my speed with that accuracy?"

The judge explained, "Young man, the Denver police are so well trained that if they were standing on the steps of this courthouse they could accurately determine the speed within two miles per hour of each of the passing cars."

To this, our gallant man in the audience responded in the only rational way possible: "Bullshit!" Our hero found himself in the mental health ward of the city hospital. His girlfriend soon found herself in my office relating the events. Within a day, the hero was released under a writ of habeas corpus. Disciplinary hearings against the judge resulted in his removal.

Elaine Leass started working as a reporter at the *Rocky Mountain Oyster* in 1978. Two years later, she owned the newspaper and retained me as its lawyer. The *Oyster* was a weekly newspaper that was distributed free at bookstores, liquor stores, bars, and adult entertainment facilities. Each issue contained two or three articles on an adult theme. The remainder of the paper was filled with advertising for massage and escort services, adult phone lines, topless and bottomless bars, adult video arcades, and movie theaters specializing in adult themes.

In 1986, based on the massage parlor ads, Elaine was charged as owner of the newspaper, with promoting prostitution. I argued that the state was unable to prove her knowledge of what transpired in the advertised businesses and introduced into evidence the *Yellow Pages*, published by the telephone company, which carried similar advertisements. Case dismissed! On the front page of the *Oyster's* next issue was a very complimentary story about its lawyer.

I focused intently on my practice, originally to establish it and make it successful. As the practice developed its unique character, appropriately described by my use of Picasso drawings of Don Quixote on my stationery, business cards, and bills, my concentration became motivated in major part by my satisfaction in fighting successfully against the establishment. It seems that I still did not play well with others.

As a lawyer, I could experience the excitement of the underbelly of society while exposing myself to little of its danger by retreating back to the safety of my middle-class, respected, suburban identity—reminiscent of *Superman* again becoming reporter Clark Kent or *Batman* as businessman Bruce Wayne.

However, there is no free lunch, and if I have any regrets in my life's path it is that my kids grew to maturity virtually without me. My practice became so much of my life that I did not participate sufficiently in my kids' upbringing. It is all to Betty's credit that they turned out so well.

Amazingly, the time between Rick's taking his first steps on that Thanksgiving Day in my first office at One West Hampden and the day we found out he was on academic probation after his first semester at the University of Colorado passed in what seemed to be just a nanosecond longer than the blink of an eye.

We had visited him several times in the basement room of his dormitory, and had met his roommates, who seemed as unmotivated in academic excellence as he was. One of his roommates was asleep each time we visited. Rick would have to improve in his second semester to stay at CU, so he enrolled in classes predominantly populated by football players. He got off probation and, with our intense prodding, found a new roommate—a straight-A student.

Linda had also gone to CU, and her only concern seemed to be that she could not decide on a major. I suggested she take whatever classes interested her, and after several years, by default or in retrospect, she would meet the requirements for a major. Not efficient, but effective. My kids named this plan "Dad's smorgasbord approach to education." Linda graduated in five years with a double major in mathematics and history.

She had taken full advantage of spending her junior year in Paris, giving us the opportunity to spend several weeks traveling through Spain with her. The most memorable product of that year was a series of her photographs of Paris. Perhaps she had developed some interest in photography because of mine.

Diane had gone to the University of Northern Colorado in Greeley, where she developed her natural skill for languages. After her first year of living in the dormitory, she moved into the Foreign Language House. She became proficient in Russian and Spanish and spent her junior year in Segovia, Spain. We visited her there, traveling throughout northern Spain and Portugal. As we remembered our early concerns, we appreciated her unique strengths as she matured into a young woman. She followed all the rules and persevered, never giving up until she reached her goal.

Linda, on the other hand, questioned every rule, challenging every one she did not willingly accept. Rick slid past the rules in his attempt to find a career that had the most generous retirement package.

Their individual approaches to life upon graduation from college seemed to work for each. Linda became a math teacher and taught for two years. Realizing she would be tenured if she completed another year, she joined the Peace Corps and served in Togo, Africa. When we visited her in the middle of her tour, she casually asked us to send her a book to help her study for the Law School Admission Test. This led to a law degree from Georgetown. Diane was still interested in foreign languages and because of her aptitude for them, she chose to go into the travel industry. Rick started out as a newspaper photographer and, after a few years, became a photography teacher in the public school system.

I began to think of my future. I probably had another ten productive years remaining. I could continue in private trial practice doing what I enjoyed immensely. But would that become repetitive? I had learned much in my twenty years as a trial lawyer. I was convinced I had talent. Would continuing in private trial practice be the best use of my abilities and experience? I had recently settled a large personal injury case; as part of the settlement, the defendants agreed to pay my fees over the next five years, which minimized any concern related to earnings in any endeavor.

In 1987, the Colorado Court of Appeals, which had accumulated an insurmountable backlog, was authorized to expand by six judges. Although I had considered teaching law, an appellate judgeship appealed to me as an opportunity to give back, in some measure, the unlimited freedom this country granted me to take my diverse career paths.

Coincidentally, the Chief Justice of the Colorado Supreme Court telephoned me for my thoughts about an administrative issue in my local trial court. In that conversation, I asked for his thoughts regarding my possible application to the appellate court. He was delighted and encouraged me to proceed. "This is the best news I have had today," the chief justice said in concluding the conversation.

I did not believe I could prepare for the interview by the Supreme Court Nominating Commission, which was composed of two residents from each congressional district, divided equally between political parties, lawyers, and non-lawyers. After answering the first question: "Why do you want to be a judge on the Court of Appeals?" I was confident my answer was as polished as any of my competitors.

The second question was more difficult: "What do you consider the most serious problem facing our society?" I thought of the Colorado economy that was in recession at the time, and there was always crime and education. After an excruciating delay, I responded—"Racism. The intractable problem of racism is not just affecting us today, but is a scourge that has persisted from the very founding of this nation. Until society cures this illness," I explained, "we will not solve the secondary problems of education, economy, or crime." I felt the tension in the room. It was apparent my answer was unexpected. There were several seconds of silence until another question was asked. For each vacancy, three names were given to the governor to consider for the judicial appointments. My name was on the list.

It was early evening. Most hallway lights in the State Capitol had been extinguished. Bright lights emanated from the governor's suite confirming his reputation for hard work. I introduced myself to the assistant in the outer lobby, and after a short wait I was ushered into Governor Romer's office.

The governor greeted me, sat down, and poured cereal and milk into a bowl, explaining that he was on a diet. I appreciated his informality. He leaned back, placed his feet on the desk, and looked at what I assumed was my file.

"I get the same comments all over the state," he said. "You are smart and hard-working, but I should not appoint you because you are too liberal."

I responded, "Let us examine how I earned that reputation. I am a criminal defense lawyer; I was active in the civil rights movement; I advocate free speech and oppose censorship; and I represented those who ran afoul of the law because of their opposition to the Vietnam War. However, I am fully aware that my responsibility as a judge on an intermediate appellate court would be to apply the law and not advance a personal agenda. I am a human being, so cannot guarantee I would not embarrass you if I am appointed, but if I did, it probably would not be because I am too liberal."

We spent the remaining twenty minutes discussing his civil rights activities and protests against the war. I suggested that if I surveyed the state, many citizens would very well say, "Governor, you are too liberal."

He reviewed some of the legal writing I had submitted as part of my application and wondered what his life would be like if he had pursued a legal rather than political career.

Betty was waiting for me in the darkened halls of the Capitol. I joined her and we went out for dinner. I told her I was not sure if he would appoint me but I certainly enjoyed the governor's interview.

– 14 –

His Honor

Adolf Hitler's 99th birthday, April 20, 1988, was the day I chose to take the oath of office as a judge on the Colorado Court of Appeals. It was a private act of contempt for the mad dictator who had had such a dramatic effect on the course of my life. I was one of the millions he wanted to destroy, and yet he unintentionally set my American Dream into motion. So, I thought it fitting to celebrate his birthday by joining the second-highest court of the state.

The gavel banged three times. The clerk of the court announced that the Colorado Court of Appeals was now in special session. The ceremony took place in the Supreme Court courtroom because its longer bench could accommodate the entire court. Rick, his fiancée Pam, Char, my mother, Betty, and I were seated at what normally would be the appellant's desk. Dignitaries were introduced, and the governor's representative was complimentary as he presented me to the court.

I sure hope the governor knew what he was doing when he appointed me, I thought. Standing at the podium, I swore to support the Constitutions of the United States and Colorado. Betty then helped me into my robe, and the junior judge escorted me to my seat on the bench. Within fifteen minutes from the fall of the gavel, I was a judge.

I expressed my gratitude to this country, which had given me the freedom to live the American dream while continually changing the direction of my life; to my mother, who literally had cleaned toilets after we arrived, penniless, in this country; to my father, no longer alive, who, as a living example, had taught me the meaning of the word *gentleman* and who, finally, would have been proud of his son; and finally, to Betty, who had stood by me through all the many twists and turns of our lives. Several people in the audience told me that my *Coming To America* speech brought tears to their eyes.

So, I could give an emotional speech, but could I do the job of an appellate judge? I had spent twenty-two years in courtrooms trying cases before trial judges and juries; and several times a year, I had argued in the appellate courts, but the qualifications of an appellate judge included the ability to work collegially with other judges. I thought of my first report card in Philadelphia: "Does not play well with others."

During the six weeks I had allocated to shutting down my private practice, the court delivered a virtual mountain of files to my office. During the day, I raced from court to court to complete any cases from my practice that could be completed. I had advised all clients of my appointment. I returned files and made referrals, for those clients who requested them, to lawyers who had my confidence. I spent my evenings going through the court files of cases that would become my responsibility immediately after I took the oath. Those six weeks were the most hectic of my twenty-two years in private practice.

I visited the court several times between my appointment by the governor and the day I actually joined the court. The chief judge was most anxious to schedule my swearing-in as soon as possible so I could start picking up my share of the workload. My new colleagues were welcoming and gave me much useful advice. I was shocked when people greeted me with "Good morning, Your Honor" at the clerk's office—I actually turned around to see whom they were addressing. The clerk of the court, who had the responsibility of implementing the administrative policies and providing for the needs of the court, treated me with such deference that I became somewhat uncomfortable.

Char had accepted my offer to join me on the court as my secretary, a confidential employee position unprotected under the state personnel system. I used my new position to negotiate the best possible starting salary for her, and found the clerk of the court very accommodating to my slightest whim.

"Your Honor, would this be a convenient time to select your chambers?" the clerk asked one day. There were four new office suites available, one for me and the remaining three for the new judges who would be selected in the summer. I chose the office with dark blue furnishings and the best view of the Capitol across the street. It seemed that I was already showing the decisiveness expected of a judge.

No one could be a specialist on the Court of Appeals. The cases were randomly assigned to divisions of three judges, without regard for their legal specialties. I felt confident in criminal, constitutional, torts, and domestic relations law, but I would never have undertaken representation in probate, corporate, real estate, or a myriad of other areas of law in which I had no experience. Although it would have constituted malpractice for me to represent a client in these unfamiliar areas of law, I would now be acting as an appellate judge in these cases, deciding whether the trial judge had erred in conducting the trial. Of course, every judge on the court faced the same problem, and all the answers were in the books.

My worst fears were now realized—in many cases, judges were less familiar with the law than the lawyers who practiced in their specialized areas daily. I had cursed the judges who had such a difficult time with my legal theories—now I was one of them.

On the Monday following my swearing-in, I was one of three judges on a division hearing oral arguments in six cases. I had distributed my initial draft of the two cases that were assigned to me, and read and analyzed the four cases that were pre-assigned to the other two judges. The oral arguments heard from this side of the bench seemed quite different from those I had experienced on the lawyer's side. Immediately after the six cases had been argued, the three judges met to conference on them. None of us had discussed the cases before the oral argument, so this would be the first time I got any reaction to my draft opinions from my fellow judges.

I was fortunate to have Lou Babcock and Don Smith—the trial judge in my *extra finger* case—as my colleagues on that first division; their knowledge and patience brought me up to speed. Training a competent trial lawyer or judge in the skills required of an appellate judge can only be an on-the-job process.

My colleagues gently pointed out some elementary precepts, which I knew, but which were not reflected in the drafts of my first opinions. I had written embarrassing sentences such as, "This court finds ..." even though I knew that an appellate court makes conclusions of law, not findings of fact that are made in the trial court. I had sweated over those early opinions, hoping to make a favorable first impression on the court, and now here I was, slinking back to my office to ask Char to change the opinions. Fortunately, my colleagues had no quarrel with my reasoning or the outcome of the cases, and word went out to the rest of the court that the new liberal judge was, in fact, a quick study.

In light of the history of my law practice, my appointment generated anxiety among some members of the court and some members of the public. A spokesperson for the anti-obscenity forces, whom I had frequently faced in legislative hearings, wrote a scathing guest editorial in reaction to my appointment. However, I saw my role as judge on an intermediate appellate court as one of applying existing law whenever possible and expanding the law as minimally as possible—only where there was no existing law precisely in point. I knew I was not on the court to further my social agenda. I am sure that came as a disappointment to many—but as a relief to many more. I was aware that I had been appointed to the Colorado Court of Appeals, not the United States Supreme Court or even the Colorado Supreme Court, and I saw my first responsibility as correcting errors made in the trial court, not setting policy.

At the time of my appointment, each judge was responsible for authoring seventy to eighty opinions a year. Since all decisions were the product of divisions of three judges, each judge participated in between 210 and 240 decisions per year—approximately one per normal working day. Even with that workload, the court was experiencing a greater and greater backlog. Certain types of cases had statutory priority, while others had none—meaning that they would never be heard.

At about the time of the court expansion that led to my appointment, several administrative changes were instituted to increase the productivity of the judges. The most positive change was the pre-assignment of cases to a judge who was responsible for reviewing the record of that case and drafting a preliminary opinion for the other two judges. Previously, the authorship had not been determined until after oral arguments. The opposition to this administrative change was the theoretical possibility of one judge, rather than the division, deciding a case and writing the opinion without participation of the other two judges. That scenario never materialized, and all judges continued to participate fully in the final opinions.

Pre-assignment alone increased each judge's output by approximately 20 percent. With the addition of the six new judges and the dedicated work of the court's entire personnel, the backlog began to decrease. As it vanished, the court found itself divided not along liberal or conservative lines, as the public and media presumed, but on how decisions should be written.

Each Court of Appeals case was completed by a written opinion. Most, probably more than three–quarters, of the opinions dealt with well-settled law, and I believe that qualified lawyers would have unanimously agreed with their reasoning and outcome. Many years earlier, the Colorado Supreme Court had decided that only those decisions of the Court of Appeals where something new was announced would be published and could be cited as precedent.

Thus, although each case was decided by a written opinion, which articulated the court's reasoning and relevant precedents, the vast majority of these decisions were not published because they said nothing new. The controversy over how decisions should be written lasted throughout my tenure on the court. Early in my incumbency, I became convinced of which side I was on. To prepare myself, I read a few texts on appellate writing, but a short article in a legal magazine made so much sense to me that I was forever on the side of the tightly written, short opinion with a minimum of nuance or ambiguity—a direct statement of the law. The short opinions that I advocated were not necessarily easier or faster to write. I was reminded of Mark Twain's letter to a friend in which he apologized for not having time to write a short letter, and so was writing a long one instead.

I strongly believed that the style of opinion writing I advocated was the most practical for the user. After all, we were writing the opinions first for the litigants who wanted to know whether they had won or lost and why; and second, for busy trial judges and lawyers who wanted to know how we interpreted the law. The reasoning had to be logical and clear; the facts of the case had to be declared without the inclusion of irrelevant facts, no matter how interesting they might be; and the conclusion of the governing law needed to be stated without ambiguity. I felt that anything unnecessary would weaken the usability of a published opinion. This brought to mind my art school days and the elegance of the precept *less is more*.

All new judges, including me, quickly realize that published opinions exist forever, as long as there is common law. Therefore, many new judges tend to write opinions for publication by emphasizing slight differences to existing precedent so the opinion would appear as new law. Usually, after a few months on the court, the burning desire for immortality abates.

After this initial period, I came to believe that if an opinion could honestly be written as an unpublished opinion—one that did not create new law—that was the preferable course for the Court of Appeals.

By statute, one secretary and one law clerk were authorized for each judge on the Court of Appeals. The law clerk traditionally was a recent, top-flight law school graduate. As one of the experienced judges on the court told me when I arrived on the court, "If you have a great law clerk, this job is a pleasure. If you don't, it's a nightmare." I was fortunate to have absolutely top-quality law clerks. Their typical tenure was one year; three of mine each stayed three years. All my law clerks made my time at the court a genuine pleasure.

When I joined the court in 1988, the use of the computer was in its infancy in law offices and the courts. Word processing was just beginning to be used to produce opinions; CDs, containing all published cases and utilizing word searches, were slowly replacing the old, familiar book-form Digests—indexes used to find relevant cases.

A concern that had been lurking in the back of my mind since my appointment, was that all actions on the Court of Appeals were decided by three judges, requiring collegial resolution. My past life had been characterized by activity where I was the sole decision maker. I had been driven by a desire to have my own law office and never to have to answer to anyone. How would I react to an environment that required joint decision-making?

Although I developed close professional relationships with my colleagues, it was never my style to meet with any of them in social gatherings outside of court. Many of the judges, along with their spouses, took vacations together and socialized on weekends. Although I thoroughly enjoyed working with all members of the court, the character of the old Peter Ney—the loner—was never going to change.

The deference given to judges, that I experienced even before I took the oath of office, always made me somewhat uncomfortable, particularly when it was displayed outside the courtroom. I appreciated that court decisions generally were complied with as part of the social contract, without the use of force, even when the result could be devastating to one of the parties. Therefore, I concluded that the elevated bench, black robes, and formalities of address probably contributed to the voluntary compliance to court orders.

Betty never let me forget who I was. When I was in private practice, I worked at the office on Saturdays. Betty, who taught five days a week, cleaned the house on Saturdays. On the first Saturday after I became a judge, I was sitting in my favorite chair reading the newspaper, while Betty was pushing a vacuum cleaner.

The roar stopped, and Betty exclaimed, "Get your honorable ass up from there and help clean this house!" Saturdays were never the same.

I rarely introduced myself, either in person or on the telephone, as Judge Ney. I was known as Peter to Char and all other court personnel. When I was on the street with a group of judges and would meet a lawyer whom I had known for many years, many times the lawyer would refer to the others as "judge" and me by my first name.

It was difficult for me not to react when I detected traces of pomposity in my colleagues on the Colorado Court of Appeals. One time, I responded, *Career options are quite limited when you have absolutely no ability in math or science, and that's why just like me all of you became lawyers and eventually judges.* But in reality, it was a conversation I was having with a mirror. I had intuitively realized my limitations in math and science early on and explored several of the remaining career options on my convoluted path to becoming a lawyer.

Shortly after coming on the court and while still its most junior member, I became interested in finding a way to increase the court's productivity without decreasing its quality. I had an idea related to the use of senior judges. I discussed my proposal with many of my colleagues and received positive feedback. Then, I put my proposal in writing and made an appointment to present it to the chief judge of the court. The more experienced judges warned against a junior member of the court proposing an administrative change to the chief judge, but I found it hard to believe that a good-faith suggestion might be considered an affront to the chief, as she could always ignore it. I was undeterred, but I did agree to have a well-respected judge accompany me to the meeting. My suggestion resulted in both of us ending up in the doghouse.

I ignored the chief's rebuff; however, other judges warned me that she might remember and retaliate against me, possibly at my first retention election. Nothing ever came of it, but the incident made me aware that judges are subject to the same ego and insecurity problems as everyone else. Courts have an inherent hierarchal structure similar to corporations, with one notable difference—judges have a term of office and cannot be arbitrarily removed or disciplined without cause. This incident gave me the undeserved label of rabble-rouser of the court, a label that I wore with pride.

Several times during my first few years on the court, my inexperience crept into my draft opinions, though I hope all the errors were caught before they were announced to the world. Once, in a full-court conference, an excellent experienced judge, Ed Ruland, asked me, "Pete, in this real estate opinion of yours, haven't you switched the purchaser and mortgagee and seller and lender?" Of course, he was right; I was humiliated at having made it obvious to everyone on the court that I had no experience in real estate matters.

A few months later, Ed came into my office and asked for my help in a criminal case since he had no experience in criminal law. I was delighted that now it was I who could demonstrate that no one comes to court familiar with all specialties, and the collegiality among the judges improves the work product of the entire court.

During my second summer on the court, I attended an intensive two-week appellate judges' training program at New York University Law School. This training, now combined with a year's on-the-job experience, made me confident that I was doing the job well.

The use of law clerks was left to the judges' discretion. Some judges had their law clerks start on the research and analysis and write the original draft of their opinions, without the judge's input. My style was the opposite: I read all briefs and written arguments submitted by the parties before my law clerks saw the cases. I then gave my view of the cases to my law clerks before they began working on them. My law clerks and I had a clear understanding that they would bring to my immediate attention any hesitancy they had with any part of my direction. We always identified issues requiring serious research at our initial meeting. Then, based on that meeting, my law clerk would work on the first draft, which I would mark up and return with comments. The process was repeated three or four times before the draft saw the light of day and I distributed it to the other two members of the division.

This process, especially the legal modifications developed during the back and forth revisions, resulted in stronger opinions than would have been possible with a single author. I had trained my law clerks to eliminate any unneeded paragraphs, sentences, and words. No avoidable subtleties or nuances appeared in any of my opinions. One result of this collaborative process was that, as I read the final draft before announcement, I was frequently unable to identify who had made what contribution.

There were three occasions when my official duties were particularly pleasurable: Over an eighteen-month period beginning in July 1989, each of my children got married, and as a judge, I was able to perform the ceremonies.

After serving two years, all judges faced a provisional retention election to determine if they would serve a full term in office. I had received generally excellent reviews in the anonymous surveys from lawyers who had appeared before me and judges who had read my opinions. However, one negative comment gave me serious concern: A lawyer accused me of treating individuals differently based on race. This accusation upset me, not because of its possible effect on my election but on its substance. What had I done that could have been interpreted as racist? A colleague, also on the ballot, mentioned that she, too, had been accused of racism.

We concluded that the accusation had originated from an African-American lawyer who had been totally unprepared at an oral argument where my colleague and I had been on the panel. The lawyer was obviously annoyed by our questioning, which highlighted her lack of preparation. We recalled that she had left the courtroom in an agitated state. My conscience was clear and I was relieved. In spite of the racist accusation, I was successful in the election and was retained for a full eight-year term.

Parallel to my strong support for short, tightly written opinions was my doubt of the value of dissents and special concurring opinions on an intermediate appellate court. I strongly believed that differences between judges on a division could be worked out by compromise and accommodation, in the majority of cases, and that the resulting opinion would be more useful than an opinion with a dissent or special concurring opinion. Further, I believed that a dissent was appropriate and unavoidable only when it was clear that no compromise could be found between my views and the majority's position. Some of my colleagues strongly disagreed with my position and believed that a dissent or special concurring opinion, even on an intermediate appellate court, added to the law.

In cases where one judge believed strongly that the result proposed by the majority was wrong, and the other two judges on the division believed just as strongly in their position, a dissent was required. I dissented in less than 1 percent of the cases in which I participated.

One of my dissents had a touch of humor. In the trial court, a lawyer had uttered, "Protracted bullshit!" toward opposing counsel, based on his and the court's opinion that a continuance was necessitated by opposing counsel's waste of time in failing to stay focused on the issues of the case. The judge asked, "What did you say?" The statement was repeated and the attorney was immediately held in contempt. The attorney appealed his contempt of court conviction, which had originally included a jail term that was later suspended.

The other two judges on the division found nothing wrong with the judge's exercise of his discretion and voted to affirm. However, I believed strongly that the judge's contempt imposition without any warning was beyond the contempt power of the court, which should be exercised only to prevent actual, direct obstruction of the administration of justice or interference with it—and not to protect the judge's dignity.

I relied on a United Supreme Court case where the utterance of "chicken shit" was found not to constitutionally support a contempt conviction when it was not directed at the judge and did not interfere with the administration of justice. An academic study, which I used in the dissent, found that shouting "bullshit" was less offensive than "chicken shit." Here, no compromise was possible, so I wrote one of my few dissents.

Special concurring opinions gave judges the opportunity to voice a reasoning that was different from the majority but arrived at the same result. Some judges believed that dissents and special concurring opinions emphasized differences that encouraged the Colorado Supreme Court or the United States Supreme Court to look at opposing viewpoints. These positions were logical, but I never saw evidence that they met those objectives.

I could not resist using some humor during my stay on the court, although I was very serious about the quality of my opinions and production numbers. After several years on the court, I found April 1, April Fools' Day, a challenge. I played an annual April Fools' Day trick on the court. Some of my victims were ensnared several times, much to their embarrassment.

On one occasion, in late March 2000, I produced what appeared to be segments of a published book. The title page of *The Independent Judiciary* showed me as the author. On the dedication page, I expressed my gratitude to my colleagues for the material they had provided, although unintentionally, without which this book could not have been written. I dated the dedication "April 1, 2000."

The first few pages of what appeared to be a memoir described—in great detail—me crossing the street to the court building while anticipating an exciting day in which I would expose secret sins of the court and its judges. It went on to say that I regretted that so many reputations would be destroyed but it was unavoidable. The faux book then skipped to its last page on which I was leaving the building, reminiscing about the exciting day that was just drawing to a close and expressing regret over the pain I had caused my colleagues.

I left my *opus* next to a photocopy machine where an assistant found it. Rushing the papers to Char, she nervously whispered, "These papers should probably not have been left near the photocopier."

Char, who was in on the joke, responded in horror, "They certainly should not! Judge Ney would be upset if he found out his secret book had been discovered."

Of course, the news that Judge Ney had written an expose of the court spread like wildfire, with everyone wondering which judges' indiscretions would be disclosed. No one appeared to have noticed the April 1 date of the dedication.

One judge, who had literary aspirations, asked to go to lunch with me to inquire about my publishing success. "How did you get an agent?" he inquired.

"Agent?" I responded. "I didn't use an agent; I just sent the manuscript to the publisher and they sent me the contract. But what really bothers me is the movie option."

"Movie option?" My poor colleague could not contain himself. "You mean they are making it into a movie?" I acknowledged they were, but that I felt I had been misled when I was told that Douglas was going to play my part, as I had assumed it would be Michael Douglas, and just recently found out that Kirk Douglas, the old man, was cast for the role, rather than his handsome, younger son. "Why, he is as old as I am!" I angrily growled. I continued the charade for another several days, until my conscience finally kicked in and I confessed.

After the tragedy of September 11, many public buildings were modified to make them more secure. It had been decided that the Colorado Judicial Building, where the Supreme Court and Court of Appeals had their offices and courtrooms, would increase security by placing triangular concrete highway dividers around the building. I objected on aesthetic grounds when the plan was announced, and when I asked the chief justice if the decision was *cast in concrete*, her glare was my answer.

The concrete barriers eventually surrounded the building. In late March of that year, I sent an e-mail to the members of the court explaining that I desperately needed their help. I told them I had suggested to some educators that the dividers would make an ideal surface for murals, to be painted by their students; that the enthusiastic teachers had concurred, requesting that I judge the murals—to which I had readily agreed, since it was my idea; and that I had just been notified that three busloads of students from all grades would be arriving on Monday morning, with judging to begin at 3:00 PM. So, I was asking for help from the court, as that was far more judging than I could do by myself.

I received positive responses from many judges, who outlined their artistic qualifications, and some cautionary queries from others, asking if the court actually owned the barriers and whether I had cleared the project with the Supreme Court. I responded with a naïve: "Do you think I should have?"

My April fool's joke ended when an administrator of public buildings, who had heard about my imaginary project, took up the matter with the chief justice. Not wishing to cause her any anxiety, I called and confessed.

The Colorado Constitution provided that judges could not serve full-time after reaching the age of seventy-two. So, in the spring of 2003, the year I reached mandatory retirement age, I sent an e-mail to the members of the court advising them of my intent to challenge the mandatory retirement provision in court the following week, on April 1. I wanted to advise them ahead of time, I stated, because I did not want them to get the news, which could affect the status and image of the court, through the media.

Many of my kind colleagues offered help and provided me with possible legal challenges. Their attitudes changed when they discovered this would be my last April 1 as a full-time judge on the court.

That spring, I had a more serious project related to my retirement— finding new employment for my assistant, Char, who had been with me since I was in private practice. Although she undoubtedly would have been able to find employment in the private sector, it was beneficial for her to remain with the state and continue to build toward her retirement. I was relieved when she became another judge's assistant, although it meant I had to have a series of temporary assistants during my last six months on the court.

One of the advantages of serving as a judge over having a private practice was that my court assignments simply ceased during my vacation periods, as senior judges absorbed the flow of the docket; when I took a vacation in private practice, I had to handle an overload before and after the vacation. My years as a judge gave Betty and me the opportunity for leisurely travel to England, France, China, Thailand, Russia, Denmark, Sweden, Greece, Turkey, Finland, Ecuador, Peru, and the Galapagos Islands.

In August 2001, Betty and I visited Linda and her family who were temporarily living in Strasbourg, France, while Linda's husband, Peter, was on sabbatical. My father's hometown, Kaiserslautern, Germany, was only about a ninety-minute drive from Strasbourg, but during the sixty years after leaving Germany, I specifically avoided setting foot again in that country. However, I decided it was more important that we experience the family roots together. To test my memory, the night before the trip I made a sketch of the house with a driveway leading from the street to a cobblestone courtyard with horse stalls on two sides. That scene had resided in my mind from the time I last saw 12 Glockenstrasse as a four-year-old.

I was concerned that when we crossed the border into Germany I might do something silly in the presence of my grandchildren. My concern was unfounded because the boundary signs had been removed since the establishment of the European Union, and the only indication I had that we were in Germany was that the highway exit signs had changed from *Sortie* to *Ausfahrt*, which my grandsons found very funny.

As the seven of us walked down Glockenstrasse, with me in the lead, I noticed that all the houses were attached to one another—no sign of any driveways. I thought we were on a fool's errand. *Why did I imagine that my memory was accurate, or that sixty intervening years and a world war had not changed the neighborhood?*

We walked past 18 Glockenstrasse, then 16, 14, and finally, at 12, there it was—the driveway with its open gates. We all walked into the courtyard. Its cobblestones had been paved over, but the horse stalls remained. I turned to look at the house where my father, as a teenager on a horse, with his sister looking out the window, had posed for the camera almost a century ago—the first picture in this book.

We learned that the house, now owned by the city was a shelter for victims of domestic violence. The stalls were used for storage.

We found the daughter of the family that had lived across the street. She had married and was still living in that house. As we introduced ourselves to her and her husband, they invited us in and insisted we have coffee and cake with them. Before we left, they gave us directions to the municipal cemetery where we found the graves of my great-grandfather and grandfather.

Many images and memories filled my mind as we left Germany that afternoon. The trip had allayed some of the anger remaining within me—perhaps someday I will visit 13 Kaulbachplatz in Nuremberg.

In spring 2003, Betty had the idea that we should celebrate our fiftieth wedding anniversary with our three kids and their eight children at a vacation site in 2004. Linda, always practical, suggested we not wait but do it as soon as we could work out the schedule for each family. So, the sixteen of us went to a ranch in Tucson, Arizona where there were activities for kids of various ages. As it turned out, Linda's let's-do-it-now idea, in lieu of planning for a year in the future, was prescient.

In the fall of 2003, I sent a letter of resignation to the governor advising him that I would be retiring on November 10. This set in motion the procedure to select my replacement on the court. Since I was overdue for my periodic physical, I arranged for a complete examination, which was completed in a series of steps over several months. The results indicated that I was in good health—until the last report, the colonoscopy.

In September, I received the news that I had colorectal cancer. This would require surgery where the cancerous section of the colon would be removed and the severed ends would be reconnected. Hopefully, all cancerous cells would be removed by the surgery. This sounded simple enough—almost routine. I was expected to be in the hospital for less than a week.

There were, of course, certain dangers associated with the surgery. As with any surgery, there was the danger of infection. If the reattached colon were to leak, the result could be an infection in the abdominal cavity. Of course, all precautions would be taken to avoid these dangers.

I rejected a surgeon who specialized in colon surgery because he would only consider opening me up completely. Describing his procedure with dramatic gestures, he explained, "I want to lay the colon out in front of me to see what I'm doing." He also insisted that I have several months of chemotherapy and radiation before the surgery. When I inquired if this would minimize the need for chemotherapy after surgery, he indicated that pre-surgical chemo or radiation would not affect post-surgical treatment. Also, responding to my questions, he answered that his recommended pre-surgical treatment had not been statistically proven to be beneficial. I wanted to get on with my life, but found myself, as most patients do, unequipped to make the medical decisions alone.

I chose another surgeon based on his specialty of laparoscopic surgery, which would require only a two-inch incision. That seemed to be the least intrusive procedure with the fastest recovery. My surgery was scheduled for the first week of October. I would be out of the hospital in less than a week and back to work a week later—two or three weeks before my mandatory retirement date of November 10.

During the latter half of September, I started to remove pictures and other personal property from my office. At that time, in addition to the scheduled surgery, I was teaching two torts classes at Arapahoe Community College. I told them there would be no class on the first Thursday in October, but that classes would resume the following week. I fully expected to resume my work as a full-time judge one month after my discharge from the hospital. Completing my pending cases, I prepared the cases scheduled for the beginning of November—the last cases I would participate in as a full-time sitting judge.

I checked into the hospital as scheduled and had a nervous get-together with Betty, Diane, and Betty's cousin Richard, who had flown in from Kansas City. The surgeon and anesthesiologist explained the procedure.

As promised, shortly after I was wheeled into surgery, everything went black. I opened my eyes in the recovery room and was taken to my hospital room where Betty and Diane were waiting. They had seen the surgeon, who had told them everything went well, with *clean margins*, and that he would see us the next day. I assumed the comment on clean margins meant the colon remaining in my body was clear of the cancerous tumor that had been removed. He must have been right—now, five years later, I am cancer-free.

Betty stayed in my room each night after the surgery. Her presence helped make my stay more comfortable. Everything seemed to be going as expected and I was due to be discharged within a week after the surgery. The one remaining goal, prior to discharge, was to demonstrate the normal functioning of my colon. To this end, I ate the evening meal with gusto, wanting to prove I was ready to go home.

During the night, as usual, I was awakened to have my vital signs checked. I was sweating, and the nurse told me my temperature was elevated; it continued to rise through the night. I was wheeled to various radiology stations where images were taken. The verdict was that I had a serious infection; there was no way I was going home that day. The infection did not subside and an infectious disease specialist, Dr. Perlman, was called in. When I did not respond to drugs, I was taken to the intensive care unit where I stayed for four weeks. I must have gone in and out of consciousness during that time.

Each nurse in intensive care had only two patients at a time, so when I was awake during the night, one of the nurses and I would speak about every conceivable subject, including constitutional law and lifestyles. One very young nurse told me that she and her husband had decided to downsize their possessions to avoid the anxieties of this acquisitive society. Even if she or her husband could not work, they would still be able to enjoy the same standard of living. I wondered how someone so young could be so wise.

One evening, my nurse told me she did not have time to talk to me because she had a new patient who had been injured in an in industrial accident and would be a permanent paraplegic. He was twenty-nine years old. During the night, I heard the family talking to the physician and nurses. *And I thought I had problems.*

Under the care of the infectious disease physician, Dan Perlman, I started to respond to new antibiotics and returned to the surgery recovery floor I had left four weeks earlier. The nurses, who, I felt, were the backbone of my treatment, welcomed me back. I now was under the care of several specialists: the surgeon, Dr. Dan Perlman, and my friend, internist Alan Bortz, who tried to coordinate the various specialties but was limited since he did not have privileges at that hospital. We hired a hospital coordinator to fulfill that function.

I continued to respond well to the new antibiotics and finally began to improve. I started to agitate for discharge before my birthday, but Dr. Perlman advised against it because he did not want me to make the change from drugs administered intravenously to orally. He told me he was treating me as he would his father. As he left the room, he turned and said. "I have some experience with cancer. I recently buried my seven-year-old son, who died of brain cancer." I never questioned him again.

I was discharged from the hospital two days after my seventy-second birthday and my retirement from the court.

– 15 –

Janus

The Colorado Constitution provides that, upon attaining the age of seventy-two, a justice or judge of a court of record shall retire. Two days after my seventy-second birthday, I came home from my six-week hospital stay no longer a full-time judge of the Colorado Court of Appeals—or a full-time anything. I was retired.

I felt that this would be the last chapter of my life. Would I spend it shuffling about the house waiting for the stage to fade to black? No, damn it! Even if I could do nothing else, I would tell my story to my grandkids, so they could appreciate their good fortune to live in a country where we all have an infinite number of chances to live the American dream, no matter how many mistakes we make.

When we got home from the hospital, walking from the car to my bed, which had never felt as good as on that day, was a major effort. Betty had arranged for the installation of grab bars in the bathroom; these now were a necessity for me. I had never felt so weak and helpless in my life. Although I remembered very little detail of my six weeks in the hospital, I did remember the gravity of the discussion the doctors and nurses had with my family when there was no progress in getting my infection under control.

I had never previously experienced a serious illness, and until then I had not fully appreciated my good health. Health crises happened to others for whom I felt sympathy but with whom I never identified. Although I never considered that this might be the end of the road for me, my family appreciated the seriousness of my condition. To me, it was just a matter of time when I would recover and come home. During my several weeks in the hospital, I complied with all the exercises prescribed, with the goal of leaving the hospital as soon as practical.

After five weeks, the infection started to subside and everyone breathed a sigh of relief. The physicians explained that their treatment, including the prescribed drugs and exercises, could not cure the infection, but only assist in my recovery—my own body was the major component of the cure. I believed that premise, and my relationship with my body changed. I, who had never exercised, had often joked that everyone was born with only a finite amount of energy and I sure was not going to waste mine on exercise.

Now, I forced myself to get out of bed and walk—first, around the house, then on the street. My strength returned so quickly that we had a family Thanksgiving dinner just two weeks after my discharge. By the beginning of January, I was participating as a senior judge. In the middle of January, I returned to teaching torts at Arapahoe Community College. I began a chemotherapy program, which knocked me out one day a week for six months, but it never interfered with my senior judging or teaching.

The court and the Bar Association each gave me a memorable retirement dinner. A humorous skit reliving my legal career was the highlight of the court's party. The three women judges played the roles of prostitute clients, and some of the male judges acted the parts of organized crime characters. It was a marvelous production with song and costumes. Many members of the court made such nice comments about me—much better than I thought I deserved.

The presenters at the Bar Association dinner were so laudatory, that it occurred to me that I would not need a funeral—everything good had already been said. Although at both dinners, the comments described someone who was much better than I remembered being, I appreciated the imaginative thoughts.

My chemotherapy regimen continued through all of this. The room was very large, with about twenty-five large leather reclining chairs, lined up in rows, all facing the same direction. On first glance, it looked as if the occupants were there to see a movie. However, on further examination, I saw an IV pole, at the side of each chair, holding a bag of chemicals intended to kill the cancerous cells hosted by the recipient's body.

Unfortunately, the killing power of the chemicals did not confine itself to cancerous cells but also attacked cells essential to a healthy body. Some patients did not look ill; others had the familiar loss of hair; and a few had the bored look of someone killing time with a magazine or book. Spouses accompanied several patients. The movement in the room was restricted to the half-dozen nurses pulling carts of supplies from one patient to another, inserting and removing IVs, and setting timers and flow meters for each patient.

My cocktail was one of the early chemical treatments that did not result in hair loss. But my body did react to the cell-killing chemicals. During the six-month weekly routine, I got to know the attendants and some of the patients. One, Jim Curran, had been a friend before our diagnoses of cancer. Sometimes we arranged to receive our chemotherapies at the same time, sitting in neighboring chairs, with our wives accompanying us. The four of us would meet as if this were a social gathering. Unfortunately, Jim's esophageal cancer caused his death shortly after he completed his chemotherapy.

Mine had a very positive outcome and I regained my strength in a few months. Every six months, I had PET scans that showed I was cancer-free, but I had one unidentified spot that never changed. I told my oncologist that if this spot proved to be a recurrence of cancer, I would opt out of any further treatment in exchange for a higher quality, if shorter, life.

Since the spot remained unchanged for four years, my oncologist became more optimistic that it was not a recurrence of cancer. After four years of periodic PET scans, a radiologist suggested the mysterious spot might be an aneurysm, which it was, and it was easily repaired. I was told that if I had never had cancer and the subsequent PET scans, it would have been unlikely that the aneurysm would have been discovered until it burst and killed me.

In 2005, we realized that the grandkids were maturing so quickly that we had very little time to take another family vacation that included all sixteen of us. If we didn't go during the next year, it would be doubtful that we ever could, as one after another, the grandchildren would be off to college and their independent lives.

It took intensive mutual planning to settle on a time that would accommodate all the families' busy schedules. We decided on Costa Rica as our destination and have never regretted that choice.

Costa Rica provided us such a broad range of activities there was no time to be bored regardless of age or interest. We were always in motion—from city to city—rainforest to ocean—volcano fields to soaking in hot spring waterfalls—and even included an exciting zip line ride over the rainforest canopy.

We had a small bus to ourselves with an excellent driver-guide. In the rainforests, knowledgeable naturalists gave each of us, regardless of age, a great appreciation for its ecology. I believe that all of us were impressed by the sophistication of this developing country—its economy, education, and growing democracy—all without an army.

I was relieved that, two years after completing my chemotherapy, I was able to scramble over rocky volcano fields, hike through the rainforest and swing over the rainforest on a zip line. Betty and I are so grateful that we did not let this opportunity for a true family vacation slip by.

Now, more than five years since my surgery, I still teach torts at Arapahoe Community College, serve as a senior judge on the Colorado Court of Appeals, do my photography, write my memoirs, travel, and see a lot of theater. Not a bad life considering how it could have easily ended five years earlier.

In 2007, Betty and I decided to travel to a part of the world we had not yet seen. Remembering that old Ronald Coleman film, *Lost Horizons*, I suggested Tibet. Again, we were fortunate that we planned quickly; a year later, the country was closed by an uprising by the Tibetans against their Chinese occupiers; and Chengdu, our jumping-off city in China, was racked by a destructive earthquake, either of which would have made the trip impossible.

Most tours of China spend only a few days in Tibet, almost as an afterthought, but we chose one that would spend most of the time there. The Chinese city of Chengdu, our entry into Tibet, was a city I had never heard of, with a population of eleven million.

We were met at the airport by our beautiful tour guide, Pearl, who told us we were the only people on the tour. Since we had flown the better part of twenty hours, she assumed that we were tired and wished to go straight to our hotel. So, when I inquired if it was possible to see the Giant Panda Research Center, which my tour book said was one of the unique attractions in Chengdu, she lit up. We immediately were driven to this remarkable research institution where we were able to see not only mature pandas, but also newborn infants.

As we left the airport, she gave us each a large document and explained that it was very important for our entry, and stay in Tibet. We were fortunate to have those papers, because even though we had visas to the People's Republic of China, and the Chinese policy was that Tibet was part of China, there were severe restrictions on foreigners entering Tibet.

After the visit to the Giant Panda Research Center, Pearl, now thinking we had unlimited energy, suggested we attend the world famous opera of Chengdu. However, by this time we had been up more than thirty hours and declined the invitation. Pearl and we became friends, even though we were together at the center for just that one afternoon, and began an ongoing correspondence.

To Betty's annoyance, an attractive tour guide, Vivian, met us at the Lhasa airport and wrapped traditional white silk-like welcoming scarves around our necks. Again, we comprised the entire tour group. So, our tour of Tibet was in a sedan with Vivian, a driver, Betty, and me.

Visualizing Tibet's occupation since the Chinese invasion of 1950, I expected to see a visible military presence. As we drove from the airport into Lhasa, we passed what obviously was a military installation—a walled complex with a soldier standing at attention by a guardhouse that had a Chinese flag flying atop it. During our week in Tibet, I saw perhaps twenty uniformed, but unarmed, Chinese soldiers who appeared to be on leave and sightseeing as we were.

On our first day, touring the landmarks of Lhasa: the Potala and the Jokhang temple, the destination of pilgrims, I asked Vivian, who had attended college in China, what she had learned at school about the history of Tibet from the 1950s to the present. She told us she had learned very little and asked what I knew about that period. I told her that most of my information came from my guidebook, which I then lent her. The next morning, she told us that she had read it all night and that the history was all new to her. In a perfectly natural tone, she said, "I can't imagine living in a country where you can purchase and read any book published anywhere in the world." I immediately gave her the guidebook.

Vivian later told us she was a great movie fan and had adopted her name based on the name of the leading actress in her favorite film, *Gone With the Wind*.

As we traveled throughout Tibet, we saw some resemblance to *Shangri-la* in the fervent devotion of the people to Buddhism. The temples were always crowded—not with tourists, but with the devout, who threw money over glass screens that protected the hundreds of ornate statues of the Buddha. Donations of currency were knee-deep behind the glass screens surrounding the statues. Betty and I were disturbed by the thought that the income from the donations in the temples, given by the obviously poor Tibetans, might be used exclusively to support the temples and the monks, rather than non-religious schools, hospitals, or the needy. Our trip to Tibet, Nepal, and Thailand reinforced, rather than diminished, my cynicism toward organized religion in general, whether Buddhist, Hindu, or Judeo-Christian.

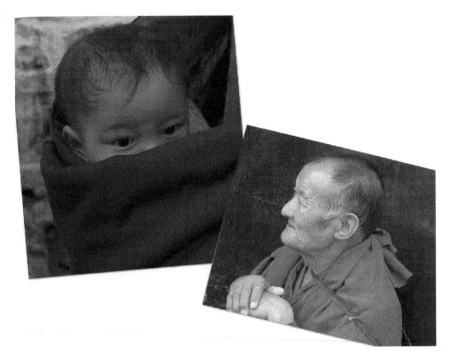

To the outsider, it looked like the Chinese had adopted a hands-off policy towards religious institutions, with one notable exception—the prohibition of the display of the Dalai Lama's image or name. So, although we saw Tibet in full color, rather than in the black and white of *Lost Horizons,* there was much resemblance.

For a multitude of reasons, I have always been grateful that, through my good fortune, I ended up in the United States as a youth, rather than any other place on earth. This gratitude is deepened whenever I return from another country. Vivian's matter-of-fact comments about freedom of expression capture only a fraction of the basis for my appreciation of the United States.

My life has been an illustration of the often-repeated description of America as the land of opportunity. Seventy years ago, I was penniless when I arrived on these shores. My parents had no money. Through the generosity of several individuals, my parents' hard work, and the structure of American society, we rose from a life of absolute poverty to one of comfort; I was able to go to college and take advantage of the American dream. I became financially secure and was privileged to serve on the Colorado Court of Appeals.

It's one thing to decide to write your life's story and quite another to actually do it. I had always thought the theme of my story would be the freedom that America gave me to change direction, sometimes recklessly, without paying a penalty. I had not considered my beginnings on the *Kindertransport,* life in England, and growing up as a part of the story. It became obvious to me, though, even before I put a single word on paper that these would need to be included.

I believe that the uniqueness of the American dream is more than the opportunities offered—this is the land of second, third, and infinite numbers of chances. I took full advantage of my allotted do-overs.

Some of the career twists and turns I took were motivated by nothing more substantial than a selfish interest in a particular subject, without regard for my responsibility to provide my family with financial security. I know of no other society that is so forgiving. I can now look back, without regret for the choices I made, even those driven by my restlessness, and never have to pay for the obvious mistakes I made. I appreciated the freedom to take every fork in the road that seemed like the right one at the time. Of course, none of this would have been possible without Betty's support. This story about the advantages of living in America is the one I wanted to tell my grandchildren.

These career changes: following an ill-defined, always-changing muse, at the time were irresponsible by any rational standard and reckless for a married man with three children. This twisted path would have led to disaster in any place on earth other than America.

In the almost seventy years I have been privileged to live in the United States, my enthusiastic love and gratitude to this country have never wavered. My good fortune to have been welcomed when I arrived here is a continual wonder to me. There is no other place in the world I would rather live. I, the only son of a successful business owner, have often thought what might have happened if my family history had been different and we had not been chased out of Germany without any assets. I firmly believe If I had had the choice, I would have chosen to start life in America.

Betty, always supportive, encouraged me to write this story. I had originally intended my theme to be the infinite number of chances to change direction in America, but it gradually expanded until it became the story of my life.

Because I was fortunate to leave Germany in the first days of 1939 and be reunited with my parents in England several months later, I never considered myself a Holocaust survivor. However, I frequently speak in schools and civic associations about my experiences on the *Kindertransport*, and I was encouraged to attend a national conference of child Holocaust survivors that was meeting in Denver. I went in spite of my belief that I did not fully belong.

At a writing workshop at the conference, the participants wrote for a half-hour, revealing a memory of the time. I described the scene in the Frankfurt train station. We were all asked to read our assignments to the group. I anticipated that I would be revealed as an outsider, as the other papers being read described horrendous events. To my surprise, my paper was well received by the participants who, without doubt, were genuine Holocaust survivors.

I attended two non-fiction writing classes primarily for the discipline of writing a regularly scheduled assignment. And the story of my life started to take form. Although I had conceived it as a chronological story, I wrote as mood and memory came to the forefront.

The exercise of taking my mind back in time was a strange but therapeutic experience. As I thought of an incident, at first I recalled only its bare outline. But, as I wrote, details presented themselves, like a movie taking place in my mind, until occurrences that had taken place before and after fleshed out the bones of the barely-remembered event. Most of my memories proved to be incredibly accurate, confirmed by documentation.

Some memories were proven to be inaccurate: for example, my memory of wandering into the countryside upon not finding the train to London when I arrived in England. I was certain that I had been lost for several days; however, in checking the postmarks on postcards I sent back to my parents, it became clear that I was lost for only one day before the policeman found me asleep. I was more surprised by what the documentation confirmed than what it contradicted.

The full-length motion picture, *Into the Arms of Strangers: Stories of the Kindertransport*, was released in 2000. Shown in the film's opening scene were some of my childhood books and games, and my silver pencil. The car from my seventh birthday gift—the prized *Autobahn*—was running down its pressed metal track as the film's title appeared.

The movie won the Oscar in 2001 as the best full-length documentary. I was pleased to have made my childhood momentos available for the film's production, and delighted to comply with the *United States Holocaust Memorial Museum's* request for the material which is now in its permanent collection. However, I kept the silver pencil.

This country has traversed good times and tough times. Administrations have been good, not so good, and terrible, but the resiliency of the American dream has sustained its spirit. This is not Pollyanna jingoism—America's 250-year-old history has proven it to be true. As a beneficiary of that promise, if there is anything I believe in, it is that dream.

I watched the 2004 Democratic convention on television and was mesmerized by its African-American keynote speaker, Barack Obama. Betty and I had never heard of the candidate for the Illinois senate seat, but within minutes we were transfixed by his charisma and powerful oratory. We both agreed he would be a great presidential candidate sometime in the future—if the country would ever be ready for a black president in that distant future. I remembered my interview before the Judicial Nominating Commission when I was asked to identify the greatest problem facing this country, and after reflection answered, "Racism." I always believed my answer, which seemed to suck the air out of the room, had assured my appointment to the bench.

In 2007, Betty and I volunteered to train immigrants for citizenship examinations. Since I had become naturalized more than sixty years earlier, I believed this was particularly appropriate for me.

In my retirement, I returned to the trial courtroom to appear as an expert witness in a murder trial. The prosecution had originally filed the case at the time of the murder, more than thirty years earlier, and it had been dismissed on the district attorney's motion. The same defendant now was charged again, and I was to testify if, under these circumstances, the defense could receive a fair trial. During almost one year, I spent six days in the courtroom listening to testimony and argument before I testified.

I experienced some nostalgia for the excitement of my previous trial practice; however, I had to admit to myself that I no longer had the energy nor the mental agility I once had to try a lawsuit.

The practice of law in general, and the judiciary in particular, are not usually welcoming to radical change, being bound up in tradition by their very nature. However, technology has revolutionized the practice of law, and, as a byproduct, dramatically changed the judiciary.

During my twenty-some years as a solo practitioner, I often thought there had been as much change in the practice of law during that period, as occurred in the more than a century that has passed since Lincoln had practiced law in Illinois. These dramatic changes were caused by the advent of the photocopy machine and the Selectric Typewriter that could miraculously lift errors off the page.

I was one of the first lawyers to use a computer in the production of documents—avoiding retyping repetitive paragraphs. When I went to the Court of Appeals, the advent of the computer increased the efficiency of the court in the production of opinions, with the use of spell-check avoiding need for manual proofreading.

Legal research also became more efficient with the use of CDs, which incorporated a word search; and later, with the use of on-line research, the efficiency of the judges, law clerks, and secretaries increased so dramatically that it became obvious that, depending on the judge, a typist could be eliminated and a judge could use the savings to hire another law clerk. At the time of my retirement, most of the judges had a staff of two law clerks rather than one law clerk and a typist or secretary.

The court's size was increased to meet the increased filing rate, resulting in the majority of the court being composed of new, highly-talented, extremely intelligent, younger judges—all wanting to prove their abilities to the world. This made my plea for short, direct, tightly written opinions a losing proposition. The capability of conducting online research and the increased legal staff encouraged each judge to include every nuance of every legal issue in every opinion—without regard for the ultimate user, busy trial judges and lawyers. I contented myself with the thought that fast-developing technology would produce software that would reveal the essence of these academic, law-review type opinions—almost as if they had been tightly written short opinions originally.

After eight years of the Bush presidency, characterized by incompetence, corruption, and cronyism and driven by muddled ideology, it was difficult for any but extreme loyalists to point to any accomplishments of that administration. This led to one of the most exciting presidential contests within a century, lasting two years. Since I now was retired, I was able to follow the campaign daily, with the news channels always playing in the background.

Because I was a Senior Judge, I was governed by the same ethical restrictions as full-time judges and barred from any political activities. Betty made up for my lack of active participation by volunteering her enthusiastic energy to the Obama campaign.

We began to believe it was possible that a person of color could become the presidential nominee of a major political party. Shortly before the Democratic convention was held in Denver, Barack Obama was assured the nomination.

Betty and I wanted to personally observe as much of the convention as possible. With gift tickets from one of my students, we were able to attend not only the pre-opening press party at Elitch Gardens, an amusement park, filled with politicos, newspersons, and other curiosity seekers like us, but also the convention the night Hillary Clinton spoke.

Her appearance created a great deal of excitement because no one was sure if she, as the unsuccessful candidate, would give merely a *pro forma* endorsement or genuine, enthusiastic support for Obama's candidacy, without which her supporters might have been left on the sidelines, splitting the support of the ticket and leading to defeat. However, she came through with flying colors, and "Unity" signs popped up throughout the crowd, as sighs of relief changed to cheers and applause at the conclusion of her speech.

At the Denver Press Club, we heard a speech delivered by Madeline Albright, the Secretary of State in Bill Clinton's administration, discussing her *Memo to the President Elect*.

As we left the Press Club, which was directly across the street from the Denver Athletic Club, we learned that Obama, who had been playing basketball inside, was just about to leave. We had an unobstructed view of the front door. As the doorman reached for the door handle, there was noticeable activity by the Secret Service. With Betty's camera framed for the image of a lifetime, the door started to open. Betty released the shutter just as a black Secret Service SUV eased into the position, blocking our previously unobstructed view, thus creating a rare treasure—our wonderful picture of the rear quarter of a black SUV—to commemorate the day when we were just across the street from the next president of the United States.

Although we were not fortunate enough to be among his 84,000 enthusiastic supporters on August 28 when he delivered his acceptance speech at Invesco field, we hung onto every word as we watched it on television.

The period from the end of the conventions to the November 4 election produced excitement that had never been experienced in American elections in my lifetime. In our house, the television was always on as we listened to the continually updated polling results. Some experts began speculating that Obama's lead in the polls might never be reflected in the election results because of some interviewees' reluctance to reveal that they would not vote for a black man. So, although the Republican candidate John McCain ran a terrible campaign and was handicapped by George W. Bush's plunging popularity, a collapsing economy, and the unpopularity of the war in Iraq, we still were holding our breath, hoping the election would turn out right—the way we wanted.

In the three months leading up to the election, as the economy appeared to be in freefall, John McCain sealed his defeat with the statement: "The fundamentals of the economy are strong." He also appeared to be a person of the last century when he readily admitted he could not use a computer, which to many voters was equivalent to functional illiteracy.

The Obama campaign garnered thousands of new volunteers. Betty joined hundreds of them in Littleton campaign headquarters, a large storefront in an older shopping center. With dozens of others, Betty registered hundreds of new voters. Arapahoe County, which had been a Republican stronghold, began to have a strong Democratic registration majority.

Betty, who had volunteered to train immigrants for their citizenship process, registered them as they were sworn in. Although I legally could not participate in the campaign, whenever I visited the storefront headquarters to bring Betty lunch, I could feel the energy in the activity of the bustling volunteers, the ringing telephones, the flashing computer screens, and the buzz of the conversations as volunteers reported back from assignments or received instructions for new ones. I had never experienced anything like this in a presidential election. The TV news reported this going on throughout the country.

Colorado, a traditionally Republican state, was now identified as a swing state that might fall into the Democratic column. In the last week of October, Barack Obama came to Denver to speak to a crowd of more than 100,000 wildly enthusiastic supporters—double the number expected. Betty and I were there. Strangers hugged each other, knowing they would barely see the stage much less the speaker; the discomfort of waiting disappeared in a feeling of common purpose. After the speech, as the surrounding streets filled with crowds of people heading to their cars, parked far away, and restaurants became sites of celebration as people believed in the impossible.

On the day before the election, Michelle Obama came to Colorado to speak at a high school gym. Although the event was held with less than a day's planning, the crowds, with Betty and I among them, were made up of highly enthusiastic strangers with a common purpose. People celebrated as they danced and hugged each other. Every square inch of the gym was filled with cheering supporters.

During the week leading up to the November 4 election, no one talked about anything but the election; the news focused exclusively on political appearances and polls. Our friends and we could not believe, or take for granted, the extension of Obama's lead in the polls as Election Day drew near.

Many voters, including us, had voted prior to Election Day, either by absentee or early voting. Throughout the country, those votes were waiting to be counted.

Most of the country experienced good weather on November 4 and reports forecast that this election would bring out the highest proportion of eligible voters in recent American history.

We had invited friends to our house to watch the election results come in. Not to miss any of the possible excitement, we set up two televisions and my computer, each tuned to a different channel.

With Obama posters displayed around the house, Betty had decorated a buffet table in red, white, and blue. The centerpiece was a chocolate cake inscribed "The Change We Need." The guests ate the cold cuts and other refreshments, but the cake remained untouched until we could be sure.

The favorable results traveled across the map from east to west but the networks could not declare a winner until all polls were closed. Within seconds of California's polls closing, the networks declared Barack Obama the next president of the United States. I broke out the champagne and proposed a toast to the forty-fourth president of the United States.

It was an emotional moment with many of us on the verge of tears. As I had four years earlier, while listening to Barack Obama deliver the keynote speech in 2004; I recalled my identifying racism, before the nominating commission in 1988, as America's greatest problem. The election of Barack Obama may have signaled that the country had now taken a step to a more perfect union.

The ten weeks between the election and the inauguration were filled with much activity for the transition to the new, era-changing administration. With the economy continuing to collapse, the new president would be inheriting a country in a total mess—a full plate.

On January 20, 2009, Barack Obama was sworn in before one million people crowded between the Capitol and the Lincoln Memorial. We were not the only ones with tears in our eyes. That evening of the inauguration, we had another party; this time the cake was inscribed, "Yes We Did!"

Barack Obama took office after a landslide victory and amid unprecedented popularity. The country believed it had taken a giant step toward *a more perfect union*, as promised by the Constitution and hope had returned. The expectations were so high, could anyone satisfy them? Again, as America had accomplished at every transition since the inauguration of George Washington, there was a peaceful transition of power without armed troops, tanks, or violence in the streets.

I know that the world in general, and America in particular, will be changed forever; not only by the election, but also by technology, and societal and economic systemic changes that began before the election. The rate of change will now be exponential compared to the previous decade. It sounds so interesting; I want to be around to see it.

It is certainly appropriate that, as I contemplate a future impossible to imagine, I bring this story to a close on July 4, 2009, the 233rd birthday of the country that gave me so much. Like the Roman god, Janus who looks forward and backward simultaneously, I anticipate the future while recalling the memories of the events and people that brought me here to live the American dream—from a seat on a train to a seat on the bench.

What a country!